W9-BHP-871

NUMBER 72

Yale French Studies

Simone de Beauvoir: Witness to a Century

Yale French Studies

Hélène Vivienne Wenzel
Special editor for this issue
Liliane Greene, *Managing editor*
Editorial board: Peter Brooks (Chairman), Ellen Burt, David
 Civali, Lauren Doyle-McCombs, Mary Lou Ennis,
 Shoshana Felman, Richard Goodkin, Christopher Miller,
 Charles Porter, Allan Stoekl
Staff: Peggy McCracken
Editorial office: 315 William L. Harkness Hall.
Mailing address: 2504A Yale Station, New Haven,
 Connecticut 06520.
Sales and subscription office:
 Yale University Press, 92A Yale Station
 New Haven, Connecticut 06520
Published twice annually by Yale University Press.

Designed by James J. Johnson and set in Trump Medieval
Roman by the Composing Room of Michigan, Inc. Printed in
the United States of America by the Vail-Ballou Press,
Binghamton, N. Y.

ISSN 0044–0078
ISBN for this issue 0–300–03897–6

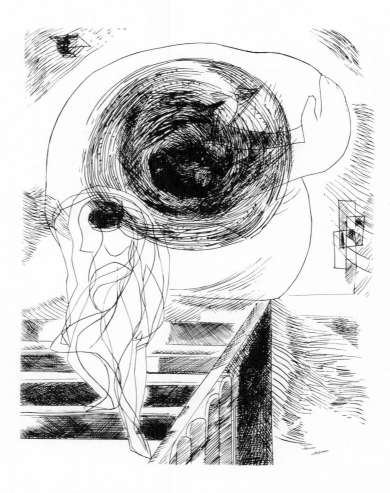

Engraving, *La Femme rompue* by Hélène de Beauvoir.
Reproduced with the kind permission of the artist.

HÉLÈNE V. WENZEL

Introduction

NOTES FROM A JOURNAL

Cambridge, MA, 12 August 1986
. . . so tomorrow it is, then: write the introduction to the Simone de Beauvoir YALE FRENCH STUDIES *issue!*

Cambridge, MA, 13 August 1986
   This morning I finished editing and typing the final list of contributors for YFS 72. *Then I proceeded to tidy up my study: I tossed out the articles I had long ago rejected; and those few first drafts of the articles accepted and reworked. Such relief at the reduced clutter! I carefully reshelved and reordered my books by and about Simone de Beauvoir— had a hard time not thumbing through the picture books yet again. Done. Well, almost. I sat down on the floor in front of the files with the proposal, my notes, and all the correspondence about the issue, expecting to finish in no time . . . .*
   Some three emotion-packed hours later, armed with pieces of those files, my Montblanc pen and a quadrille pad, I ran out of the house and up to Harvard Square; and I've ensconced myself in a cafe to "tackle" the intro. I realize, sitting here under an unusually beneficent New England sunny sky, that I've put off writing this as long as I possibly could . . . and for good reason. THIS IS THE INTRODUCTION I HAD HOPED I WOULD NOT BE WRITING! *I am reminded that as early as summer 1982, even as I went through the initial stages of outlining a proposal for an issue on Simone de Beauvoir, justifying it, having it approved by the editorial board of* YFS, *and beginning the search and inquiries about contributors, there was an underlying fear that I was working against time. "I don't want this to be a memorial issue," I*

repeated over and over again to myself, and sometimes out loud to others, with classically superstitious fears that by thinking it . . . . "Foolishness!" I would counter, silently hoping. Over these last years, this project has gone through many phases. The formal proposal letter to the YFS *Editorial Board, which I uncovered in my files this morning, was dated, coincidentally enough, 13 August 1982! But all the stages and phases and moments can now be put into only two:* BEFORE *and* AFTER *14 April 1986!*

BEFORE 14 APRIL 1986

When I first conceived of a *YFS* on Simone de Beauvoir, Sartre had already died, and the "Sartre after Sartre" issue was under way. I envisaged this as the companion issue, but a living tribute as well. The title I chose, "Witness to a Century" was deliberately open-ended: it was an explicit recognition that her autobiography "begins" back in 1908 with *Memoirs of a Dutiful Daughter* and goes up to 1970 with *All Said and Done;* and, although she claimed that *Adieux: A Farewell to Sartre* was not about herself, but about Sartre's last decade, we nonetheless have a certain account of a major focus of her life through 1980. In my title, too, was an implicit invocation that there be more to come.

Some four years, then, have gone into publication of this little volume: how to write an introduction that sketches a retrospective; how to do justice to all that has been involved in this? How, finally, to capture some essence of the energies that our hearts and minds brought to each article, and to the growing idea of a collection, a collective effort? At best this volume would be a work reflecting a spectrum of contemporary appreciations of a writer, thinker and woman whose life and works, over much of this century, and all of our lives, have become interwoven with our own. Where do I start?

Start at the beginning; start with yourself. When I first read *The Second Sex* as a freshman at Barnard College in 1961, I was not favorably impressed; on the contrary, much of what she had to say was truly terrifying to me: who would want to become one of those beleaguered creatures she called a "woman"? Almost a score of years later, this reader's response was reversed by multiple "objective" causes: a course I taught in 1978 at San Francisco State University on French Women Writers in which we studied the first autobiographical volumes of Simone de Beauvoir and Violette Leduc; the NEH Seminar I attended in Madison, Wisconsin, in the summer of 1979 on *écriture féminine* with Germaine Brée directing, and Elaine Marks close by; and the very provocative Fall 1979 conference "The Second Sex: Thirty Years Later" at N.Y.U., which catalyzed an explosion of new and revised readings of Simone de Beauvoir's work. Given my own feminist politics, I must admit that at that time I did not think hers were radical enough for me. But what fascinated me—as the interview amply illustrates—was Simone de Beauvoir, the autobiographer, and the representation of her as the muse and mentor, desired and unattainable, in the works of Violette Leduc. I wanted to know more about the literary and real-life relationship of these two antithetical contemporaries. That inquiry first found expression as a talk during the NEH seminar; and then as a more formal presentation at the December 1982 M L A special session on Simone de Beauvoir. During that time I revised my appreciation of Simone de Beauvoir's importance—thanks to the new feminist scholarship which followed the 1979 conference. This issue grew out of these significant moments. When I announced the Simone de Beauvoir issue at the 1982 M L A, I was on a panel with Yolanda Patterson, whom I knew to be at work on a book about Simone de Beauvoir, and Deirdre Bair, whom I had first heard at Harvard and who was working on an authorized biography of Simone de Beauvoir. I asked each of them to submit an article to the YFS issue. Ironically, it was to be these same two women who would share the "Simone de Beauvoir" panel table with me on 11 April 1986 at Stanford University.

In what now seems like eons ago, but was only the Spring of 1982, I read a new Yale French Department dissertation by Virginia Fichera. There, I first learned of Simone de Beauvoir's one and only play, "Les Bouches inutiles," recently translated and published as "Who Shall Die?" Later, I asked Virginia to revise and publish her study as an article. In "Simone de Beauvoir and The 'Woman Question': Les Bouches inutiles" Fichera deftly illustrates the timelessness of the themes in this play, written and produced almost a decade before The Second Sex, in occupied France.

Also at Yale another graduate student, Judith Butler, in Philosophy, was working on a dissertation in which Sartre and Beauvoir figured preeminently. In my search for multidisciplinary perspectives, I requested a piece by Butler. Her article on "Sex and Gender in Simone de Beauvoir's The Second Sex" focuses on the impact of Simone de Beauvoir's considerations of the complex interrelationships of body, nature, gender, and culture. As such, it fleshes out the more radical meanings embodied in the oft-repeated, oft-misunderstood "one is not born, but rather becomes, a woman."

Leaving Yale's halls, I cast my net wider in my search for interesting and provocative Simone de Beauvoir scholarship. Two articles sent me questing after Dorothy Kaufmann. Her "Simone de Beauvoir: Questions of Difference and Generation" gives a necessary rereading of Simone de Beauvoir's feminism as it has been called into question by contemporary theoretical writings that emerged with the French "Mouvement de Libération des Femmes" in the 1970s. She focuses particularly on Luce Irigaray and Hélène Cixous—and examines the limitations as well as the contributions of all of these theorists to the well-being of French feminisms. As would happen with many of the other new collegial relationships I made through working on the issue, I have since that first contact had occasion to meet with Dorothy at Mills College, where I was asked to speak in March 1985, shortly after that at the Columbia University "Simone de Beauvoir Colloquium" in April 1985; and most recently in another Harvard Square cafe in July when we shared grief, editorial considerations, and future work plans.

At one point shortly after the June 1983 National Women's Studies Association conference, I got two calls in one day from different colleagues urging me to get in touch with Margaret Simons whose eye-opening paper on what's missing from the Parshley translation of *The Second Sex* they said I would want to read and perhaps include. When I discovered that that paper had already been promised I asked her to follow her philosophical bent and submit something else. In "Beauvoir and Sartre: The Philosophical Relationship" Simons explores a subject that has "troubled" most scholars—feminists as well as nonfeminist: just what *was* the nature of the influence of Jean-Paul Sartre on Simone de Beauvoir's philosophical writings and, more to the point here, did Beauvoir influence Sartre, and how can we appreciate this influence on his thinking? What happened since I first contacted Peg Simons belongs to the utopia of collective feminist scholarship; we have begun a collaboration to translate and evaluate the importance of the missing, mistranslated, and otherwise loosely interpreted pieces of the original French *Le Deuxième Sexe* in Parshley's *The Second Sex*.

"Well," I thought, "surely the Beauvoir-Sartre relationship merits this special focus, but what about her relationships to women?" More specifically, what about the relationship with Violette Leduc that first prompted my own passionate curiosity? I knew that Isabelle de Courtivron was working on a book on Violette Leduc: had she, I queried, focused on the special relationship between France's most infamous "bâtarde" and her most "dutiful daughter"? Could she focus on the representation of Simone de Beauvoir in Leduc's work, so that we would see our writer/subject par excellence as the object of someone else's writing/desire? "From Bastard to Pilgrim: Rites and Writing for Madame" does just that. In addition, this unique study of a unique relationship provides vital answers to the newly opened areas of inquiry into women's enabling/writing relationships, and the attic of women's madness, even as it opens up more complex questions.

In the Spring of 1984 I decided that a special M L A session "Reading Simone de Beauvoir in the 1980s" would be an excellent forum for some of the articles whose drafts I was already reading, and for discovering others. In "Attachment and Separation in *The Memoirs of a Dutiful Daughter*" Catherine Portuges reads Simone de Beauvoir's first auto-biographical work in the light of new feminist, psychoanalytic studies of the as yet underexplored relationships between mothers and daughters, and between sisters as well. Portuges gives a fresh reading to the work and at the same time urges us to appreciate the ways in which this early text anticipates much of the contemporary theory on the subject.

The question of motherhood imposes itself in the writings of this woman who personally eschewed the role, and intellectually and politically avoided the concept. Yolanda Patterson, with whom I have shared many a platform and exchanged many a letter since our Madison seminar, has been at work on just such a book. Her article included here, "Simone de Beauvoir and the Demystification of Motherhood" carefully explores the many ways in which the author, in most of her fiction, as well as in her autobiographies, works out and assiduously reworks her own ideas and ambivalences about this multifaceted role that she has carefully avoided, but that most women assume more or less unthinkingly. Her characters are far from "unthinking" about their roles and it is difficult to say simply after reading these last two papers, that Simone de Beauvoir "rejects motherhood."

No publication on Simone de Beauvoir, written in the '80s, could be complete without the presence of something by Deirdre Bair who has been working on an authorized biography of the writer, and meeting with her regularly since the winter of 1981. In her many oral communications a certain virtuosity afforded her by frequent interviews was evident. Her article "Simone de Beauvoir: Politics, Language, and Feminist Identity" benefits from her dual roles as scholar and biographer; in it she brings Simone de Beauvoir's own voice to bear on questions of *engagement*, militancy, Sartre, writing, language, and feminism. Since she works closely with the spoken medium, Bair's article also illustrates some of the complexities involved in having a writer speak of her own writing. (These same problems obtain in an interview, of course, but there is no place for critical assessment in that genre.)

After some careful consideration, and a few chance telephone conversations, I decided to turn to some "original" sources. I wrote to Martha Evans, another NEH crony whom I knew to be working on a book of essays, in the psychoanalytic vein, about some of the writers we had studied together, including Violette Leduc and Simone de Beauvoir. Yes, she could write an article; and yes, she would be happy to participate on the M L A panel. "Murdering *L'Invitée:* Gender and Fictional Narrative" reconsiders the dichotomous relationship between textual, metaphysical creation, and physical, biological birth, as it is "narrated" in Simone de Beauvoir's first novel which, not incidentally, tells the story of a murder.

And I called Elaine Marks, whose early book, *Simone de Beauvoir: Encounters with Death* (RUTGERS, 1973), had informed my first re-readings of the author before the 1979 explosion, and whose sharp wit I had come to know more intimately since Madison. She was busily editing *Critical Essays on Simone de Beauvoir* (forthcoming, G. K. Hall), but was fascinated, she said, by the treatment of the body and of death in *La Cérémonie des adieux;* she would work on that for *YFS.* Perfect; and how would she like to participate in the special session of the M L A? I cannot think of a more fitting piece with which to close this small collection of essays than Marks's "Transgressing the (In)cont(in)ent Boundaries: The Body in Decline" in which *Adieux: A Farewell to Sartre* is read alongside Simone de Beauvoir's earlier works and contemporary critical studies of the body, to discover and offer a "new kind of content that . . . almost no one has any desire to read."

In this more or less chronological reconstruction of production then, I've reached the present. That skips over some rather major moments in the Before section, including my letter to Simone de Beauvoir, written in July 1983, in which I asked her for an interview, and her response to me, undated but postmarked 12 September 1983 from Paris. And the interview itself. Which follows this soon-to-be finished introduction.

NOTES FROM A JOURNAL:

Cambridge, MA, 14 August 1986

So much for the BEFORE *part of this introduction. I wonder, did Simone de Beauvoir have as much difficulty reconciling writing and truth and fiction when she readied her journals for publication?*

AFTER 14 APRIL 1986

Clearly BEFORE was mostly a long, gentle, joyous romp through the groves of feminism, academia, and feminist scholarship. AFTER has obviously been far from joyous, but it has nevertheless been filled with gentleness and the stronger sense of a community of scholars united by, and in spite of, forces greater than our minds or our hearts can control. In April, I went to California to participate in the conference on "Autobiography and Biography: Gender, Text and Context" sponsored by the Center for Research on Women at Stanford University, April 11–13, where I was to chair and comment at a session titled, simply, "Simone de Beauvoir." On this panel, Deirdre Bair would speak on "Samuel Beckett and Simone de Beauvoir: Toward a Methodology of Contemporary Biography;" and Yolanda Patterson would talk about "Simone de Beauvoir: Biographer of the Mandarins." "You will note," I said to a packed room in my introductory remarks, "that this is the only panel at this entire conference with one person's name as its title." And it was easy to appreciate, from the papers presented, and the commentary and discussion that followed, that we are dealing with a writer whose works loom large over all textual and contextual considerations. Planned to coincide with the conference, and executed almost single-handedly from studio to international post offices to Stanford's walls by Yolanda Patterson, (who wrote in longhand on the invitation she sent me, "I'm learning more about putting together an art exhibit than I care to know"), was a special exhibit of seventeen oil paintings and acrylics painted by Simone de Beauvoir's sister, Hélène de Beauvoir, accompanied by a series of graphics and family photographs and divided between the Office of the President, and the Center. In addition to the formal reception given for Hélène de Beauvoir at the opening of the exhibit on 10 April, there was a special banquet after the conference, at which we all honored one another. During the panel presentation I chaired, I had been deeply affected by her presence, and her uncanny resemblance to her sister. At the banquet I had further occasion to sit near her and encourage her to share family anecdotes with me and with the other conference participants, all of whom felt, as I did, that this was a privileged moment. As the memorial tributes of Bair and Patterson describe the transition between Before and After, it is clear however, that we all knew very different things at that moment.

After news of Simone de Beauvoir's death, I asked each contributor to write a personal piece for this journal: the articles, all written before, spoke for themselves, but did they wish to follow up with a personal reflection? These two, and Peg Simons's, as well as my own interspersed commentaries, reflect the various mute and voiced responses that news of Simone de Beauvoir's death provoked; and I can only shade in the textures of the conversations and their many nuances that were carried by telephone wires across the country over the next few days after the news. When, on 15 April I called my telephone answering machine in Cambridge from San Francisco, as I had been doing regularly for the days preceeding, I had a message from Elaine Marks, "Hélène, Simone has died. What shall we do?" And another from Peg Simons the next morning, "I don't think I can teach today. Call me if you can." I called Peg back, and left a message, sharing with her reflections on my own meeting with Hélène de Beauvoir, and armed with the facts of just what had been going on, which I had gotten from a very intimately involved Yolanda Patterson, I proffered them and my feelings to a voiceless machine. By the time I reached Elaine Marks two days later Jean Genêt had just died—"Hélène, they're all dead,"—prompting us to talk about the generations of French writers and thinkers we had each been "raised on." And so it went, from anecdote to anecdote, and realization to realization. At different moments we have all inspired, cheered, consoled, enlightened, and commiserated with each other, this bereaved family of American and feminist scholars.

And as I write this, I can picture the video tapes I saw at the April 1985 Columbia University colloquium, and I am reminded of how the tapes, the same ones Simone de Beauvoir had talked about during our interview, recalled her physical presence to me a year later, at the same time that they did indeed carry out her wishes to make *The Second Sex* a contemporary investigation. And I hear once more the voice which I just listened to as I translated the tapes of the interview. And I am made to think that a presence such as Simone de Beauvoir's in this twentieth century, does not cease to be a powerful force, even when the living person is no longer with us. If film and voice recording offer us the fictions of direct access and immediate presence, the written word offers us a more diffuse and timeless presence. The articles in this volume attest to the range and breadth of Simone de Beauvoir as a witness to our century, a witness who did not simply observe—as she did, perspicaciously, and more often than not observed what had gone unnoticed, or at least had remained unexamined before—but a witness who bears witness, who gives testimony, who writes of them and thereby alters commonly held notions by describing them anew; and by evaluating what she sees and what is less visible, even when it is the case more often than not, that these observations go against the grain, challenge the majority, and discover truths that unsettle the mighty, whether or not they acknowledge this. And she has made of her many readers witnesses as well.

NOTES FROM A JOURNAL

Cambridge, 18 August 1986
The intro is done! At least there's something ready for a close reading and some editing. Time to drive down to Yale with all these precious manuscript pages . . . . I wonder: does this constitute an introduction? Is it appropriate for such a publication? How did she do it! Well, I suppose if it's the memorial introduction I didn't want to have to write, it is also, in the last analysis, the introduction I simply had to write. I think, though, I need to make a more formal transition into the texts of the volume.

In this collection of articles, we have both touched upon and delved deeply into many of the different personae with whom Simone de Beauvoir identified herself, or, across time and geography, came to be identified: existentialist, socialist, companion to J. -P. Sartre, essayist, autobiographer, writer of fiction, controversial woman and, since the early 1970s, feminist. However, it is undeniable that these articles, as far-ranging and diverse as their various foci may be, when read as a collection, reflect decidedly feminist and contemporary revisions of the life, work, and influence of Simone de Beauvoir. Such is the strength, which some may call a weakness, of the collection we now must offer as a tribute, not directly to Simone de Beauvoir as we had hoped to, but to her memory, and to our readers of all schools and persuasions.

I hope I have communicated the quality of collegial collaboration that the gathering of articles for this special issue provided. As with most publications, however, this one owes at least as much to the people who helped put it together, as to those who first created its contents. I have thoroughly enjoyed working closely with Liliane Greene on the entire issue, and have learned much from her careful and judicious editing of the texts. Without Peggy McCracken's expert handling of these texts, and the all-around support of the administrative staff of the French Department—Kathy Seidel, Julie Bender and Paula Nordhem, our task would have been all the more formidable. For reading and typing from often execrably hand-scrawled notes, special thanks are tendered to

Linda Anderson, senior administrative assistant of the Women's Studies Program where my other half resides; her presence—both material and spiritual—has been of inestimable value to me over the years. Finally, I would like to thank the French Department, the Women's Studies Program faculty, and my students for providing much of the impetus and support for this project.

I. Bearing Witness

Chère Madame

Votre projet m'intéresse
beaucoup et je serai très
heureuse d'avoir un entretien
avec vous; mais le plus
tard possible, à cause d'un
long travail en cours. Si
janvier peut aller, fin janvier
serait mieux encore.

J'attends de vos nouvelles

pour que nous précisions la
date.

Tout mon soutien pour
votre projet et bien
amicalement.

S de Beauvoir

Letter from Simone de Beauvoir to the editor.

HÉLÈNE V. WENZEL

Interview with Simone de Beauvoir

We had agreed to meet at six o'clock P.M. at her home.* A few days before this meeting, I had left at her door an outline of the contents for the *Yale French Studies* special issue, and an indication of the kinds of questions and the areas of interest that I would focus on. I spent the morning and early afternoon of the day of the interview alternately reviewing and honing the script of the questions I would ask, and trying to pretend that what would take place later was not out of the ordinary.

At six o'clock, *précises*, I knocked at her door. The woman who opened it and ushered me inside was in every way, except perhaps for the speed of her gait as she went to put my floral offering into a vase, an ageless, luminous presence. She was at once familiar, from the countless pictures I had seen, and different. She was much shorter than I had expected her to be, and I had to acknowledge that the effects of her writings on me had magnified her physical size in my imagination! Framed by her light blue turban and her blue sweater, her eyes were direct and penetrating. Looking through my journal to which I've turned to help me remember, I see that I remarked on her voice ". . . how lovely and sonorous Simone de Beauvoir's voice is! Rich, sonorous, surprisingly not old or hardened. . . . 'Quelle surprise!' I think I expected a crackly, rich, but weary voice." I spent the next hours floating back and forth between two planes: the immediate situation of the interview—our questions, answers and asides; and what I call my "I am a camera"

*This interview took place on 15 March 1984, at the apartment of Simone de Beauvoir, 11 bis, rue Schoelcher, in Paris. The text, in its original French was transcribed from tape by Françoise Moinet and translated by Hélène V. Wenzel. Some extracts from this interview, translated by Hélène V. Wenzel and Linda Gardiner, previously appeared in *The Women's Review of Books* 3, no. 6 (March 1986): 11, with the permission of *Yale French Studies*.

perspective. Perched in an upper corner of the room, I had an aerial view: colors, shapes, Simone de Beauvoir on her divan, and me, seated diagonally across from her, on a little red, stuffed chair. Leaving the apartment and walking back to the metro I was still in two worlds. In my intimate world, the child in me marvelled at the distances I had traveled since I first started learning French in 1957! The feminist scholar was busily digesting what had just happened. Critics have gone so far as to criticize Simone de Beauvoir for the didacticism in her writings. In person, this assurance and certainty took on different qualities. Never had I heard anyone speak so forcefully or with such unassuming authority. She said what she thought, she would do what she thought best; and she was clearly very much at ease with her thoughts and her deeds, with herself. She was wholly and actively involved in every project that she supported; and when she didn't care, she was adamant about that, too. "Does that 'authority of experience' and that ease come to us with age?" I wondered then. As my probing and sometimes impertinent questioning reveals, and as other encounters related in this issue support, Simone de Beauvoir at seventy-six was very much a force to be reckoned with. And she still is.

Hélène V. Wenzel   Let me begin by asking you if you have any questions about *Yale French Studies*, about what we hope to present in this special issue.

Simone de Beauvoir   No, none. I should like you to explain it all to me, but I have no particular questions. . . . The subjects of the proposed articles seem interesting to me.

HVW   Good. Well, briefly, I had decided to edit a special issue of *Yale French Studies* dedicated to you, a writer, a political figure, a woman, who has witnessed and written about over half a century's worth of history. The articles and scope would be focused on your treatment of the "woman question," which has come to be called, as well, the "feminine question," the "feminist question." Which of these do you prefer as a description of the question? After all these years, is there one which pleases you more or better describes your subject matter?

SdeB   I don't know. I've spoken of women, I've also spoken of many other things. As a result, I'd prefer that a focus on my writing and my work not be absolutely limited . . . to the woman question.

HVW   How do you estimate the effects of your complete works over almost a century? It's a very broad question. But to begin . . .

SdeB   Yes, that is too broad. My complete work. . . . I'm not sure exactly what you mean. Do you mean my feminist works, or the entire body of my work?

HVW   Your feminist work.

SdeB   I think that this feminist work was not very important at the time it first appeared. It aroused much indignation among male readers; I was astonished to encounter this from Camus and from some others. I had the support of Sartre, of course, and of my best friends; but there were some men I would have expected to agree with me, like Camus, whose reactions astonished me. (Mauriac's on the other hand did not.) But there was a lot of hostility, and that's when I realized that there really was a macho hostility toward women, a very vehement hostility.

Having said that, I think that the book at that time was a success with a great many individual women. I received many letters encouraging me, telling me that the book had helped them understand their situation. I even saw some women psychiatrists who told me that they made their patients—including working-class women, women without much education—read the book; and that these women derived great benefit from it. But I would say that its success was rather private in character.

When feminism reawakened in France, around 1970, at that time women didn't have much by way of a solid theoretical basis for their beliefs, and so they appropriated *The Second Sex* and used it as a weapon in their struggle. But both in my conception of it, and in objective fact, when it first appeared it was strictly a serious study, though not an academic one, very objective and not at all combative.

HVW   What made you take up such a study in postwar France?

SdeB   Well, it was because I wanted to talk about myself, and because I realized that in order to talk about myself I had to understand the fact that I was a woman.

HVW   So might one say that a book was a kind of first stab at an autobiography?

SdeB   That's true. It was before I had begun to write my autobiography.

HVW   An embryonic autobiography?

SdeB   It was in order to understand myself, and to do so I had to understand the nature of women's lives in general. But there was nothing polemical about it, it was a very objective, very detached study.

HVW   And then there was another stage, when the translation was published in the United States, and later even, when a paperback was published. So there were successive stages of response to your book.

SdeB   Yes, that's so.

HVW   Your interest in the woman question and feminism dates back a long time before the publication of *The Second Sex*. For example, your novel *She Came to Stay*, published in 1943, and the play *The Useless Mouths*. And also the book which you've just published, *When Things of the Spirit Come First* . . .

SdeB   Yes.

HVW   Could you speak a little about *The Useless Mouths* and *Things of the Spirit?*

SdeB   Yes, it was not at all from a feminist point of view that I undertook *When Things of the Spirit Come First*. It was from my experience and my experience was obviously a woman's experience. So, in *Things of the Spirit*, I described women as I had encountered them. That's all. Because I was much closer all the same to women, my best friends were women, and I was much closer to women than to men, in spite of the fact that my primary relatonship was with a man. This didn't mitigate the fact that for understanding, sympathy, personal experience . . . and then, it was my own experience that translated itself across all these women characters whose traps I had thought to escape. I thought they lied to themselves in a certain way and that I . . . I had found a way not to lie like them. It's not about women as much as it was about my experience that I wrote *When Things of the Spirit Come First*.

HVW   And *The Useless Mouths* . . .

SdeB   It wasn't so much a question about women. It was a question which had struck me while I was reading old Italian chronicles about the coexistence of the living and those condemned to die—old people as well as children and women—which isn't a particularly feminist theme.

HVW   But there was nonetheless a difference in the attitudes of the women and the men, that is to say the young men, not the old men or the boys.

SdeB   Oh yes! It was the men who were obviously going to decide to sacrifice the useless mouths. . . . And the women were ranged among the useless mouths. But it's not a play that I'm happy about. Besides, I don't think it was a very good play, and also it's not a play to which I've attached much importance.

HVW   It's the first and the last one you wrote.

SdeB   It's the only play I've written, yes.

HVW   Was it the critical response that made you decide not to write more for the theatre?

SdeB   No, it was because I realized that the theatre wasn't my best mode of expression, that there was a kind of lie—that there are lies in literature, and that those of the theatre didn't suit me. That the lie in the novel suited me better; and finally, that the truth of autobiography suited me better yet.

HVW   Do you think that there is a genre particularly well-suited to women writers in general?

SdeB   Oh no! I think that it depends on each woman.

HVW   In the early seventies or thereabouts, you said that there was, and would probably continue to be, an explosion of autobiographical writing by women, and that this was a good thing. Do you find that this has actually happened, and that it has been a positive development?

SdeB   There has certainly been an autobiographical explosion; but very often women think that all they need do is to tell their story, which is almost always the story of an unhappy childhood. And so they tell it, and it has no literary value whatsoever, neither in its style, nor in the universality which it ought to contain. So there are many, many auto-biographies which publishers reject, which they don't want to buy.

HVW   What about the publishing of personal journals? I've found many of these disappointing.

SdeB   Very disappointing. There are extraordinary cases, like that of Violette Leduc, who, exceptionally, was wonderfully successful. . . . There have been a few remarkable cases—but really, women have gone overboard with them, it's made it too easy for them—to think that because they're women their stories will be interesting.

HVW   Exactly, it seems that women became interesting (to women) for the first time, and they believed that they could write anything at all about their lives and it would also be interesting. A propos of *When*

Things of the Spirit Come First, however, it was originally turned down by Grasset and Gallimard, and now you've decided about forty years later to have it published. Their response to the book . . . did you refuse to change something? Did they ask you to revise the manuscript?

SdeB   No, they offered criticism which I found valuable, because, really, these were separate stories, each of them more or less attached to the others, but without a really solid construction. I think it was a good thing that it wasn't published first because it was really a beginner's book, and I think that the first book they did publish, *She Came to Stay,* is really very different, much more structured, better constructed, and from my own point of view, much deeper. That is to say, in *She Came to Stay* I described an experience that was much more personal, and in which I was much more engaged.

HVW   Of course. So for the first work, *When Things of the Spirit Come First,* we had to wait some forty-odd years?

SdeB   Well, finally, that's to say, when I reread the manuscript, and when friends who like my work read the manuscript, I saw that it interested them, and I said to myself that for a certain number of people who are interested in me and in my literary career, the book could be an interesting document. It was at the time that Claude Francis and Fernande Gontier were working on a book on my works (*Les Ecrits de Simone de Beauvoir* [Paris: Gallimard, 1979]) in which they presented excerpts from everything I had written. So, everything considered, in going all the way back to the beginning, I said to myself that perhaps that manuscript deserved to be printed separately, as a document for readers who were very interested in my literary career.

HVW   Yes, it's true. I for one found a different voice in the book from the voice I thought I knew from your other works. It's a much more naive voice in some ways.

SdeB   Much younger!

HVW   Much younger, yes, that's it.

SdeB   Much more maladroit?

HVW   Let me backtrack a bit. When Sartre was in prison during the war you said that for you at that period, to write was an act of faith and an act of hope. And when he got out of prison, the two of you said that during the war writing was an act of resistance. What has writing been for you over the years? Resistance? Act of faith? What else?

SdeB   First of all, before the war writing was simply something natural for me, as I explained in my memoirs. I wanted to be a writer, I saw nothing better, especially for a woman, than to be a writer. I knew even then that there had been women writers who had succeeded quite well in gaining prestige, like Colette or Madame de Noailles and many others. And then, after all, it was my job since at the same time I was working on literature and philosophy; I was in the university. So it was absolutely normal for me to want to write.

HVW   Feminists have been raising questions about the relation of women and writing: do you think that writing, for women, is a way of wresting power from men, from the world?

SdeB   I don't think that's the way you experience things when you are a writer. You write because there is something you want to express, not so much in order to compete with men—at least in my case I never felt that. And I think that for most women, when they write important books, they don't do it in order to support a cause but to express what they have to say. The desire to communicate experience, that is something in itself; they do it as well—or badly—as they can, but I don't see at all that there is any question of power there, and I don't believe that there is.

HVW   What do you think of the notion of "écriture féminine" as it is invoked, for example by Hélène Cixous in *Le Rire de la Méduse?*

SdeB   Oh, I am not in sympathy with that at all. We need to steal the tools, women have to take back the tool that is language, but women cannot remake language. No more than the proletariat who wants the state to wither away can remake our consciousness. . . . We have to steal the tool, but not destroy it, in my opinion. And in any case, I find the word-games feminist writers play very feeble. Of course a woman will mark her work with her femaleness, because she's a woman and because when one writes one writes with one's entire being. So a woman will write with her whole being, and therefore with her femaleness too. But to feel the need to play games, to cut words up, for example, I don't like that at all, I don't find it the slightest bit interesting.

HVW   I was going to ask you what you think of the work of Monique Wittig [whose work is characterized by experimentation with grammar and page design].

SdeB   I found her first book, The *Opoponax,* very very good, written in the ordinary language everyone speaks. She knew how to get inside the skin of a child in a way that very few people, men or women, have managed to do. But I find that since then, with this doctrinaire side of her, cutting up and changing words around to show that it's "female," I don't find that interesting at all. . . .

HVW   What do you think of the work of theoreticians like Luce Irigaray and Julia Kristeva?

SdeB   I hardly know Kristeva's work; I've found very interesting things in Irigaray, but I find her too ready to adopt the Freudian notion of the inferiority of women. She's too influenced by that. Although I admire Freud on a great many points, I find that in the case of women, as he said himself, there's a dark continent; he understood nothing of what women want. Anyone who wants to work on women has to break completely with Freud. . . . But all of them, even Irigaray, they've always begun with Freud's postulates.

HVW   So these women return to Freud, which I find quite depressing, because I think there is something more to say without going backward.

SdeB   Absolutely. Freud puts woman in an inferior position, which really astonishes me on the part of feminists.

HVW   I find that there is in many feminist works, not all thank goodness, a return to masculinist thought in all the important disciplines like philosophy, psychology, and of course psychoanalysis, among others. Do you find, in the books that you are constantly sent, this kind of return, a kind of thinking that has changed in the last years?

SdeB   No, I haven't read many theoretical books on this. French women write very little in this vein. They write mostly—what I receive—about what we spoke of a little while ago, their autobiographies, or novels, often works which don't really question the problems of women.

HVW   Which of your works do you like best? Can you choose?

SdeB   It's difficult to say if one likes or doesn't like one's own books.

HVW   Well, then, which one(s) do you consider most important?

SdeB   I know that *The Second Sex* has been very successful. I think it's the most important for women. But, personally, I have a great affection for *She Came to Stay*, which is my first book, in fact, my first successful book, and also for the *Mandarins*. And then I really like my autobiography, because I feel that the ensemble of my autobiographical works wholly complements and completes my position on women. The autobiographies complete my thoughts about women by telling how I lived, how I worked, how I won on certain points and lost on others, etc. In sum, I'm very attached to the autobiographical books.

HVW   And there is a sort of continuity with, a follow-up to your autobiography, even in the book *Adieux: A Farewell to Sartre*.

SdeB   Yes.

HVW   It seems to me that your voice, your treatment of your relationship with Sartre, was much more open in this book. There was more frankness in this book than there had been before.

SdeB   That's because before I was speaking about what concerned my own life, and here, *Adieux* is a book written about Sartre. So it's very different. I've not related anything during these last ten years—what could I have done other than to be beside him? And I've recounted his story, in these last ten years, I've not told mine.

HVW   However, there is your voice, a voice much clearer, much more subjective, almost . . .

SdeB   Perhaps.

HVW   . . . than in your own autobiography, where you tried to keep some more distance.

SdeB   Perhaps. I don't see that myself. But the subject isn't the same, it wasn't my autobiography this time, it was about Sartre's last years.

HVW   In the seventeenth century, there was the "querelle des femmes" between men and women; and today we've seen debates and ruptures between women. For example, there was this complex situation of the "MLF," and the publications by Des Femmes, and Antoinette Fouque, and "Psych et Po" . . . What did you think of all this?

SdeB   Oh, it's not very interesting, all that. They were women who wanted to have a certain kind of power, and because they were very rich, they wanted to have the copyright to all the books, they wanted the trademark "MLF" all for themselves. Other women were against this. Really, I wasn't very involved in any of this, although I believe I wrote a preface to a book titled *L'Histoire d'une Imposture* [*History of an Imposture*], which my friends published about the whole affair. But I was not very impassioned over that particular story.

HVW   I went to the bookstore Des Femmes the other day, and I found an excellent and interesting collection of women's books from many countries.

SdeB   Oh yes, that's true.

HVW   There seems to be a sort of monopoly on women's writings by Des Femmes.

SdeB   I think they've done a very good job there, certainly.

HVW   Yes. And I think we have to accept the good job they've done [in collecting and making available all these women's works], in spite of their politics and what they've tried to do elsewhere.

SdeB   Certainly.

HVW   There was also a difficult situation about different political positions concerning the publication of *Questions Féministes* and *Nouvelles Questions Féministes*. [As official editor in chief, what did you think of this?]

SdeB   Yes, there were difficulties, because there were women in *QF* who didn't accept that a woman could be heterosexual and also be a feminist. So there was a big disagreement about it. There were the homosexuals, women—what did they call themselves—radical homo-sexuals, who didn't want to admit that heterosexual and homosexual women could work together. There were homosexual women who agreed that they could work with heterosexual women. And finally, there was a rupture: *QF* ceased publication and *Nouvelle QF* came about.

HVW   And you decided to remain editor in chief of *Nouvelles Questions Feministes?*

SdeB   Oh, yes!, because I was a very good friend of Christine Delphy, who had been a creator of *Questions Féministes*, and who shares my belief, that a woman can be a feminist and a heterosexual. Without that, if we limit feminism to homosexual women, then it's true that it doesn't at all interest the whole human race. . . . This was a small event without much importance.

HVW   Well . . .

SdeB   It wasn't a very big deal. Certainly it was too bad that *Questions Féministes* lost several original collective members when it became *Nouvelles Questions Féministes*. And there were some smaller ruptures, I think, with [other women who had worked closely with *QF*].

HVW   In the States over the last decade, there has been a large increase in the numbers of voices raised, and in the writings emerging, from women of color. Both individually and collectively, these loud, clear, and multiethnic voices have sought to remind us—white, predominantly university women who too often think we speak for all women and who define feminism in our writings—that the women's fight is much more complex than either we, Betty Friedan or *Ms* magazine seem to think it is, and write about it. Is there a similar situation in France, have other voices, other writings begun to manifest themselves?

SdeB   There aren't many, there aren't many women who speak. . . . Yes, there have been women who have spoken, for example, about the problem of excision (clitoredectomy), which is a particularly African problem and there have been a number of books about this. Renée Saurel, for example, has written a big book on this; Benoîte Groult, who is a very well-known woman in France, has also spoken much on this, and there have been groups, both Western and African, who have met to combat the problem of excision. And there is presently much talk about this problem.

HVW   That is very interesting, because in the States, some women have begun to write and to speak out against these manifestos decrying excision. There are Black women, and African women who have begun to say that for Western women to look at African women's problems . . .

SdeB   . . . . It has nothing to do with Western women, yes, that's it. I've heard that. But there are nevertheless African women who say that this problem belongs as much to Western women as to others, because it's a question of human rights.

HVW   Exactly.

SdeB   . . . and it's not a question . . . and there's a kind of racism, on the contrary, in not wanting to look at these sorts of conditions. . . . Because that means that deep down one doesn't care what happens to little black girls, and there are about thirty thousand a year who undergo excision, and to find that trivial, finally, not to deal with that, that proves that we think that it's fine for them, naturally, we don't want any of it. And it's much more feminist, logical and universal, and not racist, to be involved in these sorts of questions. There's a very violent movement in France about this.

HVW   That's very informative, because the movement (against clitoredectomy) has lost some of its strength in the United States because of these voices raised against the first protests. I was at an international conference where there were women from many Third World countries [1982, at the Simone de Beauvoir Institute, Montreal] And I was very disappointed by the conference, because I found that the women who were there, evidently sent by their governments . . .

SdeB   Oh, yes, that's what I was told.

HVW   . . . were the voices of their respective governments.

SdeB   Yes, that's it.

HVW   So that what we heard . . .

SdeB   . . . weren't the voices of the women, but the voices of their ministers, etc.

HVW   Exactly.

SdeB   Oh, yes. I have been keeping up to date on these sorts of meetings . . . and even in Mexico, and at many other such international meetings. Yes, it's been pretty scandalous.

HVW   I understand that as a closing of these last designated Ten Years of Women, there will be a huge conference in Nairobi. Are you planning to attend this?

SdeB   Oh, no! It's been a long time since I've left France to attend that kind of event. I find that nothing of great interest really happens at them.

HVW   It's too bad, because these are, after all, women coming together, but they represent . . .

SdeB   Yes, that's it.

HVW   . . . their governments, when it comes to it.

SdeB   Generally, they represent men.

HVW   You've been friends with several women writers (*femmes écrivains*)—I don't like the term "femme écrivain," but there's nothing better in French.

SdeB   No, there aren't many other ways to designate that, we don't say *"écrivaines"* . . .

HVW   That I don't like at all! But, for example, there was Clara Malraux, and Nathalie Sarraute . . .

SdeB   Oh, no! I was never Clara Malraux's friend.

HVW   Not at all?

SdeB   Oh no.

HVW   You did meet her, didn't you, or . . .

SdeB   Two or three times, but we never spoke.

HVW   But Sarraute, others?

SdeB   Sarraute, a very little bit, at the beginning, for about a year, I saw her often enough, but not much.

HVW   Did you feel, early in your writing career, an affinity with writers?

SdeB   No, not especially.

HVW   Not even with other women writers?

SdeB   No. With, well, with some minor writers. I was very friendly with Colette Audry, who wrote very few things. But that was because we had been friends at the lycée in Rouen; we had been there together, we had met there, she wrote, and then we had the same political ideas, and we remained friends, we saw each other a great deal. But she's not a very well-known woman writer. The one I knew the best was Violette Leduc.

HVW   Yes, and I want very much to ask you about her, but let's wait a while, because I have a great number of questions about her. Who are the women writers you prefer today, the French writers, the Americans, others?

SdeB   Oh, that's difficult to say. There are two women whom I admire a lot: the Italian writer Elsa Morante, and then, the English writer, Doris Lessing.

HVW   Oh, yes, Doris Lessing, that's a very interesting choice.

SdeB   She's one of the women who most interests me among living writers today.

HVW   No French women writers?

SdeB   Not really, no.

HVW   What about Christiane Rochefort?

SdeB   Oh! I really like her. I like certain of her books. . . . It's been a long time since I read anything of hers; I really admire *Les Petits Enfants du siècle* (Paris: Grasset, 1961).

HVW   Oh yes. I liked that book tremendously, too. And I had the good fortune to meet her in California when she came to the States. And which male writers do you read?

SdeB   Not many male writers at the moment grab my interest very much.

HVW   What about French intellectuals, those leftists who write, for example Philippe Sollers?

SdeB   Oh, Sollers, he doesn't interest me at all.

HVW   Oh. Well then let's finally get to Violette Leduc, a very special case of a woman writer and a friend of yours. She is interesting both from the point of view of her life and her work. In fact, I've presented a paper about your friendship with Leduc, as revealed in both of your books. It was much easier to speak of her feeling for you because she's really overflowing with expression of friendship while you are . . .

SdeB   . . . much more reserved.

HVW   Yes, ever so much more reserved. In *All Said and Done* you spent about ten pages describing this friendship, and you were in fact reading the proofs of the book when Leduc died [1972].

SdeB   That's true.

HVW   There has recently appeared a play from Canada called *La Terre est Trop Courte, Violette Leduc*. It appears very interesting; in fact, I just bought it here in Paris.

SdeB   Oh, yes, that's the play where there's a meeting between me and Nathalie Sarraute . . .

HVW   Yes, that's it.

SdeB   I found it very bad. I've even written quite frankly to the author that I was very disappointed. And I told her that it could not be shown in Paris, it would be . . . people would find it ridiculous.

HVW   Yes, in fact, I found that there was a certain interpretation of your rapports. . . . And because the author really wanted to say something particular about women writers, she put words in your mouth . . .

SdeB   Yes.

HVW   . . . which were very astonishing! In any event, you certainly played a very important and decisive role in Leduc's coming to writing, or at least in her birth as an author. This is a question that has haunted me over the years, and while it may be impertinent, I must ask it now that I can. You had always been her first reader: what were your intellectual and emotional reactions to your own omnipresence in her works? When you read a manuscript like *L'Affamée* for the first time, where you were inscribed as "Madame" . . .

SdeB   There had been a book before that, her first one, where I wasn't at all present . . .

HVW   Yes. *L'Asphyxie.*

SdeB   And I wasn't in that book at all.

HVW   Yes, and you took care of getting it published . . .

SdeB   Oh yes. I found it quite good. . . . I suggested some changes, which she did in a very intelligent fashion, and I proposed it to Camus, who accepted it immediately, who also found it very good. . . . There, in that book, there was a great literary quality, something I always found remarkable in Violette Leduc.

HVW   And then in *L'Affamée*, which I find incredible. . . . The emotions she describes are rather neurotic, even psychotic.

SdeB   Oh yes!

HVW   But what was your response reading these pages?

SdeB   It was mostly a defensive reaction. I defended myself against her because she was making me into a myth, and I didn't want to become her myth, understandably; it was like that, a myth.

HVW   And she continued this mythification . . .

SdeB   Underneath it all there never was a real communication between us. I couldn't talk to her about things that interested me, I couldn't speak to her about anything whatsoever.

HVW   Do you mean that in relation to her manuscripts?

SdeB   Oh, no! Oh, yes, on the subject of her manuscripts I always could. Yes, on the contrary, we could work very well on the manuscripts. But I couldn't talk to her about things that were important to me. That didn't interest her, she didn't listen to me.

HVW   Do you think that was due to a certain narcissism in Leduc?

SdeB   Oh, yes, I think she was terribly narcissistic, which resulted in her never truly being interested in anyone.

HVW   Yes, but your omnipresence in her books, that must have shocked you.

SdeB   It didn't shock me, it didn't upset me emotionally either, because it was after all a lot of literary "hype" (*truquage*).

HVW   Yes, well, I found that in all ways Leduc was your opposite. It was she who said so, in fact, in the contrast she described in your names . . . in the titles of your books. . . . In the end, it seems to me that there is a sort of response, a point/counterpoint between your two bodies of work.

SdeB   Yes, if you like, yes.

HVW   For a last question on Leduc, perhaps. In *L'Affamée* and in *La Folie en tête* [*Mad in Pursuit*], Leduc wrote of a "schoolgirl's letter," that she sent you, and of your response. She wrote that you answered her, "My life is elsewhere," and you called the feelings for you that she had described in the letter "a mirage." And that letter has always fascinated me. Was it in fact a love letter to you?

SdeB   It was that more or less, I think. . . . I don't remember it too well, it was more or less . . . in fact the beginning of the myth, so I had to tell her that it was all mythic, that it wasn't my reality.

HVW   Yes, in fact you very gently put an end to her dreams, but you never took back your friendship . . .

SdeB   Oh, no . . .

HVW   . . . your help, your support . . .

SdeB   Oh, no, never . . .

HVW   . . . for her, as a writer.

SdeB   Quite simply, I wanted to cut that mythmaking off at its start, so that it would never be a question of idolatry, and that she wouldn't come to invade me, either. Besides, she was always very, very discreet with me. It was all the others who knew her who suffered greatly from her outbursts, her exigencies . . . but she was always very, very discreet with me.

HVW   There were many other ruptures, however, with other women . . .

SdeB   With Nathalie Sarraute, for example.

HVW   And Colette Audry, too.

SdeB   And with Colette Audry, more or less.

HVW   And she wrote about all of these in her books, of course.

SdeB   With almost everyone, almost everyone.

HVW   And with Jean Genet as well, in a very . . .

SdeB   With Jean Genet, also, in a very, very tragic fashion.

HVW   But you were almost her guardian at the end of her life. Was there nobody else . . .

SdeB   There wasn't much else. She had a few friends, Madeleine Castaing, for example, and there was the guy she loved, the homosexual she loved, whose name was . . . Jacques Guérin, who was a very rich guy, but who treated her quite badly. Because she bothered him, she asked for too much, and he was a little miserly.

HVW   Yes, all true. And you knew about her cancer, while she didn't know for a time.

SdeB   No, she didn't know at first, she could hope . . . but you know: what do people know and not know in those kinds of situations? We don't know. . . . But she did have a breast removed—that she knew.

HVW   Yes, of course. Was this not a kind of rerun of what you had described in *A Very Easy Death* between you and your mother? . . .

SdeB   No, there wasn't much similarity, it was something entirely different.

HVW   Yes, of course, something else entirely, but to be you, in circumstances where you know something about someone else who is dying, that's a big responsibility.

SdeB   Yes, but that took a long time. Violette Leduc must have, I'm not sure, she must have had another five or six years of life left from the time that I first learned that she had cancer.

HVW   In the States, feminist critics have come to speak of "enabling relationships," relationships that make something else possible. It seems to me that there was this sort of rapport between you and Violette Leduc. It's you who gave her a certain kind of support . . .

SdeB   Yes, certainly I did. When she was psychologically ill, it was I who sent her to a clinic where I had her undergo sleep cures. I took charge of her, yes, surely. All the while defending myself from her, you understand . . .

HVW   Yes, that's what I could never quite understand, because I saw there was this defensiveness, a certain distancing that she even describes in her books. Because when she related what you'd said, what you'd done, there was clearly . . .

SdeB   Certainly.

HVW   And how was she able to continue in this way without there being a rupture between you?

SdeB   Oh, no, there was no such thing.

HVW   I found that very surprising. Surely an important aspect of Violette Leduc's life and her writing was her lesbianism. The question of lesbianism was also at the origin of the split between *Questions Féministes* and *Nouvelles Questions Féministes.* You talked about lesbianism in an interview with Alice Schwarzer, translated and published in *Ms* magazine [August, 1983]. And you had treated the subject of lesbianism in *The Second Sex* in 1949 in a much more equitable and comprehensive fashion than other similar studies of that period. And at that time you already knew Leduc and other lesbians in France. Did you base your own study on these acquaintances?

SdeB   Oh, no, never. I think I knew. . . . I think it was really pretty superficial, what I said about lesbianism. I did know some lesbians, but not many. I knew Violette Leduc, but she had never spoken to me about her own sexual life, because she was ambivalent . . .

HVW   Oh, yes, that was clear.

SdeB   She had also had emotional, nonsexual adventures, and sexual adventures with men. She was especially in love with homosexuals, in fact, it was all quite strange these male homosexuals. And no, *The Second Sex* was not based on any of this, but rather on more or less theoretical treatments of the question.

HVW   Did you base your study on other studies? Did you find any other valuable guides?

SdeB   No doubt I did, but I can't recall them now.

HVW   And today, thirty-five years later, how would you write that same chapter? Would it be the same, different?

SdeB   Oh, I don't know at all. I think I would write it differently, but I have no idea what I would say about it.

HVW   But there would no doubt be some changes.

SdeB   Oh yes, there would surely be changes, because I would re-think the question . . .

HVW   In light of all that has happened since . . .

SdeB   I know much more now, and based on what I now know, on my experiences of lesbians, and on many other things, of course, I would surely write it differently. . . . Besides, there's a whole lesbian literature now that didn't exist then . . . the only book I had read about it was probably *The Well of Loneliness* which is, literarily speaking, a very bad book even if it's interesting. Now there are piles of books, there's been Mallet-Joris, and Violette Leduc . . . there's been many, many others, too. I forget . . . there's been Kate Millett. . . . There have been quite a lot of books.

HVW   Yes, and it's all quite fascinating, because there has, indeed, been a pile of such books, and certain of them are worthless. Taking the question further, in matters of friendship between women, do you think that there are boundaries one can easily cross over between friendship and lesbianism. Do you find this possibility "normal," logical?

SdeB   Yes, I think there are very, very easy movements between the two. From physical tenderness to lesbianism, per se. I think one could very easily slide from one side to the other, there aren't the same barriers as between a man and woman.

HVW   Do you think that male/female relationships are extraordinarily different from female/female ones?

SdeB   That I don't know. . . . According to the books I've seen, I've seen that there are also as many stories of terrible jealousies, authoritarianism, and I'm speaking of Kate Millett's books as well, in woman-to-woman relationships as man-to-woman relationships. It doesn't seem to me to be so very very privileged, except perhaps in some particular instances. But there are also heterosexual relationships, where everything goes very well. I think that, in any event, a couple that endures, whether it be two women, two men, or a man and a woman, is a difficult enterprise. But there are some, there are; but two people of the same sex don't necessarily avoid all the traps of a couple or a married life.

HVW   And there are other problems, of competition . . .

SdeB   That's true, it seems to me.

HVW   Can a woman be friends with a man? . . .

SdeB   Oh, yes, surely.

HVW   . . . . Where there's no question of sexual relations?

SdeB   Oh, surely.

HVW   Could you speak about your friendships with women today? Are there very important women in your life, like Sylvie Le Bon?

SdeB   Yes, that's a friendship that's very important.

HVW   And what are the essential rapports between women, the things that you yourself find very important?

SdeB   Well, understanding, tenderness. . . . I don't know, the same things as in any successful relationship, finally.

HVW   You mean the same qualities?

SdeB   Yes, in all successful relationships, obviously. I don't see all that much difference between my relationship with Sartre and my relationship with Sylvie Le Bon. It's not the same thing, because Sartre and I were the same age, and she is a woman much younger than I, and so it's different. But, all the same, when there's a successful rapport, there has to be generosity on the part of each person involved, let's see, an expectation of the other person, an understanding, and all kinds of similar qualities.

HVW   And are you presently friends with other women writers? For example, whenever I have spoken of Violette Leduc, I've been reminded that you've written a preface for Claire Etchevelli . . .

SdeB   Oh, yes. I've written something for her, yes. She's a woman who is much more independent (than Leduc). She's not at all lesbian, a woman who has a great many relationships with many, many people, and a very full social life, because she's very involved with the Socialist Party. We have a good friendship, we've worked together on *Les Temps Modernes*, we get along well, we're always glad to see one another; but it's not a very intimate relationship. It's like with Colette Audry, for example; it's also a friendship that goes back to our youth, we have an entire past in common, and we understand one another well, and well, neither of these is a very intimate relationship. Not like with Violette Leduc.

HVW   Are there any other women you have dealt with in the same way as you did Violette Leduc.

SdeB   Oh, no, no. Leduc has been unique.

HVW   Was it at her death that you decided not to deal with other women unique like herself?

SdeB   Oh, no, not at all, not at all. It was a unique relationship because of her attachment to me, rather than anything else.

HVW   But you haven't sought out, or encountered other similar attachments?

SdeB   I didn't look for any . . .

HVW   Understandably . . .

SdeB   I had enough with her.

HVW   You've written about women's lives in *The Second Sex*, and yourself as a woman in your autobiographies, and then there's also your excellent work on old age. In some of the titles—*Dutiful Daughter, Prime of Life, Old Age*—you underscore a stage of life. Have you found that there are well-marked stages in a woman's life that are different from those in a man's?

SdeB   No, I don't think so. I don't think it's due to sex, it's due obviously to politics, events; there were events, I don't know, the Resistance, Liberation, the war in Algeria . . . there, those are the things that marked eras, at least for me, in any event, and for Sartre as well, and for many of my friends. That's what marked the big epochs in our lives, it's the historical events, the historical involvements one has in these larger events. It's much more important than any other kind of difference.

HVW   In the States today, there are many feminist studies on the question of motherhood: mother/daughter relationships, the education of girls. And we've come full circle to acknowledging the difference in girls and boys from infancy, as Freud did, for example. What do you think about the motherhood issue, and do you think these questions about maternity are important?

SdeB   All questions are important. But, well, from all that I have seen, it appears that mother/daughter relationships are generally bad. No matter what the mother does, because . . . the mother wants to be a friend at the same time. As she also wants to be the one to direct her daughter. Well, I've really seen some very unfortunate relationships between mothers and daughters.

HVW   Which is all very interesting, because we began this women's movement celebrating maternity, and now we've begun to call it a viper's nest. Maternity creates an entire era in the life of a woman, while there's no similar stage for paternity, no one ever speaks of paternity.

SdeB   Much less, that's true.

HVW   It's not seen as a stage.

SdeB   Much less so, yes.

HVW   At several different points in your work, you have spoken about sexuality, and at one point you said that you believed yourself to have finished with sexuality per se, with sexual relations between you and men. Nonetheless, you then found Algren and after him Lanzmann. Would you say that love, and sex, are then much more complex than we ever believe or hope them to be?

SdeB   I think they're quite complex, yes.

HVW   In your own experience, you've experienced this sort of renaissance several times.

SdeB   I think it all depends upon the education one receives. I think that now, maybe because sex is more detached from love, that there are women, now, twenty-five, thirty-years old, who can sleep with men in a very indifferent way. . . . While for myself, that would never have been possible . . . to have sexual relations without experiencing love at the same time.

HVW   What do you think of the sexual attitudes of today's young people?

SdeB   I know very little about their lives.

HVW   What about their freer sexuality?

SdeB   I know very little. I don't know if their sexual freedom is as great as it's said to be, I don't know how much that's a commonplace, I don't know.

HVW   I've been very surprised, and turned off, by the screaming sexuality, very often misogynist as well, that's flashed on the advertisements on the movie screens in France before the main film. Has it always been this bad, or is this a backlash to feminism?

SdeB   I don't know anything about it.

HVW   But you do go to the movies?

SdeB   Yes, to the cinema, but very infrequently, to see a film that I'm interested in, and . . .

HVW   . . . . And if you go at just the right time you can avoid these twenty minutes.

SdeB   Exactly.

HVW   In one of your war-years autobiographies, you wrote that the possibility of Sartre's dying before you would have been one of the most difficult, unimaginable, impossible events for you to live through. And now Sartre has indeed died. How do you go on now without him?

SdeB   I work on many things, and, then, you know, when one is old oneself, it's not the same thing. I think that if I had been fifty when he died, it would have been atrocious. But when one is already seventy-five, one feels oneself that it won't be long before, I won't say before one will rejoin the dead, because I don't think we meet again, but, well before we'll experience the same thing, so there's not so much time to wait.

HVW   Are you working on other things besides Sartre's memoirs?

SdeB   No, but for the moment I'm working on a film about *The Second Sex* that interests me a lot.

HVW   Just what kind of film will this be?

SdeB   Well, it's a film, in short, it's based on *The Second Sex*, and it will be about the condition of women, throughout the world. But there are too few programs scheduled. I'm working with a friend, who has already made a film about me, a short film you may have already seen, who's also made *A Woman Destroyed* and *Monologues*. Her name is Josée Dayan, and we've worked together to get ready four or five programs on the condition of women.

HVW   And this is to be shown when?

SdeB   Well, I think it will start being shown toward September or October [1984]. For the moment, we're filming an enormous amount, and there will need to be much cutting.

HVW   And will it be possible to see it in the States?

SdeB   I think that a channel will be linked up with the French production.

HVW   This will be a documentary on *The Second Sex?*

SdeB   It will be, yes, a sort of documentary showing the situation of women throughout the world.

HVW   And will there be interviews or discussions with you?

SdeB   Oh, yes, many discussion, certainly; and then there will be visits to child care centers, nursery schools, things like that.

HVW   You once said in an interview that you would like to see your books made into films. There's this new film *The Blood of Others* [which was shown on HBO in the summer, 1984].

SdeB   Oh, it is a very bad film.

HVW   Jodie Foster, the actress who plays the principal role in the film, is a student of mine at Yale.

SdeB   Well, she's a very good actress.

HVW   Yes, and she told me that she thought the film really destroyed the book.

SdeB   Oh! Completely! . . . I think it must be a pile of garbage. I sold the rights, well . . .

HVW   What happens then? You no longer have any rights, once- . . . the rights are sold?

SdeB   No . . . well, that is to say that I could bring a law suit, the whole thing, take back my name, the title, but you know that would cost thousands . . .

HVW   And it's not worth the aggravation.

SdeB   . . . and then it would take an eternity, it's not worth it. No, my agent steered me wrong . . . they made a six hour long film about a little book that would have taken maybe two hours which would have been quite sufficient. They invented episodes which are absolutely not in the book, and which have nothing to do with my book. It's really meaningless to me. . . . *The Second Sex*, however, that's a film I have participated in . . . and so it's even more upsetting to me, because they're only giving us four hours, and in four hours you can't talk about the condition of women throughout the world!

HVW   No, not at all.

SdeB   Four hours is just too short. But at least in that film I'll get to say what I think.

HVW   Have you ever thought about a film of *She Came to Stay?*

SdeB   Oh, I would love to do that one, and I've tried a number of times, but it never pleased producers. First, because I had a director who was Swedish, who was wonderful, who is very well known in Sweden, and not known in France. So the producers didn't want to launch something with someone unknown in France.

HVW   So there are always difficulties trying to move from one medium to another . . . you lose control when you're no longer the author.

SdeB   Yes, that's it, yes, yes.

HVW   Many women throughout the world have decided to focus their efforts first and foremost on fighting and demonstrating against nuclear madness, and for peace. What do you think about this phenomenon?

SdeB   Well, I think it's very good to protest against nuclear power, but I don't see that it should be only women protesting. . . . Simply I think we shouldn't link the idea of feminism to pacifism. Because there's always the sense that since it's women who carry life, then women should bear the message of life. I'm against that even though I've certainly signed feminist and pacifist manifestoes. Because, since I am a feminist, and a pacifist, when friends ask me to sign or to intervene . . . it's difficult to say no, but in fact my underlying thought is that that is one area where men and women should fight together, that women aren't particularly—it's not because women give birth that they have to respond particularly to nuclear power.

HVW   It seems that with the strike in Great Britain, the women in a separate encampment very near the military base, reinforce the idea of the difference between the sexes. . . . that women give life and men kill.

SdeB   Absolutely.

HVW   It's a hotly discussed issue in the States, especially during this election year campaign. . . . A propos, what do you think of President Reagan?

SdeB   [Except for laughter, the answer was inaudible and I don't remember!]

HVW   And of your own President Mitterand?

SdeB   Of Mitterand, I think much good.

HVW   And of his so-called socialist government?

SdeB   A lot of good. They have tried to do some things. And it was very difficult, because they are after all in a capitalist world, so they can't seek true socialism. But they've nonetheless done a great deal of good.

HVW   And what about the system of education in France; could you comment on it today?

SdeB   Ah! I think that education here is in a very bad way, but I don't think it's the fault of the Socialists. They inherited a rotten system, rotten for over ten years, so now they're being made to carry the weight of a situation created by all the previous reforms . . . now they have the weight of that on their shoulders, and I think that education is in very, very bad shape in France.

HVW   I've been very surprised on this visit to France to learn that in education the situation is so bad here. I've always had such enormous respect for the French system.

SdeB   No, it's in very bad shape.

HVW   And Yvette Roudy, who has just visited several campuses in the United States, do you think that she's doing good things in her position?

SdeB   Oh, yes, enormous things. She is really a feminist, she is working for women's causes. She's very sympathetic, very courageous. She fights, she gives money to women to facilitate research. She's very, very good, Yvette Roudy. I am completely behind her.

HVW And what have been some of the recent measures taken to better women's lives?

SdeB Well, Yvette Roudy has obtained free abortion for women. . . . We fought hard for it, and it's very important. She got equal salaries, too. Naturally, it's very difficult to control this, but she has just taken steps to see that it happens.

HVW And are there countermovements here, as in the States, against abortion, against equal pay?

SdeB Yes, but it's the opposition, it's a general movement by the right against everything that's done by the left.

HVW Is there any ordering in the importance of women's problems, of the solutions to these problems.

SdeB I think there is an enormous question in education, that possibilities be open to women, that careers be open to women, as open as they are to men, and Yvette Roudy is working a great deal on that. Now women have very, very little; possibilities are very restricted for women in comparison to those for men. We need more and more possibilities opened to women, to persuade parents to invest as much money for the education of a daughter as for a son; and then to offer women the same possibilities throughout their careers. For me, the essential question is that the same work be open to women as to men, in the same conditions, with as much salary, with as much chance of promotion, of success, and as much encouragement.

HVW I just heard that you paid a secret visit to the States last summer.

SdeB Secret? I didn't try to hide. . . . It's true that I spent about fifty days in the States. I went to see Kate Millett on her farm. I saw some friends, but I didn't try to hide my visit.

HVW So, did you have occasion to see important differences between the situation of women in France and the United States?

SdeB No, no. I was very much a tourist. I went to the seaside, to visit lakes, etc., etc.; but I didn't really go to study problems, except that, what most shocked me was to see, what I already knew, in fact, what people reminded me of, that there were still I don't know how many states that refused to vote for salary equity between men and women.

HVW   All too true . . .

SdeB   But that we've got in France. At least, the law has been passed. How it is applied, that's another story, but it's a law. And it hasn't yet been accepted in the States. That really struck me, scandalized me.

II. The "Woman Question": The Early Texts

JUDITH BUTLER

Sex and Gender in Simone de Beauvoir's *Second Sex*

"One is not born, but rather becomes, a woman"[1]—Simone de Beauvoir's formulation distinguishes sex from gender and suggests that gender is an aspect of identity gradually acquired. The distinction between sex and gender has been crucial to the long-standing feminist effort to debunk the claim that anatomy is destiny; *sex* is understood to be the invariant, anatomically distinct, and factic aspects of the female body, whereas *gender* is the cultural meaning and form that that body acquires, the variable modes of that body's acculturation. With the distinction intact, it is no longer possible to attribute the values or social functions of women to biological necessity, and neither can we refer meaningfully to natural or unnatural gendered behavior: all gender is, by definition, unnatural. Moreover, if the distinction is consistently applied, it becomes unclear whether being a given sex has any necessary consequence for becoming a given gender. The presumption of a causal or mimetic relation between sex and gender is undermined. If being a woman is one cultural interpretation of being female, and if that interpretation is in no way necessitated by being female, then it appears that the female body is the arbitrary locus of the gender 'woman', and there is no reason to preclude the possibility of that body becoming the locus of other constructions of gender. At its limit, then, the sex/gender distinction implies a radical heteronomy of natural bodies and constructed genders with the consequence that 'being' female and 'being' a woman are two very different sorts of being. This last insight, I would suggest, is the distinguished contribution of Simone de Beauvoir's formulation, "one is not born, but rather becomes, a woman."

1. Simone de Beauvoir, *The Second Sex* (New York: Vintage Books, 1973), 301. Henceforth, references will be given in the text.

According to the above framework, the term 'female' designates a fixed and self-identical set of natural corporeal facts (a presumption, by the way, which is seriously challenged by the continuum of chromosomal variations), and the term 'woman' designates a variety of modes through which those facts acquire cultural meaning. One *is* female, then, to the extent that the copula asserts a fixed and self-identical relation, i.e. one is female and therefore not some other sex. Immeasurably more difficult, however, is the claim that one *is* a woman in the same sense. If gender is the variable cultural interpretation of sex, then it lacks the fixity and closure characteristic of simple identity. To be a gender, whether man, woman, or otherwise, is to be engaged in an ongoing cultural interpretation of bodies and, hence, to be dynamically positioned within a field of cultural possibilities. Gender must be understood as a modality of taking on or realizing possibilities, a process of interpreting the body, giving it cultural form. In other words, to be a woman is to become a woman; it is not a matter of acquiescing to a fixed ontological status, in which case one could be born a woman, but, rather, an active process of appropriating, interpreting, and reinterpreting received cultural possibilities.

For Simone de Beauvoir, it seems, the verb "become" contains a consequential ambiguity. Gender is not only a cultural construction imposed upon identity, but in some sense gender is a process of constructing ourselves. To *become* a woman is a purposive and appropriative set of acts, the acquisition of a skill, a 'project', to use Sartrian terms, to assume a certain corporeal style and significance. When 'become' is taken to mean 'purposefully assume or embody', it seems that Simone de Beauvoir is appealing to a voluntaristic account of gender. If genders are in some sense chosen, then what do we make of gender as a received cultural construction? It is usual these days to conceive of gender as passively determined, construct*ed* by a personified system of patriarchy or phallogocentric language which precedes and determines the subject itself. Even if gender is rightly understood to be constructed by such systems, it remains necessary to ask after the specific mechanism of this construction. Does this system unilaterally inscribe gender upon the body, in which case the body would be a purely passive medium and the subject, utterly subjected? How, then, would we account for the various ways in which gender is individually reproduced and reconstituted? What is the role of personal agency in the reproduction of gender? In this context, Simone de Beauvoir's formulation might be understood to contain the following set of challenges to gender theory: to what extent is the 'construction' of gender a self-reflexive process? In what sense do we construct ourselves and, in that process, *become* our genders?

In the following, I would like to show how Simone de Beauvoir's account of 'becoming' a gender reconciles the internal ambiguity of gender as both 'project' and 'construct'. When 'becoming' a gender is understood to be both choice and acculturation, then the usually oppositional relation between these terms is undermined. In keeping "become" ambiguous, Beauvoir formulates gender as a corporeal locus of cultural possibilities both received and innovated. Her theory of gender, then, entails a reinterpretation of the existential doctrine of choice whereby 'choosing' a gender is understood as the embodiment of possibilities within a network of deeply entrenched cultural norms.

SARTRIAN BODIES AND CARTESIAN GHOSTS

The notion that we somehow choose our genders poses an ontological puzzle. It might at first seem impossible that we can occupy a position outside of gender from which to stand back and choose our genders. If we are always already gendered, immersed in gender, then what sense does it make to say that we choose what we already are? Not only does the thesis appear tautological, but insofar as it postulates a choosing agent prior to its chosen gender, it seems to adopt a Cartesian view of the self, an egological structure which lives and thrives prior to language and cultural life. This view of the self runs contrary to contemporary findings on the linguistic construction of personal agency and, as is the problem with all Cartesian views of the ego, its ontological distance from language and cultural life seems to preclude the possibility of its eventual verification. If Simone de Beauvoir's claim is to have cogency, if it is true that we 'become' our genders through some kind of volitional and appropriative sets of acts, then she must mean something other than an unsituated Cartesian act. That personal agency is a logical prerequisite for *taking on* a gender does not imply that this agency itself is disembodied; indeed, it is our genders which we become, and not our bodies. If Simone de Beauvoir's theory is to be understood as freed of the Cartesian ghost, we must first turn to her view of bodies and to her musings on the possibilities of disembodied souls.

Whether consciousness can be said to precede the body, or whether it has any ontological status apart from the body—these are claims alternately affirmed and denied in Sartre's *Being and Nothingness*, and this ambivalence toward a Cartesian mind/body dualism reemerges, although less seriously, in Simone de Beauvoir's *The Second Sex*. In fact, we can see in *The Second Sex* an effort to radicalize the Sartrian program to establish an embodied notion of freedom. Sartre's chapter, "The Body," in *Being and Nothingness* echoes Cartesianism which haunts his thinking as well as his own efforts to free himself from this Cartesian ghost. Although Sartre argues that the body is coextensive with personal identity ("I am my body"),[2] he also suggests that consciousness is in some sense beyond the body ("My body is a *point of departure* which I *am* and which at the same time I surpass. . .").[3] Rather than refute Cartesianism, Sartre's theory seeks to understand the disembodied or transcendent feature of personal identity as paradoxically, yet essentially, related to embodiment. The duality of consciousness (as transcendence) and the body is intrinsic to human reality, and the effort to locate personal identity exclusively in one or the other is, according to Sartre, a project in bad faith.

Although Sartre's references to "surpassing" the body may be read as presupposing a mind/body dualism, we need only conceive of this self-transcendence as itself a corporeal movement to refute that assumption. The body is not a static phenomenon, but a mode of intentionality, a directional force and mode of desire. As a condition of access to the world, the body is a being comported beyond itself, sustaining a necessary reference to the world and, thus, never a self-identical natural entity. The body is lived and experienced as the context and medium for all human strivings. Because for Sartre all human beings strive after possibilities not yet realized or in principle unrealizable, humans are to that extent 'beyond' themselves. This *ek-static* reality of human beings is, however, a corporeal experience; the body is not a lifeless fact of existence, but a mode of becoming. Indeed, for Sartre the natural body only exists in the mode of being surpassed, for the body is always involved in the human quest to realize possibilities: "we can never apprehend this contingency as such insofar as our body is for us; for we are a choice, and for us, to be is to choose ourselves . . . this inapprehensible body is precisely the necessity that *there be a choice*, that I do not exist *all at once.*"[4]

Simone de Beauvoir does not so much refute Sartre as take him at his non-Cartesian best.[5] Sartre writes in *Being and Nothingness* that "it

2. Jean-Paul Sartre, *Being and Nothingness: An Essay in Phenomenological Ontology*, trans. Hazel E. Barnes (New York: Philosophical Library, 1947), 329.
3. Ibid.
4. Ibid., 328.
5. Simone de Beauvoir's defense of the non-Cartesian character of Sartre's account of the body can be found in "Merleau-Ponty et le Pseudo-Sartrisme," *Les Temps Modernes*, 10:2, 1955. For a general article tracing Sartre's gradual overcoming of Cartesianism, see

would be best to say, using 'exist' as a transitive verb, that consciousness *exists* its body . . .".[6] The transitive form of 'exist' is not far
removed from her disarming use of 'become', and Simone de Beauvoir's
becoming a gender seems both an extension and a concretization of the
Sartrian formulation. In transposing the identification of corporeal existence and 'becoming' onto the scene of sex and gender, she appropriates
the ontological necessity of paradox, but the tension in her theory does
not reside between being 'in' and 'beyond' the body, but in the move
from the natural to the acculturated body. That one is not born, but
becomes, a woman does not imply that this 'becoming' traverses a path
from disembodied freedom to cultural embodiment. Indeed, one is one's
body from the start, and only thereafter becomes one's gender. The
movement from sex to gender is internal to embodied life, i.e. a move
from one kind of embodiment to another. To mix Sartrian phraseology
with Simone de Beauvoir's, we might say that to 'exist' one's body in
culturally concrete terms means, at least partially, to become one's
gender.

Sartre's comments on the natural body as "inapprehensible" find
transcription in Simone de Beauvoir's refusal to consider gender as natural. We never experience or know ourselves as a body pure and simple,
i.e. as our 'sex', because we never know our sex outside of its expression
as gender. Lived or experienced 'sex' is always already gendered. We
become our genders, but we become them from a place which cannot be
found and which, strictly speaking, cannot be said to exist. For Sartre,
the natural body is an "inapprehensible" and, hence, a fictional starting
point for an explanation of the body as lived. Similarly, for Simone de
Beauvoir, the postulation of 'sex' as fictional heuristic allows us merely
to see that gender is non-natural, i.e. a culturally contingent aspect of
existence. Hence, we do not become our genders from a place prior to
culture or to embodied life, but essentially within their terms. For Simone de Beauvoir at least, the Cartesian ghost is put to rest.

Although we 'become' our genders, the temporal movement of this
becoming does not follow a linear progression. The origin of gender is
not temporally discrete because gender is not originated at some point
in time after which it is fixed in form. In an important sense gender is
not traceable to a definable origin precisely because it is itself an origi-
nating activity incessantly taking place. No longer understood as a prod-

---

Thoman W. Busch, "Beyond the Cogito: The Question of the Continuity of Sartre's
Thought," *The Modern Schoolman* 60 (March 1983).
    6. *Being and Nothingness*, 329.

uct of cultural and psychic relations long past, gender is a contemporary way of organizing past and future cultural norms, a way of situating oneself with respect to those norms, an active style of living one's body in the world.

GENDER AS CHOICE

One chooses one's gender, but one does not choose it from a distance which signals an ontological juncture between the choosing agent and the chosen gender. The Cartesian space of the deliberate 'chooser' is fictional, but the question persists: if we are mired in gender from the start, what sense can we make of gender as a kind of choice? Simone de Beauvoir's view of gender as an incessant project, a daily act of reconstitution and interpretation, draws upon Sartre's doctrine of prereflective choice and gives that difficult epistemological structure a concrete cultural meaning. Prereflective choice is a tacit and spontaneous act which Sartre terms "quasi knowledge." Not wholly conscious, but nevertheless accessible to consciousness, it is the kind of choice we make and only later realize we have made. Simone de Beauvoir seems to rely on this notion of choice in referring to the kind of volitional act through which gender is assumed. Taking on a gender is not possible at a moment's notice, but is a subtle and strategic project which only rarely becomes manifest to a reflective understanding. Becoming a gender is an impulsive yet mindful process of interpreting a cultural reality laden with sanctions, taboos, and prescriptions. The choice to assume a certain kind of body, to live or wear one's body a certain way, implies a world of already established corporeal styles. To choose a gender is to interpret received gender norms in a way that organizes them anew. Rather than a radical act of creation, gender is a tacit project to renew one's cultural history in one's own terms. This is not a prescriptive task we must endeavor to do, but one in which we have been endeavoring all along.

The predominance of an existential framework has been criticized by Michele Le Doeuff[7] and others for resurrecting "a classical form of voluntarism" which insidiously blames the victims of oppression for 'choosing' their situation. When the doctrine of existential choice is used in this context, it is assuredly insidious, but this uage is itself a misusage which diverts attention from the empowering possibilities of

---

7. Michele Le Doeuff, "Simone de Beauvoir and Existentialism," *Feminist Studies* 6, no. 2 (1980):278.

the position. The phenomenology of victimization that Simone de Beauvoir elaborates throughout *The Second Sex* reveals that oppression, despite the appearance and weight of inevitability, is essentially contingent. Moreover, it takes out of the sphere of reification the discourse of oppressor and oppressed, reminding us that oppressive gender norms persist only to the extent that human beings take them up and give them life again and again. Simone de Beauvoir is not saying, however, that oppression is generated through a series of human choices. Her own efforts in anthropology and history underscore her awareness that oppressive systems have complicated material origins. The point is rather that these systems persist only to the extent that gender norms are tacitly yet insistently taken up in the present through individual strategies which remain more or less disguised. Over and against a less sophisticated view of 'socialization', she is using the existential apparatus to understand the moment of appropriation through which socialization occurs. Through this emphasis on appropriation, she is providing an alternative to paternalistic explanatory models of acculturation which treat human beings only as products of prior causes, culturally determined in a strict sense, and which, consequently, leave no room for the transformative possibilities of personal agency.

By scrutinizing the mechanism of agency and appropriation, Beauvoir is attempting, I believe, to infuse the analysis with emancipatory potential. Oppression is not a self-contained system which either confronts individuals as a theoretical object or generates them as its cultural pawns. It is a dialectical force which requires individual participation on a large scale in order to maintain its malignant life.

Simone de Beauvoir does not directly address the burden of freedom[8] that gender presents, but we can extrapolate from her view how constraining norms work to subdue the exercise of gender freedom. The social constraints upon gender compliance and deviation are so great that most people feel deeply wounded if they are told that they are not really manly or womanly, that they have failed to execute their manhood or womanhood properly. Indeed, insofar as social existence requires an unambiguous gender affinity, it is not possible to exist in a socially meaningful sense outside of established gender norms. The fall from established gender boundaries initiates a sense of radical dislocation which can assume a metaphysical significance. If existence is always gendered existence, then to stray outside of established gender is

---

8. A term commonly used by Sartre to describe the experience of having to make choices in a world devoid of objective moral truths.

in some sense to put one's very existence into question. In these moments of gender dislocation in which we realize that it is hardly necessary that we be the genders we have become, we confront the burden of choice intrinsic to living as a man or a woman or as some other gender identity, a freedom made burdensome through social constraint.

The anguish and terror of leaving a prescribed gender or of trespassing upon another gender territory testifies to the social constraints upon gender interpretation as well as to the necessity that there be an interpretation, i.e. to the essential freedom at the origin of gender. Similarly, the widespread difficulty in accepting motherhood, for instance, as an institutional rather than an instinctual reality expresses this same interplay of constraint and freedom. Simone de Beauvoir's view of the maternal instinct as a cultural fiction often meets with the argument that a desire so commonly and so compellingly felt ought for that very reason to be considered organic and universal. This response seeks to universalize a cultural option, to claim that it is not one's choice but the result of an organic necessity to which one is subject. In the effort to naturalize and universalize the institution of motherhood, it seems that the optional character of motherhood is being denied; in effect, motherhood is actually being promoted as the *only* option, i.e. as a compulsory social institution. The desire to interpret maternal feelings as organic necessities discloses a deeper desire to disguise the choice one is making. If motherhood becomes a choice, then what else is possible? This kind of questioning often engenders vertigo and terror over the possibility of losing social sanctions, of leaving a solid social station and place. That this terror is so well known gives perhaps the most credence to the notion that gender identity rests on the unstable bedrock of human invention.

AUTONOMY AND ALIENATION

That one becomes one gender is a descriptive claim; it asserts only that gender is taken on, but does not say whether it ought to be taken on a certain way. Simone de Beauvoir's prescriptive program in *The Second Sex* is less clear than her descriptive one, but her prescriptive intentions are nevertheless discernible. In revealing that women have become "Other," she seems also to be pointing to a path of self-recovery. In criticizing psychoanalysis, she remarks that,

> Woman is enticed by two modes of alienation. Evidently to play at being a man will be for her a source of frustration; but to play at being a woman is also a delusion: to be a woman would mean to be the object,

the *Other*—and the Other nevertheless remains subject in the midst
of her resignation. . . . The true problem for woman is to reject these
flights from reality and seek self-fulfillment in transcendence. [57]

The language of "transcendence" suggests, on the one hand, that Simone de Beauvoir accepts a gender-free model of freedom as the normative ideal for women's aspirations. It seems that Beauvoir prescribes
the overcoming of gender altogether, especially for women, for whom
becoming one's gender implies the sacrifice of autonomy and the capacity for transcendence. On the other hand, insofar as transcendence appears a particularly masculine project, her prescription seems to urge
women to assume the model of freedom currently embodied by the
masculine gender. In other words, because women have been identified
with their anatomy, and this identification has served the purposes of
their oppression, they ought now to identify with 'consciousness', that
transcending activity unrestrained by the body. If this were her view,
she would be offering women a chance to be men, and promoting the
prescription that the model of freedom currently regulating masculine
behavior ought to become the model after which women fashion
themselves.

And yet, Simone de Beauvoir seems to be saying much more than
either of the above alternatives suggest. Not only is it questionable
whether she accepts a view of consciousness or freedom which is in any
sense beyond the body (she applauds psychoanalysis for showing finally
that "the existent is a body"), (10, 38) but her discussion of the Other
permits a reading which is highly critical of the masculine project of
disembodiment. In the following analysis, I would like to read her discussion of Self and Other as a reworking of Hegel's dialectic of master
and slave in order to show that, for Simone de Beauvoir, the masculine
project of disembodiment is self-deluding and, finally, unsatisfactory.

The self-asserting 'man' whose self-definition requires a hier-
archical contrast with an "Other" does not provide a model of true
autonomy, for she points out the bad faith of his designs, i.e. that the
"Other" is, in every case, his own alienated self. This Hegelian truth,
which she appropriates through a Sartrian filter, establishes the essential interdependence of the disembodied 'man' and the corporeally determined 'woman'. His disembodiment is only possible on the condition that women occupy their bodies as their essential and enslaving
identities. If women *are* their bodies (which is not the same as 'existing'
their bodies which implies living one's body as a project and bearer of
created meanings), if women are only their bodies, if their consciousness and freedom are only so many disguised permutations of bodily

need and necessity, then women have, in effect, exclusively monopo-
lized the bodily sphere. By defining women as "Other," 'men' are able
through the shortcut of definition to dispose of their bodies, to make
themselves other than their bodies, and to make their bodies other than
themselves. This Cartesian 'man' is not the same as the man with
distinct anatomical traits, and insofar as a 'man' is his anatomical traits,
he seems to be participating in a distinctively feminine sphere. The
embodied aspect of his existence is not really his own, and hence he is
not really a sex, but beyond sex. This sex which is beyond sex must
initiate a splitting and social projection in order not to know his own
contradictory identity.

The projection of the body as "Other" proceeds according to a peculiar rationality which relies more on associative beliefs and conclusions
which defy the laws of commutativity than on sound reasoning. The
disembodied 'I' identifies himself with a noncorporeal reality (the soul,
consciousness, transcendence), and from this point on his body becomes Other. Insofar as he inhabits that body, convinced all the while
that he is *not* the body which he inhabits, his body must appear to him
as strange, as alien, as an alienated body, a body that is *not* his. From this
belief that the body is Other, it is not a far leap to the conclusion that
others *are* their bodies, while the masculine 'I' is a noncorporeal phenomenon. The body rendered as Other—the body repressed or denied
and, then, projected—reemerges for this 'I' as the view of Others as
essentially body. Hence, women become the Other; they come to embody corporeality itself. This redundancy becomes their essence, and
existence as a woman becomes what Hegel termed "a motionless
tautology."

Simone de Beauvoir's use of the Hegelian dialectic of self and Other
argues the limits of a Cartesian version of disembodied freedom and
implicitly criticizes the model of autonomy upheld by masculine gender norms. The masculine pursuit of disembodiment is necessarily de-
ceived because the body can never really be denied; its denial becomes
the condition for its reemergence in alien form. Disembodiment becomes a way of living or 'existing' the body in the mode of denial. And
the denial of the body, as in Hegel's dialectic of master and slave, reveals
itself as nothing other than the embodiment of denial.

THE BODY AS SITUATION

Despite Simone de Beauvoir's occasional references to anatomy as transcendence, her comments on the body as an insurpassable "perspec-

tive" and "situation" (38) indicate that, as for Sartre, transcendence must be understood within corporeal terms. In clarifying the notion of the body as "situation," she suggests an alternative to the gender polarity of masculine disembodiment and feminine enslavement to the body.

The body as situation has at least a twofold meaning. As a locus of cultural interpretations, the body is a material reality which has already been located and defined within a social context. The body is also the situation of having to take up and interpret that set of received interpretations. No longer understood in its traditional philosophical senses of 'limit' or 'essence', the body is a *field of interpretive possibilities,* the locus of a dialectical process of interpreting anew a historical set of interpretations which have become imprinted in the flesh. The body becomes a peculiar nexus of culture and choice, and 'existing' one's body becomes a personal way of taking up and reinterpreting received gender norms. To the extent that gender norms function under the aegis of social constraints, the reinterpretation of those norms through the proliferation and variation of corporeal styles becomes a very concrete and accessible way of politicizing personal life.

If we understand the body as a cultural situation, then the notion of a natural body and, indeed, a natural 'sex' seems increasingly suspect. The limits to gender, the range of possibilities for a lived interpretation of a sexually differentiated anatomy, seem less restricted by anatomy itself than by the weight of the cultural institutions which have conventionally interpreted anatomy. Indeed, it becomes unclear when one takes Simone de Beauvoir's formulation to its unstated consequences, whether gender need be in any way linked with sex, or whether this conventional linkage is itself culturally bound. If gender is a way of 'existing' one's body, and one's body is a "situation," a field of cultural possibilities both received and reinterpreted, then gender seems to be a thoroughly cultural affair. That one becomes one's gender seems now to imply more than the distinction between sex and gender. Not only is gender no longer dictated by anatomy, but anatomy does not seem to pose any necessary limits to the possibilities of gender.

Although Simone de Beauvoir occasionally ascribes ontological meanings to anatomical sexual differentiation, her comments just as often suggest that anatomy alone has no inherent significance. In "The Data of Biology" she distinguishes between natural facts and their significance, and argues that natural facts gain significance only through their subjection to non-natural systems of interpretation. She writes: "As Merleau-Ponty very justly puts it, man is not a natural species; he is a historical idea. Woman is not a completed reality, but rather a becoming, and it is in her becoming that she should be compared with men; that is to say, her *possibilities* should be defined (40).

The body as a natural fact never really exists within human experience, but only has meaning as a state which has been overcome. The body is an *occasion* for meaning, a constant and significant *absence* which is only known through its significations: "in truth a society is not a species, for it is in a society that the species attains the status of existence—transcending itself toward the world and toward the future. Individuals . . . are subject rather to that second nature which is custom and in which are reflected the desires and fears that express their essential nature" (40).

The body is never a self-identical phenomenon (except in death, in the mythic transfiguration of women as Other, and in other forms of epistemic prejudice). Any effort to ascertain the 'natural' body before its entrance into culture is definitionally impossible, not only because the observer who seeks this phenomenon is him/herself entrenched in a specific cultural language, but because the body is as well. The body is, in effect, never a natural phenomenon: "it is not merely as a body, but rather as a body subject to taboos, to laws, that the subject is conscious of himself and attains fulfillment—it is with reference to certain values that he evaluates himself. And, once again, it is not upon physiology that values can be based; rather, the facts of biology take on the values that the existent bestows upon them" (40).

The conceptualization of the body as non-natural not only asserts the absolute difference between sex and gender, but implicitly questions whether gender ought to be linked with sex at all. Gender seems less a function of anatomy than one of its possible uses: ". . . the body of woman is one of the essential elements of her situation in the world. But that body is not enough to define her as woman; there is no true living reality except as manifested by the conscious individual through activities and in the bosom of a society" (41).

THE BODY POLITIC

If the pure body cannot be found, if what *can* be found is the situated body, a locus of cultural interpretations, then Simone de Beauvoir's theory seems implicitly to ask whether sex was not gender all along. Simone de Beauvoir herself does not follow through with the consequences of this view of the body, but we can see the radicalization of her view in the work of Monique Wittig and Michel Foucault: the former self-consciously extends Simone de Beauvoir's doctrine in "One is Not

Born a Woman";[9] the latter is not indebted to Simone de Beauvoir (although he was a student of Merleau-Ponty) and yet promotes in fuller terms the historicity of the body and the mythic status of natural 'sex'.[10] Although writing in very different discursive contexts, Wittig and Foucault both challenge the notion of natural sex and expose the political uses of biological discriminations in establishing a compulsory binary gender system. For both theorists, the very discrimination of 'sex' takes place within a cultural context which requires that 'sex' remain dyadic. The demarcation of anatomical difference does not precede the cultural interpretation of that difference, but is itself an interpretive act laden with normative assumptions. That infants are divided into sexes at birth, Wittig points out, serves the social ends of reproduction, but they might just as well be differentiated on the basis of ear lobe formation or, better still, not be differentiated on the basis of anatomy at all. In demarcating 'sex' as sex, we construct certain norms of differentiation. And in the interest which fuels this demarcation resides already a political program. In questioning the binary restrictions on gender definition, Wittig and Foucault release gender from sex in ways which Simone de Beauvoir probably did not imagine. And yet, her view of the body as a "situation" certainly lays the groundwork for such theories.

If 'existing' one's gender means that one is tacitly accepting or reworking cultural norms governing the interpretation of one's body, then gender can also be a place in which the binary system restricting gender is itself subverted. Through new formulations of gender, new ways of amalgamating and subverting the oppositions of 'masculine' and 'feminine', the established ways of polarizing genders becomes increasingly confused, and binary opposition comes to oppose itself. Through the purposeful embodiment of ambiguity binary oppositions lose clarity and force, and 'masculine' and 'feminine' as descriptive terms lose their usefulness. Inasmuch as gender ambiguity can take many forms, gender itself thus promises to proliferate into a multiple phenomenon for which new terms must be found.

Simone de Beauvoir does not suggest the possibility of other genders besides 'man' and 'woman', yet her insistence that these are histor-

9. Monique Wittig, "One is Not Born a Woman," *Feminist Issues*, 1, no. 2 (1981) and Wittig, "The Category of Sex," *Feminist Issues*, 2, no. 2 (1982).

10. See Foucault's introduction to the volume he edited, *Herculine Barbin, Being Recently Discovered Memoirs of a Nineteenth Century Hermaphrodite*, trans. Richard McDougall (New York: Pantheon, 1980). Also, Foucault, *The History of Sexuality*, vol. 1, (New York: Bantam, 1979).

ical constructs which must in every case be appropriated by individuals suggests that a binary gender system has no ontological necessity. One could respond that there are merely various ways of being a 'man' or a 'woman', but this view ascribes an ontology of substance to gender which misses her point: 'man' and 'woman' are *already* ways of being, modalities of corporeal existence, and only emerge as substantial entities to a mystified perspective. One might wonder as well whether there is something about the dymorphic structure of human anatomy that necessitates binary gender arrangements cross-culturally. Anthropological findings of third genders and multiple gender systems suggest, however, that dymorphism itself becomes significant only when cultural interests require, and that gender is more often based upon kinship requirements than on anatomical exigencies.

Simone de Beauvoir's own existential framework may seem anthropologically naive, relevant only to a postmodern few who essay to trespass the boundaries of sanctioned sex. But the strength of her vision lies less in its appeal to common sense than in the radical challenge she delivers to the cultural status quo. The possibilities of gender transformation are not for that reason accessible only to those initiated into the more abstruse regions of existential Hegelianism, but reside in the daily rituals of corporeal life. Her conceptualization of the body as a nexus of interpretations, as both "perspective" and "situation," reveals gender as a scene of culturally sedimented meanings and a modality of inventiveness. To become a gender means both to submit to a cultural situation and to create one, and this view of gender as a dialectic of recovery and invention grants the possibility of autonomy within corporeal life that has few if any parallels in gender theory.

In making the body into an interpretive modality, Beauvoir has extended the doctrines of embodiment and prereflective choice that characterized Sartre's work from *Being and Nothingness*, through *Saint Genet: Actor and Martyr* and his final biographical study of Flaubert. Just as Sartre in that last major work revised his existential assumptions to take account of the material realities constitutive of identity, so Simone de Beauvoir, much earlier on and with greater consequence, sought to exorcise Sartre's doctrine of its Cartesian ghost. She gives Sartrian choice an embodied form and places it in a world thick with tradition. To 'choose' a gender in this context is not to move in upon gender from a disembodied locale, but to reinterpret the cultural history which the body already wears. The body becomes a choice, a mode of enacting and reenacting received gender norms which surface as so many styles of the flesh.

The incorporation of the cultural world is a task performed incessantly and actively, a project enacted so easily and constantly it seems a natural fact. Revealing the natural body as already clothed, and nature's surface as cultural invention, Simone de Beauvoir gives us a potentially radical understanding of gender. Her vision of the body as a field of cultural possibilities makes some of the work of refashioning culture as mundane as our bodily selves.

Simone de Beauvoir in 1945. Reprinted from *Simone de Beauvoir et le cours du monde* with the permission of Janine Niepce/Rapho.

VIRGINIA M. FICHERA

Simone de Beauvoir and "The Woman Question": *Les Bouches inutiles*

Simone de Beauvoir's only play, *Les Bouches inutiles*, was first produced on the Paris stage in November 1945.[1] Although it is a major
work exploring the relationship between gender and power predating
The Second Sex by about four years, unfortunately it has been almost
completely neglected by critics and scholars of her work. However, in
1945, critic Marc Beigbeder wrote of *Les Bouches inutiles*, "It has been a
long time since we have seen a play of as great scope as that of Simone de
Beauvoir; alongside it even *Caligula* and *The Flies* appear to be bourgeois psychological dramas."[2] Simone de Beauvoir herself recalls the
play in several brief passages of her memoirs in which she gives it short
shrift, depreciating the play's originality and ground-breaking themes.
She records in *Force of Circumstance* that Genet sat next to her for one
of the performances and kept whispering, "This isn't what the theater's
about! This isn't theater at all. . . ."[3] In the end, she dismissed the play
(though not, she added, without reservation), saying, "My mistake was
to pose a political problem in terms of abstract morality."[4] In spite of
this early and seemingly categoric dismissal, a reading of *Les Bouches
inutiles* today raises serious philosophical and political issues which are
of growing concern in our nuclear age. The themes of war, gender, and
society are conjoined in a situation far more poignant and realistic than
the legendary *Lysistrata*. Simone de Beauvoir's play poses the following
questions: in a world of scarce resources, in a crisis of political legitima-

1. Simone de Beauvoir, *Les Bouches inutiles* (Paris: Gallimard, 1945).
2. Marc Beigbeder, "Le Petit et le grand," *Les Etoiles* 29 (27 November 1945):6.
(Translation mine.)
3. Simone de Beauvoir, *Force of Circumstance*, trans. Richard Howard (New York:
Putnam, 1965), 51.
4. Beauvoir, *The Prime of Life*, trans. Peter Green (Cleveland: The World Publishing
Co., 1962), 465.

tion where the stakes appear to be life or death, how shall people govern themselves? How is power defined and established? How is power shared? How are societal values determined? Are some persons seen as having more intrinsic worth than others? On what basis? What does it mean to be useful or useless to society? How do the governed consent to their rulers? Can they participate in their fate to ameliorate it? Or is it only possible to perpetuate a democracy at the intervention and the decision of the governing?

Inspired by the Italian chronicles of Sismondi, the play presents the town of Vaucelles in Flanders as having freed itself from the rule of the tyrannical Duke of Burgundy and established a form of representative government. As the play opens, the Burgundians have Vaucelles under heavy siege in the winter and the town is running out of rations. The King of France promises to aid them but only in the spring. The soldiers are constructing a belfry to symbolize their achievement and to pass the time until the king's arrival. Everyone is slowly starving: spring is three months away and the town has rations for only six weeks. The all-male Town Council and magistrates decide that the survival of the town depends upon sacrificing "the useless mouths": the women, children, the old and the infirm. The play is a dramatization and analysis of the effects of such a decision.

The play centers around the reactions of the family of the chief magistrate, Louis d'Avesnes. Catherine, his wife, and his daughter Clarice confront not only the betrayal of the Town Council but also of their son and brother, Georges, who reveals a penchant for incest and political opportunism. The Council will not be swayed from this path, however, until Jean-Pierre and Louis reveal Georges's and another magistrate's murder and plot to take over the town. The Council then votes to share the remaining food with all of the town's inhabitants, to burn the town, and attack the Burgundian camp together. With the townspeople prepared for the counterattack, the gates of the town open as the play ends.

Les Bouches inutiles owes much of its cool critical reception to the conditions and time of its composition and performance. Just as the French were trying to put the Vichy government behind them, Simone de Beauvoir's play posed the question "has one the right to sacrifice individuals for the general future good?"[5] Although the play is set in fourteenth-century Flanders, the plot revolves around a town under siege and the compromises among which the government must choose in order to survive despite the scarcity of food. The author and her

5. Simone de Beauvoir, *The Prime of Life*, 465.

VIRGINIA M. FICHERA   53

audience knew those conditions only too well. She wrote in *Force of Circumstance* that even after the war, in 1945, "It was still difficult to find food and lodging. . . ."[6] Her play would thus have very likely been perceived, consciously and unconsciously, as an allegory for Paris and France only, here, the role of the Jews was played by women, children, and old people. The title, "the useless mouths," would have rung in everyone's ears as the translation of the infamous Himmler slogan "nutzlose Esser."[7]

The play could not have been without resonance for the French who had collaborated with the invading Nazis in the establishment of the Vichy government, and its many parallels with the events of World War II explain the discomfort with which it was first received. Although there was a Resistance movement in France, recent work has shown that the Paris intellectual was not very vocal in protesting the collaboration government.[8] Simone de Beauvoir's play presents several slippery "we's," collectives with allegorical implications. Sacrificing French Jews to the Nazis as though they were not French was not a democratic solution to France's state of siege. If you were French, during the war itself, were you really other than a supporter of the Resistance movement? The "we" of collective "reality" thus shifted. *Les Bouches inutiles* is, in a sense, a critique of the French who did not really resist the Nazis or the Vichy government (and was perhaps, for Simone de Beauvoir, a self-critique). It is also, by extension, an ironic critique of the so-called liberated France which never, until recently, considered the real liberation of women from their subordinated position. The plight of the women of Vaucelles is potentially the plight of all women, the play seems to say. And a proper solution of "the woman question" will determine whether a society is truly just and democratic.

Les Bouches inutiles may thus be read as a play about women and power: it addresses issues directly related to the role of women in society, women's expectations of society, and society's debt to women. The play underscores the clear sex division in society between the governed and the governing. Women (and those who share womanlike qualities by association with them, i.e., children and the aged) are the governed, "les bouches inutiles." Men, the warriors and builders, govern. But

6. Beauvoir, *Force of Circumstance,* 35.

7. Hannah Arendt, *Eichmann in Jerusalem: A Report on the Banality of Evil* (New York: Viking Press, 1964), 105. I am grateful to Jeffry Larson for identifying the slogan and bringing it to my attention.

8. Cf. Herbert R. Lottman, *The Left Bank: Writers, Artists and Politics from the Popular Front to the Cold War* (Boston: Houghton Mifflin Co., 1982).

while the play thematically concerns women, depicting women as the major interest group, it nevertheless sees its audience as imbued with male values. It pleads the cause of women, in a real sense explains and defends women's perspective, yet does not address women collectively. The play almost seems to be in search of enlightened men, men who have a sense of honor which includes women. It is conscious of power in society, of who has it and who does not, and it seems to be asking those who have it not to abuse it.

Les Bouches inutiles was an early exploration in the then relatively uncharted territory of modern feminism, and as such it contains the seeds of many of the most challenging and important debates of our modern and postmodern culture. Simone de Beauvoir's play presents a society not unlike our own in that male experience is publicly valorized, taken by the men and often by the women to be the norm of personhood and even of humanity or humanness. Men are the public actors with many women in the wings, to be sure, but not at the sites of social and political organized power: the Council is male; the magistrates are male; and power is male. It is therefore a disturbingly logical extension of this monopoly for the male identity to consider itself the essential identity, supported by replaceable, interchangeable beings whose primary duty is to ensure its survival and well-being. Simone de Beauvoir's play, therefore, only concretizes the societal, psychological, and even linguistic dominance of the male by giving it its most absolute possible form: the power of life or death over the "other," the non-male, in the name of the survival of the city and the state. *Les Bouches inutiles* rises from the ashes of World War II to protest that a democratic collective cannot legitimately be formed by the mechanism of opposition to and destruction of an "other." The play's underlying objectives are to present, to critique, and ultimately to change relationships which are based on dominance rather than interdependence.

The male characters of the play are a mixed group, and function much like an emblematic sampling of the men of a society. There are common workmen and noble magistrates, a good father but an incestuous brother, loyal citizens and traitors. What they have very obviously in common is a sense of their importance to their city, their absolute, unquestioned usefulness. Lest even the lowliest mason question his ultimate usefulness, the Council has mandated the construction of a belfry to make all of the men useful. Of course, even setting aside all possible Freudian implications of the construction of a tower, in the context of a limited food supply, of limited resources, the construction of a celebratory (and therefore ultimately *useless*) tower is an obvious case of conspicuous consumption and an effectively ironic symbol of the subjective nature of male self-perception in the play.[9] Last but not least, the play presents Jean-Pierre, an existentialist intellectual, who hopes to lose all responsibility by refusing to claim any, but who eventually assumes the role of a magistrate.

The women of the play are equally emblematic. Catherine is the good mother, the noblewoman, first lady of the city who is there to support the men, to help guide the women and children, and who, despite her lack of any real political power, is truly convinced of her equality with the men. Clarice is the sceptic or, rather, the realist. When condemned to die against her will, she decides in a somewhat existentialist manner that freedom lies in choosing one's own death. Nevertheless she is often quite properly scornful of male-defined goals, authority, and protocol. She has fallen in love with Jean-Pierre and is carrying a child by him, but she is unwilling to accept his view that life is without commitment or responsibility. Neither she nor Catherine feels there are options for resisting the male survival plan. When women of the town join together to ask Catherine to intercede for them, she does not attempt to organize a revolt or some other form of collective action. Both Catherine and Clarice respond individually rather than collectively to the command to die. Clarice contemplates suicide; Catherine decides to try to kill Louis so that they can be together in death. At this point the women are locked into the classical position of believing they are powerless against a male-defined government and accepting its terms.

Catherine very poignantly spells out the injustice of the men's position, attacking the sleight of hand which renders the women invisible, makes them victims and robs them of whatever freedom they may have had:

> Come closer. Look carefully at these men. They assembled with thirty other men, and they made a declaration: we, MEN, are the Present and the Future, we are the whole town, we alone exist. We declare that the women, the old men and the children of Vaucelles are now nothing more than useless mouths to feed. Tomorrow they will all be led through the city gates and condemned to perish of hunger and cold in the ditch at the foot of the fortifications.[10]

9. Cf. Thorstein Veblen, *The Theory of the Leisure Class* (New York: Modern Library, 1934), especially chapter 4: "Conspicuous Consumption."

10. Simone de Beauvoir, *Who Shall Die?*, trans. and intro. Claude Francis and Fernande Gontier (Florissant, MO.: River Press, 1983), 39. One regrets that the translators did not retain Simone de Beauvoir's title. The force of the Himmler reference is diminished for the English-speaking reader. (Hereafter, page references will be given in the text.)

There is more at stake here than a question of justice in this particular instance of the exercise of the male power prerogative. First of all, what Simone de Beauvoir has isolated is a fundamental problem of the establishment of identity. Catherine states that the men have defined all political and social reality from the starting point of the male sex. Men alone are subjects; all other beings in the social and physical order are objects to be acted upon. The entire plot of the play is contrived to illustrate this one basic observation concerning male subjectivity.

To many contemporaries, the plot must have seemed a sweeping generalization, a *reductio ad absurdum,* an oversimplification. At the time of the play's production, Simone de Beauvoir had not yet written *Le Deuxième sexe* and, although the French public was doubtless aware of suffrage movements, it was in no way seriously acquainted with the basic tenets of feminism.[11] Yet it is just such generalized observations which have become the point of departure for many serious philosophical, sociological, and psychological studies of gender roles in society. Four years later in *The Second Sex,* Simone de Beauvoir wrote, echoing Catherine:

> But women do not say "We," except at some congress of feminists or similar formal demonstration; men say "women," and women use the same word in referring to themselves. They do not authentically assume a subjective attitude.[12]

It is interesting to note that in both passages it is the collective subjectivity, not an individual man's or woman's ability to say "I," which determines identity. The degree and nature of verbal participation in a "we" appears to play the decisive role.

Since drama is the art form which most completely embodies the major components of human communication (precisely because it literally embodies language), a communications approach provides useful concepts for an analysis of the paradoxes and binds of the play's global structure. The late Gregory Bateson, perhaps the best-known proponent of communication theory, developed a basic classification model describing human interaction patterns as symmetrical or complementary relationships. A simple summary of the behavior patterns the model describes can be found in his article, "The Cybernetics of 'Self' ":

> If, in a binary relationship, the behaviors of A and B are regarded (by A and B) as *similar,* and are linked so that more of the given behavior by

11. Women voted in France for the first time only a month before the play's opening on the Paris stage.
12. Simone de Beauvoir, *The Second Sex* (New York: Knopf, 1952), xix.

A stimulates more of it in B, and vice versa, then the relationship is "symmetrical" in regard to these behaviors.

If, conversely, the behaviors of A and B are *dissimilar* but mutually fit together (as, for example, spectatorship fits exhibitionism), and the behaviors are linked so that more of A's behavior stimulates more of B's fitting behavior, then the relationship is "complementary" in regard to these behaviors.[13]

If this communications model is used to examine the relationships in this play, several interesting observations result. First of all, it would seem accurate to say that the women of the play basically view their relationship to the men as complementary. They perceive themselves as acting in a manner quite different from the men, as having unique and important roles to fulfill in the town. But they also believe that their behavior complements that of the men and furthers the common good of the town. For example, in the first act, Catherine explains this to Jean-Pierre:

> It was I who laid the first stone of this Belfry. The banner that floats above City Hall was embroidered by these hands. Will you ever know the joy of looking around and saying to yourself: This I have achieved? [28]

The men, on the other hand, do not seem to see themselves as engaged in complementary but rather in a more symmetrical mode of behavior. They view their role not simply as dissimilar from the role of the women, but as more important, more essential, in fact, essential to the town's existence. The women are clearly subordinated in the political sphere: the town is governed by thirty artisans and three magistrates, all men.

A major consideration in the plot is the fact that the inhabitants of Vaucelles have overthrown a tyrannical duke and have instituted a new, model democratic government. Obviously, all of the inhabitants of the town found the old regime, which denied them participation in their destiny, oppressive and unjust. In defending this new government against attack, the inhabitants are confronted with the harsh reality of finite resources. In this crisis situation, the new form of government finds itself under intense scrutiny and it thus finds itself tested from within. If it can equitably deal with the pressures in a manner qualitatively different from the old regime, if the democracy can, in short, survive, then it will have proven itself a model town.

13. Gregory Bateson, "The Cybernetics of 'Self': A Theory of Alcoholism," in *Steps to an Ecology of Mind*, (New York: Ballantine, 1972), 323.

But in order to survive, given its situation, the town must first establish its priorities, which, in a manner of speaking, entails a form of self-definition. The reality of political power, however, ensures that the definition, or the perception of the definition, held by the powerful will become apparent and crystallize since these perceptions will guide decision making. Thus, the men of the town consciously or unconsciously perceive themselves as the town. The less powerful find that such times of crisis rob them of their illusions concerning their perception of self-definition inasmuch as their perceptions do not coincide with those of the powerful.[14] For example, Catherine, who considered herself equal but complementary to the men, discovers that she is not equal in political power where she does not find herself really represented as a woman. Equality based on complementarity is found to be a male fiction which, from the male make-up of the Council, could have been foretold.

The men, on the other hand, continue to propagate the fiction of complementary equality, while reserving and exercising the power to define equality. The women are thus told that since they are the equal partners of the men in the establishment of the town, they cannot object to being condemned to die for the survival of the town. One learns from the title, *Les Bouches inutiles*, that the basic perception of the men is that the women, by eating, use up the finite amount of food which the men want for themselves. Thus, upon hearing the Council's decision, Clarice remarks, "So this is what you have come up with? You are going to murder us in order to gorge yourselves with food!" (39). Since, in a zero-sum game (i.e., where there are a finite number of elements), competition for resources is evidence of a symmetrical relationship, it is clear that the men do not view the women as complementary partners. Their elaborate justification of their competitive, symmetrical behavior, however, assumes the disguise of a complementary partner.[15]

In his article on "The Cybernetics of 'Self,'" Bateson also notes that:

> Various sorts of "double binds" are generated when A and B perceive the premises of their relationship in different terms—A may regard B's behavior as competitive when B thought he was helping A, and so on.[16]

14. Cf. Elizabeth Janeway, *Powers of the Weak* (New York: Knopf, 1980).

15. Of course, in some cultures and subcultures, there is no effort at disguise in the competition for food. Cf. for example, Maxine Hong Kingston, *The Woman Warrior: Memoirs of a Girlhood Among Ghosts* (New York: Vintage Books, 1977), 54, in which she recounts the Chinese adages which haunted her American childhood: "Feeding girls is feeding cowbirds" and "There's no profit in raising girls. Better to raise geese than girls."

16. Bateson, "The Cybernetics of 'Self': 323–24.

According to Bateson, a double bind is said to occur when, in the context of an intense, important relationship between two or more persons, a message is communicated which both asserts something and denies its assertion, while forbidding metacommunication and escape from the situation.[17] The basic communicational structure of *Les Bouches inutiles* can be described as a double bind in which the men of Vaucelles assert the equality of all the town's inhabitants, then deny it by condemning to death all the women, the aged, and the children as useless and inessential to the town's survival. The men refuse to see that simultaneously to categorize the women (and those non-males associated with the women) as their equals yet to keep the power to treat them as subordinates or even, in this case, as non-persons, is to establish a paradox which generates a schizophrenogenic state. Although metacommunication is not totally blocked in that the women attempt to discuss the situation, it is effectively blocked since, with the exception of Jean-Pierre and eventually Louis, their complaints are completely ignored by the men. The women cannot escape the situation since the men intend to force them out of the gates of the town.

Viewers and readers of the play are perhaps quite tempted to consider the basic situation contrived and unrealistic, assuming that no men would really be foolish or egocentric enough to equate their survival alone with that of their town, government, or civilization. Yet events of relatively recent history confirm Simone de Beauvoir's dramatic imagination. A 1982 article in *The Washingtonian*, discussing evacuation plans of the United States government in the event of nuclear attack, reported:

> Just who is on the lists to be saved is among the most closely held of government secrets. The First Lady has a pass, but other spouses do not. When the late Chief Justice Earl Warren learned his wife was not included, he is supposed to have said: "If she's not important enough to save, neither am I." And he gave up his pass.[18]

As the fear of a nuclear holocaust spreads, the question of survival, the issues of government and women's role and participation become ever more timely. Simone de Beauvoir's play openly and directly questions the survival strategy of men. The men of Vaucelles appropriate women's reproductive labor. But the women are replaceable; only male sur-

17. Gregory Bateson, Don D. Jackson, Jay Haley, and John H. Weakland, "Toward a Theory of Schizophrenia," in Gregory Bateson, *Steps to an Ecology of Mind*, 208.

18. Howard L. Rosenberg, "Who Gets Saved?," *The Washingtonian*, November 1982, 110.

vival and possession of the town matter. For the women, on the other hand, all of the townspeople physically embody the continuity of the town. Male detachment from the physical reproductive survival process prompts the men to eliminate their children, too, form the Vaucelles to-be-saved list. Women, children and the aged are replaceable commodities. The men would appropriate (make into property) other women and have other children. Moreover, the only significant property for the men is material property (the town), and only such property is equated with power. Such egocentric callousness has been seen to have its roots in the male lived experience of alienation from reproduction. As Mary O'Brien argues in her book, *The Politics of Reproduction,* "The fact is that men make principles of continuity because they are separated from genetic continuity with the alienation of the male seed."[19] Simone de Beauvoir understood this basic *lived* difference and set up, in her play, a political confrontation of the female and male *lived* perspectives on reproduction and the survival of society.

"Les Bouches inutiles" are, in addition, the organs of language, and the play possesses an equally paradoxical linguistic component which both summarizes and embodies these issues of identity, power, and survival in its concern with the semantic and political rules for the interpretation of the phrase, "we, the town." The dissimilar use of personal pronouns cited earlier effectively polarizes the disjunctive concepts of identity. The women, in using the first person plural pronoun "we," assume or presume a cooperative complementarity with the men. Their use of "we" before the Council's decision is inclusive of all the inhabitants of the town, i.e., not referring to themselves as women collectively and as distinct from the men. The Council's decision destroys this inclusiveness and establishes a total exclusiveness based on the already established absence of the women from the official modes of government. "We, Vaucelles" shifts ground and the men declare that "we" is male and Vaucelles is male. The women are then trapped in the men's language game, for as they refer to the town as "other" in discussing or debating the decision, they are granting the men their premise. Louis composes the formula thus, addressing Catherine: "This community was built by you as much as it was built by us, and you want its final triumph as much as we do. We have the right to ask you to give up your life for Vaucelles" (38).

The plight of the women is, of course, highly ironic. They have

19. Mary O'Brien, *The Politics of Reproduction* (Boston: Routledge & Kegan Paul, 1981), 33.

worked side by side with the men to build a new existence, believing they were important and essential, only to discover that their subordination in government undermines their participation in all other aspects of the town's life. The play presents this double bind as the touchstone, the crucial test of democracy. The play's argument is, in a sense, a metacommunication concerning this issue, a search for a viable solution. But breaking a double bind is never easy. If the survival strategy applied to all, and if the persons deciding truly represented the persons bound by the decision, that is, if all of the collective uses of "we" had the same inclusive referent or subject, then the double bind would not exist.

But the play's greatest irony lies in the fact that it "solves" the problem without really breaking the double bind. And of course, any solution which does not alter the double bind leaves the system basically unchanged, and therefore offers no lasting solution. First of all, the new decision is reached without the women's participation; their distress is real and their expression of distress is heard, but ignored. Jean-Pierre is very clearly upset with the Council's decision even before hearing any of the women's objections. He is, in many ways, the single deciding factor in the reversal. Louis does change sides on the issue, ostensibly after confronting Catherine's extreme passion and emotion. But the context of his decision is not the isolation of one man against the multitude. He is aware of Jean-Pierre's support and thus finds himself more easily able to change his mind. One may speculate as to whether he would have even considered an alternative without the leadership of another man, or at least a sense of male bonding.

Secondly, even when presented with strong arguments from Louis and Jean-Pierre, the Council does not immediately abandon its project. It is only with the revelation of François's treason that the Council is put in the position to change its vote. The men are not swayed so much by the moral arguments of their chief magistrate as by the fact that their original plan must have been flawed if another magistrate could so quickly take advantage of the situation. The realization that the equality of all the men was jeopardized by the decision, making them vulnerable to the possible despotic rule of François, turns the tide.

Third, when confronted with the fact that their system of self-governing is not perfect, since the treason would not have been easily found out, the men do not question the form of government but only the individual in power. Ironically, the treason is discovered by a woman, Jeanne, but it is her brother Jean-Pierre who bears the message since she is murdered by the traitors because of her fidelity to the town. The men do not hold a memorial for her, nor does she really receive full credit for her information and her sacrifice. Instead of learning from this episode that women deserve to participate in the exercise of power, the men simply continue to perpetuate their familiar structure. Jean-Pierre becomes the third magistrate and the Council does business as usual.

Lastly, the decision to share the food and plan a counterattack by all of the inhabitants appears to include the women, aged, and children, but in reality it simply repeats the structure of the earlier decision. An exclusive group, "we, the men," has decided the fate of the inclusive group, "we, the townspeople." One might object that it is not obvious that the women, if given political power, would have decided otherwise. Although it appears that reversing the decision was the primary concern of the women, the female characters' preoccupation with their equal status implies that their value in society and the form and process of government are indeed the central issues. At one point, Clarice, when addressing Jacques van der Welde, clearly states, "If I were in your position or in my father's position, I would not let thirty workmen rule the town" (19). Catherine also protests: "You have made your decision without me, and all the words that I could pronounce would only be the words of a slave. I am your victim, you are my executioner" (53).

In a very real sense, a male democratic government can only legitimately impose obligations upon the male population. The male ordering of women's lives is illegitimate and achieves its ends only through the creation of double binds like those we have been examining. Simone de Beauvoir's play, by recreating the situation of the Vichy government's participation in the Holocaust using women in the place of Jews, adds a new dimension to an analysis of legitimation and government. The characters of the play do not spend very much time debating the fairness of an all-male council; only the morality of an order which does not include the men is questioned. In fact, the legitimacy of the order is not disputed at any length. It is as if the play did not dare to attack seriously the fact of men's governing provided they ultimately treat men and women equally. The inhabitants of Vaucelles recognize, on the one hand, that the situation is hardly democratic if laws do not apply to all. On the other hand, the situation is not democratic if the governed do not participate in the making of the law. There is no true democracy unless both conditions obtain. In short, although the women have won this battle, they have lost the war.

In the final scene, Catherine is obviously disturbed by the entire outcome, but seems unable to identify her malaise. Jean-Pierre credits her with saving the town, saying, "Vaucelles owes you its salvation" (64), but the town and we, the readers-spectators, know that officially the town's fate has been decided by Jean-Pierre and Louis. Catherine reveals her confusion, replying:

> Maybe I should have let them throw me in the ditch. Have I saved these children and these women? Have I condemned these men to die? [64]

In fact she has done neither, since she has never been allowed to claim full responsibility for any of her thoughts, or actions. The play ends with Jean-Pierre and Louis summing up the situation, giving the orders. But there is nowhere any other evidence that something is amiss, that democracy has not really had a victory at all. Perhaps the enemy, stunned by the town's desperate yet open willingness to annihilate itself rather than surrender, will retreat.[20] More likely, as most of them fear, the inhabitants will be killed. The uncertainty of the ending is most appropriate. Simone de Beauvoir was grappling with the evolution of individual and collective feminist consciousness. A positive solution would have ratified the decision of the Council, crowned the outcome with a certain victory, and denied the dilemma.

About four years after the play's first production, in *Le Deuxième sexe*, Simone de Beauvoir abstracted the action of her play into a theoretical discussion of the dialectical structures involved. She describes male subjectivity as resulting from a Hegelian master-slave dialectic, but with the added twist that there are two types of "other": the slave and the woman.[21] As O'Brien points out, in *The Second Sex*:

> It is only women, she [Beauvoir] argues, who take no risks and gain no recognition. She does not consider the risk inherent in childbirth, for women do not choose (or did not choose) to take these risks. She also implies that no known society grants recognition to women as the reproducers of the people who must be born before history or value can have any meaning at all.[22]

Interestingly enough, objections to *The Second Sex* on these grounds do not apply as directly to *Les Bouches inutiles*; Simone de Beauvoir appears to have been more radical in her play than in her theoretical work. For the women of Vaucelles do indeed argue that their work, though different, is of comparable worth, and they imply that their reproductive

---

20. In a similar, but historical situation, the Duchess of Tyrol abandoned her siege of Hochosterwitz in 1334. Cf. Paul Watzlawick, John Weakland, and Richard Fisch, *Change: Principles of Problem Formation and Problem Resolution* (N.Y.: W. W. Norton & Co., Inc., 1974), xi.

21. Cf. *The Second Sex*, 66–81.

22. O'Brien, *The Politics of Reproduction*, 70.

labor has value for the town. Indeed, the lesson of the play is that human interrelationships form society. In part, the men of Vaucelles confront their alienation from reproduction and achieve an understanding of the value of women, children, and the aged. If the play's ending does not completely satisfy Catherine, Simone de Beauvoir, or today's reader, it is because it fails in the end to address the issue of women's need for a collective consciousness and collective action. Although Clarice questions the legitimacy of the male government, the women of Vaucelles do not demand to determine their own fate. Simone de Beauvoir consciously understood, wrote about, and acted upon this issue in the 1970s and 1980s.[23]

Les Bouches inutiles is remarkable in that it was and is a very contemporary play. Feminists of the eighties find dramatized the issues of comparable worth and the continuing struggle for democratic justice. But we also find a parable of the betrayal we experience if we accept to be governed by the principles of the New Right. If we trust that men will recognize our worth and grant us equality, we will be disappointed, for recognition will be achieved only with our collective struggle. A few enlightened men under certain conditions may be reasoned with, but government is illegitimate if women cannot participate. Projected into the past rather than the future, the play does not present radical solutions because it fails to present new, collective action by women. Its unsettled ending is, however, conscious of these flaws. Simone de Beauvoir's theoretical achievement here is nonetheless significant. She sensed that male alienation from reproduction affects political decision making and is thus a crucial issue for feminism to address. Attempting to present the dilemma and choices of an entire town, she used the theater as a medium for exploring gender relations in society rather than the plight of a single "hero." Simone de Beauvoir thus began a critique of subjectivity and legitimacy in government which is continued in her later work. In so establishing the terms of "the woman question," *Les Bouches inutiles* is a powerful forerunner to *Le Deuxième sexe.*

23. Cf. especially the interviews entitled "I am a feminist" (1972) and "A vote against his world" (1980) in Alice Schwarzer, *After the Second Sex: Conversations with Simone de Beauvoir,* trans. Marianne Howarth (New York: Pantheon, 1984).

III. Women's Life Today: Revisions of Formation

MARTHA NOEL EVANS

Murdering *L'Invitée:* Gender and Fictional Narrative

The telling of stories has always been in a way the telling of the first story—the story of how we got here and why we are here. As retellings of this original tale, all stories will have something to do with myth, something to do with the puzzle of the relationship between birth (of the individual) and creation (of the world, the text). Since creation has become a male affair in the Western world, this relationship between biological birth and metaphysical creation has become a particularly tricky question, the move from one to the other inscribing the long history of the claims to patriarchal preeminence.

The dichotomization of birth and cultural creativity turns writing into a potentially self-contradictory activity for women; for if they tell stories, they find themselves in the absurd position of having to deny their biological potential in order to replace it with another order of generation. Writing becomes for women, therefore, a kind of cultural contraception, a peculiar but effective birth control device.

In reality, of course, things are not so simple, and certain forms of cultural inventiveness have been allotted to women all along: telling certain kinds of stories, for instance. Especially with the institution of the novel as a recognized—but frivolous—genre in the eighteenth century, this area of writing has commonly been recognized as a proper domain for women. Domestic, private, having to do with the everyday tales of the salon and boudoir, novels were right up their alley.

It will come as no surprise that as Simone de Beauvoir began to write and, specifically, to tell stories, she conceived her activity in the terms her culture presented to her. What is perhaps surprising is that this woman who considered herself iconoclastic and out of the ordinary adopted these traditional ways of looking at her art with such apparent wholeheartedness.

BIOLOGY VS. LITERATURE

As Simone de Beauvoir recounts the birth of her vocation, she represents it as a preeminent value, a kind of sacred task whose goal is not so much perhaps to save others as herself: "Through literature, one justifies the world by creating it anew, in the purity of the imaginary, and by the same token, one saves one's own existence."[1] The mythological function of writing as a substitute birth could not be more clearly stated. Literature is "pure," a clean creation in contrast to, one must suppose, the impure, dirty process of physical birth in the domain of the real. This purity associated with writing, its status as a cleansed version of biological life, endows it for the writer not only with a moral prestige, but with a strong redemptive force as well. Everything pales for her in the clear light of this scriptorial salvation: "I never regretted not having children to the degree that what I wanted to do was write."[2]

Given that Simone de Beauvoir experiences existence as in need of redemption, her minute documentation of her life is understandable.[3] What is less understandable is her almost equally abundant commentary on her own writing. Not only is her life doubled by its own chronicle, her writing as well is documented and shadowed by a second writing as if the first were insufficient and incomplete.

DOUBLE WRITING: FACT AND FICTION

As it turns out, there is for Simone de Beauvoir a kind of writing that approximates the impurity of life which she now contrasts to "reality" in the philosophical use of the term: "It's a little boring to make up stories. So many people think it's better to be very close to reality and to recount one's life as it is rather than . . . to fictionalize, as they say, that is to transpose, and therefore to cheat."[4]

In this truly remarkable statement, Simone de Beauvoir (or is it "so many people," the "they"?) envisages nonfiction as somehow closer to

1. *The Force of Circumstance (La Force des choses)*, trans. Richard Howard (New York: Putnam's Sons, 1976), 237.
2. Quoted in Serge Julienne-Caffié, *Simone de Beauvoir* (Paris: Gallimard, 1966), 215.
3. *Memoirs of a Dutiful Daughter (Mémoires d'une jeune fille rangée)*, trans. James Kirkup (New York, Harper and Row, 1974) [first published by World Publishing Co., 1959]; *The Prime of Life (La Force de l'âge)*, trans. Peter Green (New York, World, 1962); *Force of Circumstance*, op. cit.; *All Said and Done (Tout compte fait)*, tr. Patrick O'brian (New York, Putnam, 1974). Beauvoir has also documented other specific events in her personal life: the death of her mother in *A very gentle death (Une mort très douce)*; and the death of Sartre in *La Cérémonie des adieux*.
4. Alice Jardine, "Interview with Simone de Beauvoir," *Signs* 5 (Winter 1979), 234.

reality than fiction and therefore as a superior mode of expression. According to the Platonic model implied here, fiction is a distortion, a cheat, "reality" twisted out of shape. She thus sets up a hierarchy of kinds of writing with nonfiction—her autobiography, essays, and published interviews—at the top, and fiction coming after as a less true version of the truth.

At other times, she speaks in a more positive mode about fiction and its role. She calls it the "privileged locus of intersubjectivity," where separation is overcome and people—namely she and her readers—can come together.[5] Fiction is the arena of feeling and connection, the same domain as that allotted to women in our society. Nonfiction, as she defines it, is the sphere of reason, lucidity, truth, the province assigned to men.

Writing is thus dichotomized by Simone de Beauvoir into two modes which correspond to the traditional division of human experience according to gender. She goes on to arrange these modes of experience in a hierarchy which also reflects traditional values. While the work of Eros accomplished in fiction is defined by Simone de Beauvoir as one of her most "comforting" experiences as a writer,[6] she still sees it as an inferior mode when compared with the more direct expression of reality accomplished in nonfiction writing. Nonfiction corresponds finally to what so many "people" value—rigor and veracity—while fiction, comforting as it may be, is messy, distorted, a cheat.

While her nonfiction comments on her fictional writing, thus forming a kind of companion text, the complementarity of the fiction/-nonfiction couple is only apparent. The secondary text—the commentary—is actually primary in importance: nonfiction supplants fiction whose connection with the female mode of intersubjectivity makes it the expression of doubt and distortion.

In a secondary development and extension of her thinking about writing, Simone de Beauvoir duplicates the traditional attitude toward novels as a less worthy genre of writing and as a genre associated with a female mode of being. Fiction, like being a woman, is a cheat or what is perhaps even worse, a bit of a bore.

Even women writers of fiction are tainted by their *genre* (gender): in her view they are in general "inferior to men," good only when they

5. "My Experience as a Writer" ("Mon expérience d'écrivain"), lecture given in Japan in 1966, reproduced in Claude Francis and Fernande Gontier, *Les Ecrits de Simone de Beauvoir* (Paris: Gallimard, 1979), 459.

6. Ibid.

have been pushed and encouraged by their fathers.[7] Literature is in itself an inferior mode of knowledge, and it sinks even lower when it is not animated by male seriousness and ambition.

As we can see, while Simone de Beauvoir has an intense and elevated sense of her vocation as a writer, she has a highly ambivalent and conflicted view of herself as a writer of novels. On the one hand, she regards fiction as an inferior form of writing, in fact a form of lying. On the other hand, she also views fiction as the place where all the mess and complexity of life can be exposed; the place where her need to be recognized and loved in all her confusion can be met. Furthermore, this ambivalence toward fiction is inextricably linked with her ambivalence toward her own gender. The question of writing cannot remain for her a neutral, or rather, a neuter one.

What will happen when a woman with such mixed feelings about herself and her writing actually writes a novel? The very attempt to read these crossed and double messages in her fiction is a project loaded with aggression by Simone de Beauvoir's peremptory reading of her own texts. The effect of her (male) commentaries is to rationalize the confusions of her (female) fiction and thus to preclude the reader from facing the trouble that is there. This pre-emptive move by Simone de Beauvoir in respect to the interpretation of her fictions turns the task of the critic, whose place has already been taken by the author, into an act of antagonism. While we try to come to terms with the turbulent complex of vulnerabilities and defenses that roils in her first novel, we are obliged at the same time to tangle with her as the protector of her own duplicity.

THE RIGHT TO WRITE

She Came to Stay, Simone de Beauvoir's first published novel,[8] is itself a story of love turned into antagonism and violence. She tells us in her autobiography that she drew heavily on her own experience for the plot of the novel. In 1933, she and Sartre formed a trio with one of her students, Olga Kosakievicz, to whom the novel is dedicated. For more than three years, they worked on this relationship as an existential

7. "Women and Creation" ("La Femme et la création"), lecture given in Japan in 1966, reproduced in C. Francis and F. Gontier, 465.

8. Published as *L'Invitée* (Paris: Gallimard, 1943); English translation by Yvonne Moyse and Roger Senhouse (London: Martin Secker and Warburg, 1949). All quotations will be from this edition. Where I have modified the translation, this will be indicated by the letters, TM. The title itself is infelicitously translated; the French means simply, "the guest."

enterprise, trying to move beyond the bourgeois notion of love as possession in a generous extension of the couple. This unusual network of attachments proved to be highly unstable, however, and depended for its survival on a certain amount of self-sacrifice on Simone's part. She says, in fact, that she was never happy with the trio but attempted to make it work because she did not want to thwart Sartre's wishes; he was at that time, she says, highly unstable, on the brink of psychosis.[9] This attempt to realize a new kind of intimacy ultimately failed in 1936. But while Simone and Olga continued to be friends in real life, in the fictional transposition of this experience, that is in the messy, female domain of writing, Simone de Beauvoir's counterpart murders the younger woman.

The murder that ends the book is also a reflection of Simone de Beauvoir's fantasy of what writing means to her. She states in *The Prime of Life* that her writing this book was part of an attempt to separate herself emotionally from Sartre, to feel and express her own autonomy. Curiously, she associates this gesture of individuation with the commission of a crime.[10] The only way, she reasoned, to establish her independence was to commit a crime so heinous that she alone would be willing to take responsibility for it.

The reference of Simone de Beauvoir's remarks is oddly ambiguous, extending not only to the plot of the novel but to the writing itself. Writing may be a sacred vocation, but as the only means she can conceive of an idea to declare herself a separate, autonomous being, it is also a crime. Without registering the import of her statement, she implies that a woman's autonomy is a profound violation of some rule. For woman, for fiction, for woman as fiction to stand on her own two feet, violence must be done.

These radical implications linking female authority and female authorship to the transgression of a taboo are borne out in the plot structure of the novel. While *She Came to Stay* appears to present a conventional love triangle, the passions usually aroused in such a situation are strangely muted. On the one hand, although Pierre and Françoise (the protagonist) have been deeply committed lovers for a long time, there is essentially no depiction of physical passion or erotic connection between them. That part of their relationship is simply absent. Likewise, in their relationship with Xavière, the young student, erotic attraction, while present, is never acted on. The coupling of intense

9. *The Prime of Life*, 204.
10. Ibid., 270–71.

emotional involvement with an absence of eroticism creates an aura of uncanniness, not to say perversity, around this trio. They seem to operate in a world predating sexual passion as they play out with extreme intensity a drama that makes sense as a childhood fantasy but not as an adult enterprise. The plot gives the impression, then, of an acting-out in which all the reasoning and talk seem to be a front, a rationalization of another deeply hidden and denied drama.

We are in a world in which the issues are in fact more primitive than those of erotic connection, in which, to speak the language of psychoanalysis, the problem is not which "object" to love, but rather whether there are "objects" at all. What looks like an adult, erotic trio, or even an Oedipal triangle, turns out be rather a series of superimposed dyadic relationships in which the dynamics of fusion and separation create a fatal power struggle over the individual's right to survive. The principal drama does not involve, then, the establishment of equality and love among three people, but rather the self's right to be at all. The triangle flattens out into a straight line stretched tautly in a tug-of-war between Self and Other.

Although Simone de Beauvoir has always spoken with great serenity about her vocation as a writer, the pseudotriangle of *She Came to Stay* uncovers authorial conflicts of the most fundamental sort: conflicts not between male and female, but about the possibility of being female at all; conflicts not between life and death, but about the right to live at all. And so this first fiction, *She Came to Stay*, stands at the crossroads between life and writing, the place where Simone de Beauvoir's most fundamental conflicts about her right to exist, her right to be female are intimately linked with conflicts about another right: the right to write.

THE (UN)CONVENTIONAL COUPLE

As a reflection of Simone de Beauvoir's fantasies and fears about writing in this her first novel, the dynamics of the relationship between Françoise and Pierre will reveal some of the contradictions and hidden assumptions that are involved in this dangerous enterprise of self-assertion. Françoise is a writer. During the course of *She Came to Stay* she is working on a novel. At least she says so. We never actually see her working on it, nor does she talk about what it means to her to be writing a book. While Françoise's work, on the one hand, is thus (self)effaced, on the other, Pierre's work in the theater is constantly foregrounded.

Françoise and Pierre bill themselves as an unconventional couple because they are not married, but in practice their relationship displays many traditional characteristics. The fading of Françoise occurs not only on a professional level, but on a personal one as well. Although their relationship is founded on a pact of mutual independence, in fact they operate as if they were fused into one:

> "It's impossible to talk about faithfulness and unfaithfulness where we are concerned," said Pierre. He drew Françoise to him. "You and I are one. It's true, you know. Neither of us can be defined without the other." [21, TM]

Pierre and Françoise have one rule: to tell each other everything. There is to be nothing hidden between them, no dark corners, no silences. Their relationship is perfectly transparent and "pure," to use Françoise's word (21), and, as such, it reflects the same transparency as the world of male discourse described by Simone de Beauvoir in her "other" writing.

Françoise becomes in effect Pierre's writing. Her relationship to him expresses the clarity of his relationship to reality. So while Françoise seems to be the center of the text's consciousness, it turns out that her own consciousness is not centered in her. Her own story does not belong to her: "As long as she hadn't told Pierre about it, no event was altogether real" (21, TM). Her consciousness is not split, rather it resides altogether in Pierre. Without him and his discourse, his formulations of things, she is empty, or at least just a swirling mass of unstructured impressions. As long as her union with Pierre is perfect, however, as long as the fusion of the two continues, Françoise does not *feel* empty; she suffers no sense of loss from this displacement of self-consciousness.

Françoise's liberty and power do not reside in her but in Pierre. This ostensibly iconoclastic couple is, in fact, oddly traditional. Pierre's wishes, desires, words, work, dominate the life of the pair. Pierre speaks with assurance, never doubts himself, dallies with other women to please his vanity, and it is his idea to form the trio with Xavière. Like the female partner in the traditional heterosexual couple, Françoise is living as a kind of parasite.

As presented on the surface of the text, the male is the possessor of language and creativity. Flowing from this possession, his power at once creates and validates his authority. Although Françoise may make up stories, they do not seem true until she tells them to Pierre. The male is the source of "reality." So although it seems that we are reading a "female" text, in fact we are facing a divided discourse. The voice of

Françoise is a kind of dummy voice with Pierre playing the role of ventriloquist.[11] Françoise specializes in feeling, in giving support, in mediating, while Pierre is the authority, the consciousness, the voice of the couple. Françoise's words are not validated until they pass through the checkpoint of male discourse.

THE IMPERIOUS "I"

While on one level Simone de Beauvoir depicts Françoise as a selfless echo of Pierre, on another she represents her as breaking out of this effacement and speaking for herself. This self-assertion is dramatized in the narrative by the use of the authorial "I." In the first chapter of *She Came to Stay*, Beauvoir introduces an unusual technique that she will continue to use sporadically in her later fictional works as well: the interspersing of the first-person pronoun "I" in an otherwise traditional third-person narrative. Every now and then an "I" will burst through the texture of the narrative creating the impression of an eruption of self-consciousness in an otherwise mediated discourse:

> She turned over a page. Two o'clock has struck a short time ago. Usually, at this hour, there was not a living soul left in the theatre: this night it was alive. The typewriter was clicking, the lamp threw a rosy glow over the papers. And I am here, my heart is beating. Tonight the theatre has a heart and it is beating. [5, TM]

These incursions of the "I" are infrequent and occur principally in the opening sections of the novel. They usually appear at moments when Françoise ecstactically experiences herself as the living center of the world or as the consciousness that bestows vitality on lifeless objects: she is the beating heart of the otherwise "dead" theatre. A godlike source of life, Françoise is situated at the center of a mass of inert, abandoned, silent "things." If she did not bring them to life in her consciousness, if she did not structure and express them, they would remain inanimate forever. The world does not live in and for itself: without the consciousness of the "I," it is dead.

Not only things, but other people as well play the role of objects in her landscape. Without her consciousness of them, they would come undone, lapse back into some original inertness. This kind of imperi-

11. Over twenty years ago, Hazel Barnes presented a similar reading of *She Came to Stay*, interpreting it as a kind of defense and illustration of Sartre's *Being and Nothingness*, published the same year as Beauvoir's novel (cf. *The Literature of Possibility* [Lincoln: University of Nebraska Press, 1959], 113).

alism characterizes the attitude of Françoise during the entire first section of the novel. She deals with other people in a condescending way, talks about them as if they were to be humored, controlled, used— rather like pets. With these existences annexed to hers, Françoise creates stories. In fact, she alone knows the whole story:

> Xavière's gestures, her face, her very life depended on Françoise for their existence. At this very moment, for herself, Xavière was no more than a taste of coffee, a piercing music, a dance, a light feeling of well-being; but for Françoise, Xavière's childhood, her days of stagnation, her disappointments made up a romantic story as real as the delicate contour of her cheeks. And that story ended up precisely here in this cafe . . . where Françoise was turning toward Xavière and contemplating her. [15–16, TM]

The world, things, other people's lives are inert, disconnected, ungraspable until the consciousness of Françoise, the observer, the writer, tells their story for them. And for Françoise at this point, there is no separation between fact and fiction. Her stories are real; they are, in fact, the only reality.

At the end of everyone else's story, we return, as at the end of this passage, to the gaze of Françoise, the seeing eye, the "I" whose contemplation creates and maintains the world's reality. What she creates never really has a life of its own; she works by a process of annexation and possession.

THE GAZE RELAYED

Although this imperious "I" that bursts unpredictably into the narrative of *She Came to Stay* remains unthematized and thus strangely disconnected from the explicit issues of the text, it nevertheless plays an important role as an instance of a hidden, unstated level of meaning. It reveals, for instance, a secret agenda in Françoise's deference to Pierre. By channeling her perceptions and initiative through him, she can enjoy the prerogatives of power without having to take responsibility for them. While in one sense Pierre mutes Françoise, she in turn uses him as a front for her own passion for power.

Simone de Beauvoir's putting the authorial "I" in the mouth of Françoise also raises the possibility of an analogous relationship between herself as author and her protagonist. On the one hand, the use of the "I" seems to suggest a fusion of character and author: Simone and Françoise speak with one voice. On the other hand, pursuing the analogy with Pierre and Françoise, this fusion can also be seen as a decoy hiding the dark divisiveness of power and aggression.

The sporadic pattern of the use of the first person in *She Came to Stay* throws the third-person narrative into a curious profile. Each time the switch is made from first to third person, it has the effect of a withdrawal, of emphasizing the difference and distance between the two, between protagonist and author.

While the centering of consciousness in Françoise and the occasional use of the first person suggests a direct and positive link between protagonist and author, the flickering of this fusion puts this relationship into a new light. The third person takes on a negative aura, and Simone de Beauvoir's representations of Françoise are transformed into instances of the ironic narrative device; *le style indirect libre*.[12]

The technique of *style indirect libre* allows the author to identify with the characters of her novel but in an ironic, disrupted way that points up their self-delusions. Every statement the author makes about a character or in that character's name may either be taken at face value or it may be read as an implied criticism of the character's bad faith. It activates, then, a doubly charged connection between author and character, a relationship that hovers unspecifiably between identification and condemnation. When, for instance, at the beginning of the novel, Simone de Beauvoir reports Françoise's reflections on her relationship with Pierre, it is difficult for the reader to evaluate the status of these declarations:

> Before, when she found Pierre intimidating, there had been a number of things that she had brushed aside in this way: uncomfortable thoughts and ill-considered gestures. If they were not mentioned, it was almost as if they had not existed at all, and this allowed, underneath her true existence a shameful, subterranean vegetation to grow up where she felt utterly alone and in danger of suffocation. And then, little by little, she had yielded everything; she no longer knew solitude, but she was purified of those chaotic swarms. [21–22, TM]

It is important for us as readers to know whether we are meant to take these statements at face value or whether we are intended to read

---

12. There is no equivalent term in English for this technique by which an author reports directly the thoughts or words of a character, but in the third person and without indicating specifically that they are the character's. While the use of this technique is sometimes used in traditional fictional discourse as an extension of the omniscient narrator, its ambiguities open up possibilities of irony amply developed and exploited by Flaubert, especially in his novel *The Sentimental Education* (1869).

them as ironic signposts pointing to Françoise's ability to fool herself. The tone of this passage hinges on the word "purified"; in order to interpret the meaning of the text, we have to decide whether this word is used as a straightforward purveyor of a message or whether it is meant to emphasize the erroneous belief on Françoise's part that she can ever be pure. The apparent transparency of the language is put into question, and we are called on at each moment to judge the degree of clouding that is taking place.

Any one instance of the *style indirect libre* cannot be used as a decisive illustration; its ironic effects are inevitably cumulative, resulting from subtle but repeated examples of discordance between a character's thought and actions. This lack of coincidence between the character and herself, this bad faith, creates, however, as an inevitable logical aftermath, a parallel bad faith on the part of the author. At one with her character or her ironic judge, Beauvoir can manipulate Françoise as a mouthpiece or an object of scorn without having to declare her own position. Like her predecessor Flaubert, who used *le style indirect libre* to such advantage, Simone de Beauvoir is nowhere and everywhere at once.

While this kind of ambiguity and indeterminacy characterize much of modern fiction, it is put to particular use by Simone de Beauvoir in *She Came to Stay*. By maintaining an indeterminate relationship to her discourse, flipping in and out between emotional fusion and moral judgment, Simone de Beauvoir as author finally displaces the text as object of desire. In order for the reader to take up a well-defined relationship to the text, we must finally interrogate, not the text, but the deflected reflections we find there of the mind and will of the author.

We are, in other words, in the same relationship to Simone outside of the text as Françoise is to Pierre inside the text. As the author, she is the only one who holds the secret of the "correct" attitudes to take toward her book. This mythology of the all-knowing and all-judging creator suggested here is doubly reinforced by her comments and commentary on the book in her autobiography. If only we can "yield everything" as Françoise did to Pierre, we can be rid of all that "shameful, subterranean vegetation" of doubt, and become one with the author, the "purified" consciousness of the text, the only one who knows what is "real" in this fiction.

By setting herself up as the implied authority outside of the text and by maintaining the reader in an enforced state of perplexity, she establishes a model of writing-reading based on the dynamics of the traditional heterosexual couple. She is thus able to distance herself, as the "male" author who knows all, from the tangled thicket of her own "female" fiction.

Although Simone de Beauvoir eventually calls into question the imperious nature of Pierre's relationship to Françoise, she never directly addresses the issue of Françoise's bad faith (nor, by implication, her own). The possibility that a woman's yielding to a man's dominance may satisfy a secret appetite for power is never made part of the thematic equation of the plot. Rather, like this secret agenda itself, it is blatantly present without its implications being registered. The startling likelihood that the heterosexual paradigm may be a pretext for a discourse of female power proliferates unchecked in another place, in the shameful, subterranean vegetation of Françoise's relationship to Xavière.

WOMAN-TO-WOMAN

In many respects, Françoise reproduces in her relationship with Xavière a reversed version of the power structure that shaped her relationship with Pierre. As we have already seen, in her relationship with the younger woman, Françoise plays the role of the powerful authority, the ratifier of mutual experience, while Xaviére is the murky, unfinished *oeuvre*. But, we must suppose that since the two players in this drama of creation are women, the male metaphors defining this relationship gradually but irresistibly yield to another vocabulary.

From the outset, Françoise takes pleasure in Xavière's youth and dependency. She pays Xavière's bills and enjoys feeling protective. By the middle of the novel, the suggestions that have been latent become explicit; Simone de Beauvoir has Françoise reflect on "this little sleek, golden girl whom she had adopted" (216). The male model of authority collapses, then, under the metaphor of maternity. Writing and having children—reproducing—are no longer mutually exclusive. The structural analogy that makes either one a substitute for the other surfaces as the major metaphorical vehicle she uses to explore her relationship as a woman to her own reproduction in writing. Using her own mother's name, Françoise, Simone de Beauvoir replaces the lucid idealist male language of authority with the messy, biological female language of maternity. But when this replacement takes place, something curious happens; feelings flood in, and what was called a sacred vocation looks more like another, more radical kind of fusion, a fusion that is indistinguishable from a grandiose and ferocious attempt to control another being, or perhaps an unruly part of herself. In the following passage, she emphasizes the unresolvable puzzle of connection and separation that makes motherhood an unusual, if not unique, model of merged relationship:

> Whether she wanted to be or not, Xavière was bound to her by a bond stronger than hatred or love. . . . Françoise was the very substance of her life, and her moments of passion, of pleasure, of covetousness could not have existed without this firm web that supported them. Whatever happened to Xavière, happened through Françoise, and even if she wanted to or not, Xavière belonged to her. [267]

Reading Xavière as Simone's child-text, we see that even in the derived, metaphoric version of motherhood which adoption or literary production represents, the dynamics of identification and possessiveness seems irresistible. Like her "child" Xavière, writing seems to "belong" to Simone de Beauvoir. As her offspring, her production, they cannot possibly resist her or pose any obstacle to her expressive needs. There is no sense here that this child, this text, might be playful, elusive, or stubborn; that it might grow up to have an independent life of its own.

Nevertheless, the logic of this biological metaphor of motherhood introduces the possibility, here the danger, of development and growth. Françoise is indeed troubled by any signs of independence in Xavière, any evidence that her daughter might be growing up: "Françoise looked at her a little uneasily; it seemed sacrilegious to think of this virtuous little austerity as a woman, with the desire of a woman" (196, TM).

Besides raising the troubling possibility of sexual rivalry or even of sexual desire between the two women, Xavière's sexuality represents for Françoise another danger of even greater proportions: a sacrilege, the profanation of her belief in a possessable, transparent child-language which, like Pierre's love, will justify and redeem the inadequacies, the distortions, the cheat of female life. Françoise's dream of a symbolic maternity, an adoption in and of language, uncovers the secret script of her liaison with Pierre. Françoise loves Xavière because she can use her as an expression, a witness of her own power. Xavière's virtue, both as a character and as a text, is to be vacant. This "sweet sacrificed figure" (420) is sweet because she is sacrificed, sacred because she is void.

Françoise's relationship to Xavière uncovers, then, the agenda perversely expressed/hidden in her relationship to Pierre. Her loving and yielding to him was an indirect and finally misguided attempt to possess herself. Françoise's search for herself through a man founders, however, in the politics of gender and in her own bad faith. So cut off from herself that she is no longer aware of her own dispossession, Françoise's desperate yearning to belong to herself is thus deflected in a desire to belong to Pierre. It is only when a reflected version of herself—another woman, a child, a text—actually belongs to her that Françoise's fierce need to be her own can take shape in the mirror of her gaze.

These needs to possess and protect herself that she offers to Xavière have been denied and confined so long, however, that they have become volcanic. When the power of her desire, now through long deprivation become a voracious desire for power, begins to break out of its altruistic casing, Françoise is troubled and frightened. And when her "generosity" bounces off the increasingly recalcitrant Xavière, when the reflexive aspect of her metaphoric maternity ineluctably surfaces, Françoise begins to panic and to withdraw.

Not only does Françoise balk at attributing any adult sexual desire to Xavière, she blanks totally when she tries to imagine desiring her herself. She cannot conceive the possibility of giving shape or expression to a desire for another woman as an autonomous being, to her own desire as an autonomous woman. Françoise (Simone de Beauvoir?) questions herself: "But what did she desire? Her lips against hers? Her body surrendered in her arms? She could think of nothing" (263).

The possibility that there is *another* desire, a specifically female desire not mediated by the laws of transparent male language, this possibility overwhelms Françoise with terror, sets her adrift. The difference of no difference threatens to put her directly in touch with that "shameful, subterranean" world of her own desire—the desire of a woman, but precisely as a "nothing," unknowable and unpossessable, suffocating and alone; the desire of a woman who is at once her substance and yet not her. The child of her desire, Xavière, reveals to Françoise that she is a frightening stranger to herself; she knows for the first time the terror of having to desire herself as an other.

Françoise retreats in panic when Xavière puts her face to face with her own desire of and as a woman. The blank Françoise draws becomes a yawning chasm that threatens to engulf her. Although she attempts to circumscribe the danger by confining Xavière in the image of a pure child, Xavière—this part of Françoise that eludes her own possession and control—continues nightmarishly to expand:

> Françoise stiffened, but she could no longer simply close her eyes and blot out Xavière. Xavière has been growing steadily all through the evening, she had been weighing on her mind as heavily as the huge cake at the *Pôle Nord*. [68]

Like the unappetizing cake, Xavière grows too big to take in, to engulf, to swallow. And because she represents this unswallowable gob of existence, she seems herself voracious:

> For a second Françoise looked with horror at this delicate but implaca-
> ble face in which she had not once seen reflected any of her own joys
> and sorrows. . . . Sobs of revulsion shook her: her anguish, her tears,
> this night of torture. belonged to her and she would not allow Xavière
> to rob her of them. She would fly to the end of the world to escape the
> avid tentacles with which she wanted to devour her live. [313, TM]

As she looks into the implacable face of her own unsentimentalized desire, Françoise sees the little angel as a "witch" (253), a voracious monster ready to eat her up.

The dynamics of identification and doubling engendered by the difference of no difference between mother and daughter makes desire transferable and finally unlocatable. This encounter with her own hidden, unspeakable desire in the reflection of another woman's being means, then, that Françoise experiences this contact not as a confrontation, but as an implosion. The nonmediated avidity of her own desire sucks her into an infinite, wordless emptiness:

> It was like death, a total negation, an eternal absence, and yet, by a
> staggering contradiction, this abyss of nothingness could make itself
> present to itself and make itself exist for itself in all its fullness. The
> entire universe was engulfed in it, and Françoise, forever dispossessed,
> was herself dissolved in this void whose infinite contour no word, no
> image could encompass. [310, TM]

This reflection of herself in her adopted daughter that mirrors the inadequacy of her own words, this unendurable experience of her own femaleness as a simultaneously imperious and uncontrollable desire, is what drives Françoise to murder Xavière.

While Françoise was able to tell (almost) everything to Pierre, here she can say nothing at all. Words fail her, she says. But in truth what has failed her is her ability to imagine a female discourse that would emerge out of her terror as its embodiment. Since language represents for her the purity of an idealized male desire—the fully adequate and transparent correlation between a statement and "reality"—and because all writing thus ideally approaches nonfiction, anything that intrudes in the purity of that correlation must inevitably seem to her a blotch, a shame. According to Beauvoir, then, a specifically female discourse must by definition be morally and philosophically impure, dirty. To wish to construct a dirty discourse, in the clean world of "Beauvoir," of seeing everything as beautiful, would be, quite simply, absurd.

The murder of Xavière comes as the substitute for, the acting out of this absurdity. This senseless act fills up the empty place of Beauvoir's female words; it replaces her encounter with language as a sullied, intractable, hungry version of her own desire. Instead of yielding to the maelstrom of that desire, to the frightening meaning of her gender as confusion, Beauvoir simply kills it off.

The banishment of metaphor that this murder represents paradoxically makes the murder itself seem strangely unreal. As Elaine Marks has pointed out, "When at the end of the book, Françoise kills Xavière by turning on the gas . . . , we are conscious neither of a real murder nor of a real death."[13] This is a ritual murder emptied of reality precisely because its meaning lies elsewhere, because it is finally a failure of meaning. So although Beauvoir represents the murder as a triumph for Françoise, as an affirmation of herself, on another level it seems to be a cop-out, an abdication of the author's desire to write—as a woman.

THE CORPSE

But something seems wrong here. This has been too easy, proving that Simone de Beauvoir is a coward, that she does not like herself as a woman. It occurs to me that I have just killed off Simone de Beauvoir the way Françoise kills Xavière, to avoid anxiety, to cut off some meaning. I have been drawn into the confused and confusing position of a dependent female reader who crazily identifies, merges with the characters of a book. Perhaps, like Françoise, I have fallen into the trap of fusing with my double and then having to kill her, to demolish Simone de Beauvoir, to protect my identity as an authoritative (male) critic.

I have refused an encounter with Simone de Beauvoir as a messy, cheating female.

Instead of taking Beauvoir at her word and accepting the priority of her explanation of this text in her autobiography, let us allow this female-authored book to speak for itself. In spite of her repeated assertions that she put herself in Françoise—in her (the mother?)—that she limited her point of view to that of her characters,[14] we have already seen that her identification with these fictional intelligences wavers

13. Simone de Beauvòir: *Encounters with Death* (New Brunswick: Rutgers university Press, 1973), 77.
14. *The Prime of Life*, 251, 253, 271.

often into irony and moral judgment. What's more, if Françoise as a character in the book experiences a radical dispossession, a failure of language in the face of a female counterpart, the author does not; she puts that failure precisely into words.

In other words, words have *not* failed, and the acting-out of hostility in the murder of the threatening fictionality of her femaleness is, contrary to the message of the book, subsumed in and by language. Simone de Beauvoir has managed to articulate a tale in the chaotic space of her panic, a tale that distances her from that very panic, that conjures and contains it.

The murder is indeed unreal, a cheat and a lie—and in more ways than one. Not only is it a switch to allegory in a realistic novel, not only does it misproclaim its own message, it is not even "really" a murder. It is not only not a murder in the sense that it is made up of words, but it is not even a murder in the plot of the story. Françoise has decided to kill Xavière; she has turned on the gas and knows that she will be dead in the morning. But when the novel ends, Xavière is still alive. The "murder"—as everyone, including the author, calls it—is incomplete. As far as the novel is concerned, it will never be finished. Moving always toward completion outside the book, it is forever frozen in its own process: not a murder but a murdering. Xavière will always be this woman in the process of becoming a corpse; her death, her disposal, her apotheosis are forever deferred.

It is this body on the way to being a corpse, this fake murder moving endlessly toward its completion and definition outside the confines of the words on the page, this expression of a female will always postponed—this is the *abyme* where Simone de Beauvoir and her writing come together. At once language and its symbol, hidden and yet crazily blatant, this unfinished murder, this woman becoming a corpse embodies Simone de Beauvoir's writing as a false resolution

Simone de Beauvoir does not confront her vision of her own gender as sullied and dangerous, as contingent, as fictional, as something made up of a woman's own words, but neither does she entirely kill off, or silence, her own femininity. She sets up rather a protective, negative logic of preserved ambiguity and permanently false resolution. This is not the either/or logic associated with maleness, nor the both/and logic often associated with femaleness, but rather a strange neither/nor logic that simultaneously incorporates and denies both of them. By neither fully espousing nor fully repudiating her gender, Simone de Beauvoir leaves her writing hovering somewhere between life and death, male and female, never finished, never completed, always in need of being

recommenced, restated, rewritten. And as long as her writing is unfinished, her own death, like Xavière's, is deferred.

Writing does not replace or debase life, and Simone de Beauvoir's
own statements about the precedence of male lucidity over female distortion are themselves distorted. Her yearning for clarity and repose on
the one hand, and her ravenous desire to plunge into and possess life on
the other remain in an unresolved tension. And as long as that tug-of-
war continues, as long as the crime of writing, of self-definition, is not
completed, as long as the corpse, the corpus is unfinished, then its
author, by definition, cannot die. As long as the murder of this uninvited
guest, the fear and temptation of writing as a woman, remains a present
participle, a process—not a murder, but a murdering—Simone de Beauvoir is here to stay.

To write is to assert oneself, one's Self. It implies, therefore, authority, a
sense of justification. But what if the Self one wishes to assert turns out
to be confused, guilty, soiled? In that case, writing becomes an exhibition of just those qualities one wishes most to hide. Simone de Beauvoir
attempts to solve this dilemma she feels as a woman by projecting and
enclosing the messy parts of herself into the female characters in her
books, thus preserving the "purity" of herself as author. As Henri Peyre
points out in his introduction to Jean Leighton's book, *Simone de Beauvoir and Woman:* "As an imaginative writer, she has not once, strangely
enough, presented a female character whom we might admire, or merely remember lastingly as a complex, winning, mature, true woman" (7).
Simone de Beauvoir herself corroborates this pattern: in *The Force of
Circumstance* she describes how in writing *The Mandarins* she at-
tributed her own negative qualities to Anne while endowing the male
protagonist, Henri, with her positive characteristics (268).

This effort on the part of Simone de Beauvoir to remove all evidence
of moral or emotional taint, that is, all trace of femaleness, from her
writing has resulted in a style known for its no-frills quality. As one
critic put it, Simone de Beauvoir maintains a "doctor's outlook on the
world," always maintaining "her distance, her self-control and an entire
lucidity."[15]

This distance from her female self in her writing has led many
critics to comment on the "virility" of her style.[16] Konrad Bieber, for
instance, notes with much relief:

15. Jacques Ehrmann, "Simone de Beauvoir and the Related Destinies of Woman and
Intellectual," *Yale French Studies* 27, (Spring–Summer 1961):29.
16. Cf. "Interview with Alice Schwarzer," *Ms. Magazine*, August, 1983, 90.

Whatever qualms the male critic might have, Simone de Beauvoir puts his mind at rest: she speaks and writes in such a way that one might forget about the sex of the novelist.[17]

Bieber's appraisal is curiously echoed by Simone de Beauvoir's own statements about herself: "I don't think very much about my gender, I don't think about the fact that I am a woman writer."[18]

In another echo of her own writing, thirty-six years after the publication of *She Came to Stay*, Simone de Beauvoir explicitly asserts the impossibility of constructing a specifically female discourse. Language, she states, belongs to the collectivity; but this collectivity is in her eyes exclusively male: "It's hard to imagine that women can invent within the universal language a code that would be all their own. As it happens, they are doing no such thing. They are using men's words, even if they do twist the sense of them."[19]

Paradoxically, this failure of the imagination, this blank she draws when she tries to conceive a women's language, this "twisting" that femaleness represents, all these things she thinks of "very little," are blatantly revealed in her writing. Like the letters that Françoise had written to Xavière's lover Gerbert and locked up in her desk, like those guilty letters revealing that—in a reverse of the Oedipal scenario—she, the mother, had stolen her daughter's lover, the shameful truth hidden behind and in and by her writing comes spilling out for everyone to read. While in the "purified" trio of Françoise, Pierre, and Xavière, Françoise is generous and long-suffering, in the subterranean level of this other triangle, Françoise reveals herself to be a guilty, selfish, passionate, erotic woman.

This is precisely the inscription of herself as a writer that Beauvoir seems most eager to lock up in her writing. But this message has left its mark everywhere in the debased and murdered heroines, in the failed sisterhood, and the hostile mother-daughter relationships in her novels. Women, Beauvoir has said in response to a criticism of her negative presentations of female characters, women are "divided."[20] Herself, it seems, most of all.

In her public behavior, Simone de Beauvoir has challenged traditional values and has been a strong champion for the cause of women. But in her writing, the traditional definitions of gender and her own

17. *Simone de Beauvoir*, (Boston: Twayne, 1979), 17.
18. "Interview with Madeleine Chapsal," in C. Francis and F. Gontier, 381.
19. "Interview with Catherine David," *Vogue*, May 1979, 295.
20. "Interview with Madeleine Gobeil," in S. Julienne-Caffié, 213–14.

strivings as a female writer have remained in conflict. Beauvoir presents us with a model of female writing haunted by a history of bad faith and denial. The encounter with herself as a confused, erotic, angry, powerful woman who writes from within those feelings simply never takes place. Taking up a position of mastery with respect to her own femaleness, her writing is thus bleached of the enriching power of its own vulnerability. The metaphoric language that might emerge from confusion as its expression and its transcendence is sapped of its vitality and cast aside. To make up stories—that "boring" female activity—seems to threaten Beauvoir with the possibility of imagining the unimaginable: that she is not only Françoise but also Xavière, that sweet sacrificed figure who is "so hungry to . . . conquer and so eager to sacrifice nothing" (399, TM).

The writing of Simone de Beauvoir, this contemporary model of a liberated woman, demonstrates ironically that the mere fact of writing is not necessarily a liberating experience in itself. The prevailing debased models of women and of relationships between men and women may easily become paradigms for reading and writing even in the works of women authors. But when these models are maintained, as they are largely in Beauvoir's work, they have the tragic effect of splitting the author's gender off from the powers of her own creativity. Rather than becoming a free zone of the imagination in which she might create new images of wholeness, Beauvoir's writing is the re-inscription of the divisions that separate her from herself.

This inability to construct with pride a female model of writing and reading finally produces the most devastating split of all: the split between Beauvoir and her own writing—the vocation that has been the sustaining enterprise, the "salvation" of her life. All those millions of words that she has aligned with such care and tenacity finally do not belong fully to her. They are strangely stiff and empty, severed from their own inspiration. Because Beauvoir fails to establish a relationship of reciprocity with her own writing as a reflection of her female self, it continually drifts away from her and must endlessly be recommenced in a second, shadow writing. She is thus caught in a never-ending process of subversion and attempted recuperation of her own texts.

It seems no accident that Simone de Beauvoir's debut as a writer tells the story of a "murder." The most anguishing and criminal aspect of that murder is that it is a suicide.

YOLANDA ASTARITA PATTERSON

Simone de Beauvoir and the Demystification of Motherhood

From early childhood, Simone de Beauvoir observed with penetrating insight the role which has been foisted upon mothers by twentieth-century society. Her own mother, Françoise Brasseur de Beauvoir, exercised a profound influence on her development, providing a warm and affectionate atmosphere in which the young and precocious Simone was encouraged to make full use of her talents. Her mother also represented, however, a domineering authority figure, one intent upon molding her daughters' lives to fit her own specifications and those of the traditional bourgeois milieu in which she herself had been raised. The author's loss of religious faith at age fifteen established a barrier between her and her mother which was not removed until the final weeks of Françoise de Beauvoir's life, poignantly recounted in *A Very Easy Death* (1964), in which she described her relationship with her mother as "a dependence both cherished and detested."[1] Beauvoir's ambivalence about her mother, reinforced by her perception of the mother of a best friend Zaza Mabille, who died at the age of twenty-one, convinced her that the traditional family relationships touted as ideal by contemporary society could be devastating both for the mothers locked into their maternal molds and for the children whose supervision often became their sole raison d'être. As a young girl, Simone de Beauvoir dreaded the prospect of being caught in the same uninspiring routine of daily chores which she saw draining her mother of energy and vitality. At age sixty-eight, in an interview with Alice Schwarzer, she still equated a woman's decision to marry and have children with selling oneself into slavery.[2]

1. Simone de Beauvoir, *Une Mort très douce* (Paris: Gallimard, 1964), 147.
2. "Même si une femme a envie d'avoir des enfants, elle doit bien réfléchir aux conditions dans lesquelles elle devra les élever, parce que la maternité, actuellement, est un véritable esclavage." Alice Schwarzer, *Simone de Beauvoir aujourd'hui. Six entretiens* (Paris: Mercure de France, 1984), 77.

The problem of establishing an effective balance between self-fulfillment and family obligations is one which has plagued women throughout the centuries. In *L'Amour en plus* (1980), Elisabeth Badinter has traced the history of maternal devotion in France from the 1600s, noting that it was long fashionable for mothers to hand over their infants to a wet-nurse immediately after their birth and to have minimal interaction with them as they were growing up and maturing. Badinter argues convincingly that it is societal expectations rather than maternal instinct which determine the degree of responsibility a woman is willing to assume for the children she produces and pays tribute to Simone de Beauvoir who, thirty years earlier, questioned the validity of the concept of maternal instinct.[3] As long as women were valued for their participation in the life of the court and the salons, children were considered a necessary evil to be kept out of sight and away from home as long as possible. Once the state began to look upon children as future citizens and soldiers, their care and nurturing became a matter of general interest to men and women alike.

For more than sixty years of the twentieth century, Western society conditioned women to become wives and mothers and made those who rejected those roles feel somehow inadequate and incomplete. The ambivalence of creative women who have attempted to meet these expectations has been eloquently expressed by a number of writers. Betty Friedan, Smith College class of 1942, admits, "I married, had children, lived according to the feminine mystique as a suburban housewife. I could sense no purpose in my life, I could find no peace."[4] Sylvia Plath, Smith class of 1955, wrote to her mother that she and her new husband Ted Hughes planned on having seven children, "after each of us has published a book and traveled some."[5] Adrienne Rich confided wrenchingly to her journal in 1960:

> My children cause me the most exquisite suffering of which I have any experience. It is the suffering of ambivalence: the murderous alternation between bitter resentment and raw-edged nerves, and blissful gratification and tenderness.[6]

Rich found herself torn between the very real love she felt for her three sons and her need to write poetry: "For me, poetry was where I lived as

3. Elisabeth Badinter, *L'Amour en plus* (Paris: Flammarion, 1980), 27.
4. Betty Friedan, *The Feminine Mystique* (New York, W. W. Norton and Company, 1963), 70.
5. Sylvia Plath, *Letters Home* (New York: Bantam, 1975), 289.
6. Adrienne Rich, *Of Woman Born* (New York: W. W. Norton and Company, 1976), 21.

no one's mother, where I existed as myself."[7] Shirley Radl's ominously titled book *Mother's Day Is Over* chronicles the feelings of guilt and inadequacy which plague the woman who has accepted the myth of idyllic motherhood perpetrated by the media and found herself enmeshed in "the struggle to pursue her own interests against overwhelming odds."[8]

In addition to the focus on the mother's ambivalence about the duties and sacrifices demanded of her when she gives birth, modern literature has also produced many testimonies to the ambivalent feelings of daughters and sons about the woman responsible for their existence and their early nurturing. Hervé Bazin's 1948 novel *Vipère au poing* is a chilling account of a young boy who pits himself against the tyranny of an insensitive and unyielding mother determined to break his spirit and who thrives on the constant conflict which is the essence of their relationship. Nancy Friday begins *My Mother/ My Self* with the dramatic statement "I have always lied to my mother. And she to me."[9] Luce Irigaray opens her 1979 essay "Et l'une ne bouge pas sans l'autre" with the equally dramatic declaration "With your milk, my mother, I imbibed ice. And here I am now, frozen inside."[10] The trauma of the mother-daughter relationship has been brought to the screen by Ingmar Bergman, in "Autumn Sonata" where Eva (Liv Ullmann), after a night of soul-searching discussion, launches out at her mother, a concert pianist (Ingrid Bergman) with the words:

> People like you are a menace. You should be locked away so you can't do any harm. . . . A mother and a daughter. What a fierce terrible combination of failings, of confusion, of destruction.[11]

The Oscar winning film "Ordinary People," based on a novel by Judith Guest, examines the interaction between mother and son as the viewer follows the adolescent Conrad Jarrett (Timothy Hutton) from his return home after a suicide attempt to his acceptance of the fact that his mother (Mary Tyler Moore) is simply incapable of being as affectionate and articulate with him as he would like.

In the last twenty years, much literature and film footage have brought the enigma of modern motherhood to the attention of the public. However, it was as early as 1949, that Simone de Beauvoir scan-

7. Rich, 31.

8. Shirley Radl, *Mother's Day Is Over* (New York: Charterhouse 1, 1973), 10.

9. Nancy Friday, *My Mother/ Myself* (New York: Delacorte Press, 1977), 1.

10. Luce Irigaray, *Et l'une ne bouge pas sans l'autre* (Paris: Les Editions de Minuit, 1979), 7.

11. Ingmar Bergman, director. "Autumn Sonata" (Sweden: 1978).

dalized her readers by devoting the first fifteen pages of the chapter of *The Second Sex* entitled "The Mother" to a discussion of abortion and contraception. Simone de Beauvoir had long since decided that motherhood was not for her and felt an obligation to warn other women about the entrapment it represented. In a heated argument with her best friend Zaza Mabille, one of nine children in a devout and conservative Catholic family, the adolescent Simone had once disagreed vehemently with Zaza's assertion that producing a large number of offspring was just as creative as writing books. Simone de Beauvoir stated in numerous interviews that she never had any desire to have children of her own and that she never regretted her decision to remain childless. In an interview published in Betty Friedan's *It Changed My Life*, she categorically advised feminists to avoid motherhood, causing Friedan to comment that Simone de Beauvoir did not seem to be dealing with women's lives as they were lived in the real world. Yet several articles which appeared after Simone de Beauvoir's death on April 14, 1986 proclaimed her the mother of the women's movement, the mother of all liberated women, whether or not they know her name or her work. Women working at the Centre Audiovisuel Simone-de-Beauvoir in Paris were quoted in *Le Monde* as saying "We are all orphans now."[12] When I suggested in a September 1985 interview that many feminists look upon her as a mother figure, Simone de Beauvoir laughingly pointed out that the analogy was erroneous because people don't tend to listen to what their mothers are telling them.

It is apparent from the recurring focus on her own mother, on Zaza's mother, and on mother figures in both her autobiographical and her fictional works that Simone de Beauvoir could not simply dismiss the maternal role as one which held no particular interest for her. She approached the whole question of motherhood obliquely in her fiction before theorizing about it in *The Second Sex* or talking about her own mother in *Memoirs of a Dutiful Daughter* (1958) and *A Very Easy Death* (1964). Her fictional works contain a vast spectrum of mother-child relationships which become more nuanced as the author matures, and which move from a sense of anger and outrage to one bordering on pity for victims of a system not of their making. In interviews and essays Beauvoir frequently reaffirmed her conviction that the early years of children's existence are critical to their ability to find fulfillment and happiness in adult life. Just as she was grateful to her own mother for

12. Le Centre Audiovisuel Simone-de-Beauvoir, quoted in *Le Monde*, Wednesday 16 April 1986, 19.

providing an atmosphere in which she and her sister Hélène flourished during their early childhood, so was she hypersensitive to the detrimental influence of mothers who were overly manipulative, self-effacing, seductive or perfectionistic with their children. These are the mothers who populate her fictional works and who constitute a chilling ensemble of personalities guaranteed to cause many a young woman to think twice before joining their ranks.

When her best friend Zaza Mabille died at age twenty-one of a high fever and undetermined medical causes, Simone de Beauvoir was convinced that it was bourgeois society, and more specifically the emotionally manipulative Madame Mabille, who had assassinated her. Seething at maternal control masked as concern for a child's soul and salvation, she attempted numerous fictional transcriptions of the tragedy of Zaza's death, and ultimately vented her anger both on Madame Mabille and to some degree on her own very pious mother in the vicious portrait of Madame Vignon which occupies the central story of the early collection of stories *When Things of The Spirit Come First* (written between 1935 and 1937, but unpublished until 1979). For five and one half pages, Madame Vignon prays to the Good Lord for guidance in raising her children according to His will, and more specifically in pushing her daughters toward arranged marriages which will undoubtedly prove as loveless as her own. She assumes that her daughters have been designated by both the Lord and the State to become wives and mothers and therefore considers it her maternal duty to torment the intellectual and vivacious Anne with social obligations which would expose her to appropriate suitors. This "prayer," laden with irony and hypocrisy, is a broadside attack on the devoutly Catholic milieu in which Françoise de Beauvoir brought up her daughters, a milieu whose psychological hold was loosened forever when the adolescent Simone lost her faith. For Zaza Mabille as for the fictional Anne Vignon, however, the stranglehold remained, because devotion to God was equated with love of and obedience to mother, the original source of information about this God. Like Zaza, Anne writhes in agony under the emotional strain of attempting to maintain her close relationship with her mother while striving at the same time to assert her independence. Her dilemma is eloquently stated when she admits to her friend Chantal:

> I had sworn to myself that I would never hurt Mother in any way, and I am a continual source of torment to her. When I give in to her, I have no self-respect; when I resist, I hate myself . . .[13]

13. Simone de Beauvoir, *Quand prime le spirituel* (Paris: Gallimard, 1979), 160.

Raised in a tradition of Christian obedience, Anne can neither bring
herself to defy her mother openly nor can she endure the thought of
adopting the lackluster life style which Madame Vignon is trying to
foist upon her. Her premature death seems to be the only way out of this
labyrinth of conflicting emotions.

Simone de Beauvoir presents this particular mother-daughter relationship as a trap preventing an intelligent and talented young girl from
progressing beyond the limited confines of existence prescribed by the
older generation to which her mother belongs. Like Zaza, like the young
Simone de Beauvoir herself, Anne Vignon is grateful to her mother for
the happy and secure childhood with which she provided her. The desire
to keep things from changing, to perpetuate a relationship which proved
so gratifying during her early years, is a strong counterbalance to the
thrust toward independence for Anne, particularly when mother, God
and salvation are inextricably bound together in the mind of the young
woman striving for maturity. Madame Vignon is fully aware of the
variety of chords she can strike to keep Anne firmly under her sphere of
influence, and she never hesitates to make use of them. If she can force
her daughters to become devout middle-class wives and mothers like
herself, her existence will somehow seem justified. The story leaves the
reader with a haunting image of a self-centered mother who, even after
Anne's untimely death, manages to avoid facing reality by persuading
herself that she has been a mere instrument in the hands of a God who
has selected her daughter for martyrdom and sainthood. Her final prayer
is addressed to her deceased daughter rather than to God:

> Anne, my little saint . . . pray for me, a poor sinner. Help me accept
> without complaint the fact that I have been the instrument of your
> suffering and of your salvation.[14]

The poignant irony of Beauvoir's portrait makes Madame Vignon a
strong candidate for the role of the female Tartuffe of the twentieth
century. The writing of this story, which was completed before Beauvoir turned thirty, undoubtedly had a cathartic value for the author who
needed to deal with her lingering grief over the loss of Zaza, with her
sense of guilt at having been so involved in her own life that she was
unable to help her friend fight more effectively for her freedom and
happiness, and with her anger at Madame Mabille for having made the
final months of Zaza's life so miserable.

The reader does not find another incarnation of the destructively

14. Ibid., 188.

manipulative mother until the publication of the 1954 Goncourt Prize winning novel *The Mandarins*. Although a relatively minor character in the narrative, Lucie Belhomme is an outrageous caricature of the pushy stage mother who goes so far as to lift up her humiliated daughter's skirt at a cocktail party to show off her lovely legs to a theatrical producer. It is assuredly not by chance that Simone de Beauvoir chose the name "Belhomme" for this mother who spends much of her time pushing her very attractive daughter Josette into the arms of any gentleman, "bel" or otherwise, who may prove useful to either or both of them. Josette whines about the way in which her mother dominates her life but does not appear to have either the energy or the initiative to break away. Like Anne Vignon, Josette has been paralyzed by the past which she has shared with her mother, in this case a rather sordid past which included intimate relationships for both of them with German soldiers during the Occupation. Just as Anne and Zaza continue to share religious convictions with their respective mothers, Josette shares an apparent lack of ethics and morals with Lucie, and the attitudes that lies and perjury are justifiable means to an end. Josette complains that even after she becomes a successful actress her mother continues to talk to her as if she were a child, yet does not hesitate to use tears and feigned innocence to get men to respond to her every wish. She internalizes her mother's ruthlessness and justifies it in her own conscience by her determination never again to be without the material necessities, indeed the luxuries of life.

A final example of a domineeringly manipulative mother is to be found in the second story of the 1967 collection *The Woman Destroyed*. In "Monologue," the reader spends New Year's Eve and the dawn of the incoming year with Murielle, who rants and raves about the injustices of her life. At forty-three, she has had two husbands and two children, none of whom is living with her at the moment. Feeling abandoned and alienated from the social circles in which she would like to move, she imagines unorthodox methods of forcing her second husband to move back in with her, and derives a sadistic glee from the thought of opening her veins in front of her eleven-year-old son and splattering her blood everywhere. This is the same child whom she is eager to take to the circus, the zoo, the Ice Capades, in order to prove to the rest of the world that she is indeed a model mother. Murielle is decidedly one of the most emotionally unstable of Simone de Beauvoir's fictional characters.

Murielle's obsession with death and suicide becomes more understandable when we learn that her seventeen-year-old daughter Sylvie killed herself five years earlier to escape from her mother's intolerable domination. Much of what is said throughout the monologue is an attempt by Murielle to prove that she was in no way responsible for Sylvie's death, which she considers an act of egregious ingratitude, aimed primarily at ruining her reputation as a conscientious and caring mother. Accused by her own mother of having murdered Sylvie, Murielle protests that she insisted on maintaining strict control over her daughter precisely because she wanted to prevent Sylvie from becoming "a whore like my mother."[15] These strong words reflect Murielle's resentment of her mother's affectionate and perhaps seductive interaction with her younger brother. They also suggest the degree to which, coming from an unhappy and unstable childhood situation, Murielle is essentially incapable of being an effective mother to her own children.

All of the metaphors used by Murielle when she talks about her theories of raising children indicate that she equates this process with the training of a performing animal. Her major problem is that no one here on earth will allow her back in the circus ring with her whip. In a seethingly sarcastic parallel to Madame Vignon's prayer for divine intercession, Murielle appeals to one final authority in the last words of her monologue:

> My Lord! Let it be that You exist! Let there be a heaven and a hell where I will stroll along the paths of paradise with my little boy and my beloved daughter and the rest of them will all be writhing with envy in flames. I'll look at them roasting and moaning. I'll laugh and laugh and the children will laugh with me.[16]

It is on this sardonic image of an eternally triumphant Murielle reunited with her children in heaven that "Monologue" ends. Murielle's vulgarity, her self-deception, the torment she must have caused her daughter, all make her an unsavory character with whom the reader cannot at all identify. Along with Madame Vignon, she is an exquisitely drawn caricature of the tyrannical mother. Her final prayer is a rather ironic variation on a comment Françoise de Beauvoir made in a letter to a friend which was found by the Beauvoir sisters after their mother's death. In it, Françoise de Beauvoir admitted that while she herself would certainly like to go to heaven, she would not want to be there without her two daughters. This comment apparently underlined for Simone de Beauvoir the wide gap between the certainty that there is no existence

15. Simone de Beauvoir, "Monologue," *La Femme rompue* (Paris: Gallimard, 1967), 95.

16. Ibid., 118.

beyond death, no reunion in an afterlife with loved ones (which she so wrenchingly expressed in the final sentences of *Adieux: A Farewell to Sartre* (1981)[17] and Françoise de Beauvoir's religious faith, which remained to the end an obstacle to complete communication between mother and daughter. The exaggerated and almost painful image of mother and children gleefully prowling through paradise is perhaps a telling indication of the extremes of emotion which characterized Simone de Beauvoir's relationship with her mother.

The daughters of all three of these fictional mothers desperately seek ways of escaping from their control. The devoutly Catholic Anne Vignon would never consider actually committing suicide, yet the emotional pressure imposed upon her by her mother causes her, like Zaza Mabille, to lose all desire to live, to abandon herself to a physical disease which might well have been curable had she been psychologically strong enough to offer it some resistance. Josette abandons the struggle in a different way by adopting the life style her mother inflicts on her. She may have moments of lucidity, of thinking about rebelling against Lucie's iron hand, but the fact that she has not done so by the time she is twenty-six suggests that she probably never will. Sylvie has chosen the most direct and most tragic means of escaping permanently from her mother through her suicide. These daughters are driven to separate physically, by death if necessary, from a controlling figure with whom they can no longer cope, or to allow their own identities to be totally absorbed and thereby to abandon their struggle for independence.

The chronology of Simone de Beauvoir's early fictional works suggests the degree to which writing helped her make the necessary break from her family and the milieu in which she was raised, and most particularly from the mother she both loved and resented. In *When Things of the Spirit Come First,* irony and cynicism help her make the transition from the protected, maternally dominated atmosphere of the Beauvoirs' Parisian apartment to a world of infinitely expanding horizons. The vindictive tone, the sarcasm, the unsympathetic portrayal of many of the characters in the throes of spiritual confusion imply a breaking away which was an extremely painful period in the author's own life, a reflection of her late adolescence from which she had to distance herself by the passage of several years before she could effectively deal with its traumas even on paper. The minimal role played by Madame Miquel, the only biological mother who figures in Simone de Beauvoir's first published novel *She Came to Stay* (1943), is a fairly clear

17. Simone de Beauvoir, *La Cérémonie des adieux* (Paris: Gallimard, 1981), 159.

indication of the degree to which Françoise de Beauvoir had receded into the background at this stage of her daughter's development. In her second novel, *The Blood of Others* (1945), Beauvoir devotes several key passages to the masochistic Madame Blomart, a maternal martyr par excellence.

Madame Blomart is the type of submissive, passive woman whom Simone de Beauvoir would later label a "relative being" in *The Second Sex*. Like Françoise de Beauvoir, she is timid and self-effacing, filled with an overabundance of love and energy for which she has difficulty finding an outlet. Her adeptness at playing the martyr keeps her son Jean vacillating between feelings of guilt and resentment as he reacts to the unspoken accusations he senses behind his mother's resigned exterior façade.

Our entire impression of Madame Blomart is formed from what we learn of her through her son. Jean Blomart predates ten-year-old Catherine of *Les Belles Images* by two decades in his concern for poverty, for misery, for the plight of the workers. It is of interest that in the early 1940s Beauvoir chose a male character to bear the burden of concern for human suffering, whereas in the 1960s it is a young girl, also influenced by her mother's sensitivity, who carries the standard for her creator. In the interim, Beauvoir's hopes for a socialistic world which would cure the ills of humanity had begun to fade, and her awareness of male dominance in the struggle for all causes promising a better tomorrow had sharpened.

Like Françoise de Beauvoir, Madame Blomart has instilled in her impressionable child a sense of Christian duty toward those less fortunate than his comfortably fixed bourgeois family. As a boy, Jean trotted along behind her as she visited "her" sick, "her" poor people. Her days are still filled with the charitable activities expected of a well-off middle-class matron, yet Jean senses a frenetic quality in them, a busyness calculated to make her forget the basic injustices of class distinction. When he decides to help change the inequities of the social class system by joining the Communist party, his mother is extremely upset:

> It was crazy to want to change anything about the world, about life; things were already miserable enough if you were careful not to touch them. . . .The thing to do was to crouch in a corner, to make oneself as inconspicuous as possible, and, rather than try something doomed to failure from the start, to accept everything.[18]

This passage undoubtedly reflects the attitude Simone de Beauvoir saw her own mother adopt in a society in which she felt uncomfortable and

18. Simone de Beauvoir, *Le Sang des autres* (Paris: Gallimard, 1945), 21, 22.

ineffectual. In *A Very Easy Death*, the writer recalls the provincial Françoise de Beauvoir's method of agreeing with all opinions expressed, no matter how divergent they might be, in order to avoid calling attention to herself in the sophisticated Parisian social circles which seemed so alien to her upbringing.

Simone de Beauvoir recreates the hurt she must have sensed in her own mother's reaction to her decision to live away from home, albeit only as far away as her grandmother's Parisian apartment, in a poignant scene in which Madame Blomart berates Jean for his ingratitude toward his father in abandoning the family printing business. Jean is attuned to another, more authentic voice inside of his mother begging him not to leave her, a voice which never surfaces audibly during their conversation. Overtly, Madame Blomart is not a domineering mother. "We were free, free to sully our souls, to ruin our lives; the only liberty she took was to suffer from what we did."[19] Psychologically, she is a more stifling personality for her three children than a mother who makes continual demands on them. As he packs his things, Jean cannot shake off the image of his mother isolated in the satin and velvet decor of their expensively appointed home, realizing that with both of his sisters living elsewhere he is all she has left. One wonders if Simone de Beauvoir felt a similar twinge of guilt when she moved away from home, knowing that her father was essentially indifferent to her mother's psychological and material needs, and that her younger sister would also be declaring her independence soon. Jean Blomart has no idea how to go about defending his mother against herself, a self which continually denies its own impulses and desires in order to fit inconspicuously into a traditional middle-class routine. The portrayal of Madame Blomart in this passage parallels Simone de Beauvoir's description of her mother in *A Very Easy Death*, her body, her heart and her spirit "corseted" in the values and restrictions imposed upon her during her childhood.

The pain of growing up, of separating from one's mother, is dramatically conveyed in a scene in which Jean, exhausted and overwhelmed by his leadership role in the French Resistance, has just finished having dinner with his parents:

> . . . suddenly I'm five years old, I'm afraid and I'm cold. I would like my mother to tuck me into my bed and give me a big long hug; I would like to stay here: I would stay in my old room, curled up in my past, and maybe I would get a really good night's sleep.[20]

He knows, of course, that this is impossible. The assumption of the

19. Ibid., 32.
20. Ibid., 294.

responsibilities of adulthood places a return to childhood security forever out of reach. Jean must now live not only with his mother's silent suffering but also with her unarticulated disapproval of his responsibility for the taking of human lives during the Occupation.

The Blood of Others takes the reader from the entanglement of interpersonal relationships in *She Came to Stay* to the collective experience of World War II in France. Madame Blomart represents a kind of collective conscience forcing the members of the younger generation to think hard about the taking of any human life, be it that of enemy or of countryman. Throughout the narrative, Jean has railed against the "senseless" caution he has inherited from his mother, a caution which almost paralyzed him because of his fear of hurting other people. His final confrontation with Madame Blomart in the novel seems to pit concern for human life against regrettably necessary violence, with the latter prevailing. The maternal thrust toward preserving life represented by Madame Blomart and her generation appears outmoded in an era in which action is valued over passivity.

Madame Blomart is a likeable human being with admirable instincts who has become a martyr precisely because she has accepted an unspoken dictum that women, and most particularly mothers, are meant to sacrifice their own needs and desires to those of their families, and especially those of the next generation. Several decades later, she is joined by Monique, protagonist of the story "The Woman Destroyed" in the collection of the same name, who has given up her own medical studies in order to marry a doctor and raise two daughters. Monique is perhaps the most haunting incarnation of Simone de Beauvoir's warnings about the pitfalls of marriage and motherhood: she prides herself on her success as a wife, mother and housekeeper until the night she discovers that her husband is having an affair with a younger woman. Then her world begins to crumble around her as she probes frantically through her past for indications of what she has done wrong. She blames herself for discouraging her older daughter from pursuing a promising career by her example as a homebody, for driving her more independent younger daughter off to New York by being overly protective and solicitous with her. The younger Lucienne's assurance that no individual ever has that much impact on any other makes Monique feel even more desperate, negating as it does the entire rationale behind her years of devotion to her husband and children. She gradually comes to see herself as "some sort of bloodsucker nourishing itself on the lives of others."[21] After her husband moves out, she will

---

21. "La Femme rompue," *La Femme rompue,* 237.

at last be obliged to abandon her secondary role as wife and mother and to live primarily for herself. It was precisely the courage to do just that which Simone de Beauvoir admired in her own mother after her father's death. A widow at fifty-five, she found herself an apartment, learned to ride a bicycle, worked part-time at a library, attended lectures and learned both German and Italian. As Monique returns to an empty apartment in the final scene of "The Woman Destroyed," the reader hopes that she too will find the energy to recuperate from illness and depression and to reconstruct an independent life for herself.

Unlike the manipulative mothers, the maternal martyrs of Simone de Beauvoir's fiction are loved by their children, but also cause the more sensitive of them to feel guilty about the sacrifices of time, energy and identity which their mothers have made for them. From the thousands of letters Simone de Beauvoir received from readers of *The Second Sex*, and from her observation of her own contemporaries, she knew that women who had invested themselves entirely in the raising of their families suddenly found themselves without any focus to their lives once their children left home. In the final chapters of *The Second Sex*, Simone de Beauvoir urged women to pursue careers, and three of the fictional works which she wrote after the publication of *The Second Sex* focus on mothers who are also career women.

The 1954 novel *The Mandarins* occupies a special place in the canon of Simone de Beauvoir's work, appearing midway between her extensive study of women in *The Second Sex*, and the first volume of her autobiography. In 1954, the author was in her midforties and was listening to what her friends who had children were saying about raising them to adulthood. After World War II, the reader begins to see the action of Simone de Beauvoir's fiction presented from the point of view of the mother rather than from the point of view of the daughter or son.

One of three protagonists in *The Mandarins*, Anne Dubreuilh is a psychiatrist approaching her fortieth birthday as the narrative begins. She is gradually losing faith in her ability to help people adjust to the turbulence of the modern world and is at the same time uneasy about her relationship with her only child, Nadine. She blames her maternal ambivalence partly on the hostility she feels toward her own mother, who does not appear at all as a character in the novel. The void represented by the generation of Anne's parents seems to correspond to the minimal emotional involvement Simone de Beauvoir herself had in her own mother's life during this exceptionally productive decade of her career.

Hostility toward her own mother, indifference toward herself: these are the focal points of Anne's explanation of her alleged ineptitude at mothering. Having sought her identity in her husband Robert's protective and mature arms—he was her professor at the university—Anne had anticipated that marriage would be a one-to-one relationship which would make her feel both secure and needed. She therefore interpreted Robert's immediate desire to have a child as an indication of her inability to fulfill his needs herself. Simone de Beauvoir uses Anne Dubreuilh as an example of an intelligent woman who does not fit the modern myth of maternal instinct, who is quite articulate about her resentment of the child she produced against her will: "I didn't want her. It was Robert who wanted a child right away. I resented Nadine for intruding upon our intimacy."[22] Nadine's birth interrupted Anne's search for her own identity by putting unwanted demands on both her time and her energy. Anne has spent many years analyzing her feelings toward her daughter, which appear to be a mixture of discomfort, resentment and guilt.

The fact that Nadine Dubreuilh has been a difficult, rebellious child to raise has added to Anne's problems. Anne is sure that Nadine has consciously avoided associating herself with anything feminine because she does not want to admit to belonging to the same sex as her mother. Nadine taunts Anne by pointing out that, despite her success as a psychiatrist, she will never be Freud. "All women can do is vegetate,"[23] she declares defiantly. Both mother and daughter are agonizing over sex roles in the late 1940s, when options for women were still quite limited. Despite her sexual promiscuity and her tomboy temperament, Nadine admits resignedly to her mother one day, "I suppose I'm meant to have a husband and children like all women. I'll scour my pots and produce a brat a year."[24] This is hardly a romanticized view of woman's destiny, and it is undoubtedly designed to provoke a reaction in Anne by reducing the role Anne has assumed in their family to one which appears insignificant and uninspiring.

Despite her psychological sophistication, Anne Dubreuilh apparently accepts the myth of the perfect mother-daughter relationship. She is all too ready to interpret Nadine's recalcitrance as an indication of her failure at motherhood. She realizes that none of the traditional expectations of earlier eras can be applied to a generation whose adolescence corresponded to the World War II years and has allowed Nadine complete freedom to choose her own life style with a minimal amount of maternal advice or involvement. Like Jean Blomart, however, Nadine can always sense when her mother disapproves of something she is

22. Simone de Beauvoir, *Les Mandarins* (Paris: Gallimard, 1954), 48.
23. Ibid., 171.
24. Ibid., 201.

doing and she resents the unarticulated judgment this implies. Anne is quick to assume the blame for the vicious circle this situation has created:

> If I had loved her more, our relationship would have been different. Maybe I could have prevented her from leading a life of which I cannot approve.[25]

A rare moment of relief occurs when Anne compares Nadine to the "faded virgin" she observes serving coffee at her mother's social get-together. Nadine, Anne realizes, is at least acting out all of her obsessions, sexual and otherwise, while this overprotected young woman is caught in a web of repression and middle-class convention.

In the final chapter of *The Mandarins*, Anne Dubreuilh lies on her bed fingering a vial of poison she once confiscated from a suicidal friend and contemplates suicide herself. She realizes she has been fleeing from death since she was fifteen, and is simply too tired to continue the struggle. Simone de Beauvoir herself first experienced the anguish of death when at fifteen she lost her religious faith and along with it the assurance of an afterlife in which one would reap the rewards of one's accomplishments here on earth. Simone de Beauvoir and her protagonist Anne Debreuilh have been through the emotional intensity of affairs with the real Nelson Algren and the fictional Lewis Brogan, respectively, and have returned to France wondering about what to do with the rest of their lives. Anne Dubreuilh no longer considers herself essential to the well-being of either her daughter or her husband. In her newborn granddaughter she sees the inevitability of her own decline and demise, of the oblivion which eventually awaits us all. Just as in an earlier section of the novel Anne remained immobilized waiting for Nadine to summon her in to have tea with her friends, she is now called back to life by the sound of Nadine's irritated voice asking why Anne has left her new granddaughter unattended in the garden. Could something have happened to Maria? Anne is jarred out of her detachment by the concern she still feels for the members of her family. Her inbred sense of responsibility makes her realize the full implication of committing suicide:

> I imagined Nadine's voice, loud and indignant: "You shouldn't have done that! You had no right!" . . . . I cannot inflict my cadaver and everything associated with it on their hearts: Robert bending over this bed, . . . Nadine's infuriated sobs.[26]

25. Ibid., 61.
26. Ibid., 578.

Anne would have to agree with Nadine's predictable reaction: no one has the right to inflict such a psychological burden on her family. In the last analysis, it is Nadine's opinions and feelings which count more than anything else for Anne. All of her life Anne has tried in her ambivalent but well-intentioned way to bring happiness and security to her daughter. At the end of the novel she reverts to the self-sacrificing maternal role which has both ensnared and justified her existence. Her successful career and her sexual freedom distinguish her from the long suffering Madame Blomart and Monique, but Anne Dubreuilh finds herself attached more strongly than she had previously realized to the child to whom she so reluctantly gave birth.

Twelve years and four volumes of autobiographical works separate *The Mandarins* from Simone de Beauvoir's next fictional work, *Les Belles Images* (1966). The focus on mothers and motherhood is ever present in these autobiographical works. Laurence, the protagonist of *Les Belles Images*, is a modern career woman caught between the needs of a fifty-one-year-old mother to whom she has never felt particularly close and those of a ten-year-old daughter who is beginning to ask probing and often unanswerable questions. Whereas Françoise de Beauvoir had an emotionally deprived childhood during which she yearned for affection from an undemonstrative mother, Dominique Langlois had a financially deprived childhood which made her intent upon turning both of her daughters into the picture perfect little girls she never was. Her daughter Laurence associates her impeccable childhood with the tale of the king who turned everything he touched, including his child, into gold, and blames her mother for turning her into a metal doll incapable of emotion. Yet in many ways Laurence is oversensitive and she fears that her older daughter Catherine has inherited this trait. She feels threatened by the questions Catherine is asking, and would prefer not to think about them:

> Why do we exist? That's not my problem. We do exist. The thing to do is to take no note of it, to keep moving along straight toward death. . . .
> My problem is this sense of falling apart from time to time, as if there were a frightening answer to Catherine's question.[27]

In this determination to avoid unpleasantness and unsettling thoughts at all cost we find a reflection of the attitudes of both Françoise de Beauvoir and the fictional Madame Blomart, passive women afraid to take too close a look at reality.

Like Anne Dubreuilh, Laurence is conscientious in her attempt to achieve an effective balance between her career and her family respon-

27. Simone de Beauvoir, *Les Belles Images* (Paris: Gallimard, 1966), 44.

sibilities. She is both extremely fond of her two daughters and resentful of the commitment their existence demands of her:

> It's frightening to think that one marks one's children merely by what one is. . . . Daily moods, a chance word, a silence, all of these contingencies which should be erased immediately become inscribed upon this child who ruminates and who will remember, as I remember the inflexions of Dominique's voice. It seems unfair. One cannot be responsible for everything one does or doesn't do.[28]

What Laurence gradually realizes is that she must indeed assume that responsibility. This point is driven home to her as she watches a little Greek girl totally absorbed in her dancing and contrasts her with her bovine mother who is completely insensitive to the passion inside of her child. Laurence does not want that little girl to grow up to resemble her mother any more than she wants Catherine to grow up to resemble her. When Laurence, desperately seeking something to eat in an impoverished Greek town, can only locate two rotten eggs, there is an implication that these eggs may parallel those produced both by Dominique and by Laurence unless the latter acts quickly to reorient the course of her daughters' lives. Literally nauseated by her life and its lack of purpose, Laurence is jolted out of her anorexic indifference at the end of the novel by her determination to provide her daughters with a more lucid and sensitive upbringing than the one Dominique so carefully arranged for her and her sister. Just as the thought of Nadine kept Anne Dubreuilh from committing suicide at the end of *The Mandarins*, Laurence is shaken from her torpor by her very real concern for Catherine's future and by her awareness that she can do something to influence it.

The perfectionistic protagonists of Simone de Beauvoir's fiction who are striving to be successful as wives, mothers and career women share feelings of responsibility and guilt with the martyred women who do not try to extend their sphere of influence beyond their own homes. Both career women like Anne Dubreuilh and Laurence and domestic types like Monique show a tendency toward illness and self-destruction when faced with crises in their lives. Less manipulative than the Madame Vignons and the Lucie Belhommes of the world, they turn their frustrations inward upon themselves rather than venting them on their offspring. Intellectually accepting of modern permissiveness in the rearing of children, mothers like Anne and Laurence nonetheless feel uneasy about remaining detached and uninvolved, unsure of whether or not they are doing a properly conscientious job of raising their daughters.

28. Ibid., 135, 136.

Many of the families in Simone de Beauvoir's fiction are drawn from her own experience growing up in a household with two daughters. In the opening story of *The Woman Destroyed*, however, Beauvoir deals with an overly seductive mother of a grown son. The sixty-year-old unnamed protagonist of "Age of Discretion" is lost and depressed when she finds her teaching career and her maternal influence coming to an end at the same time. In the first scene of the story, as she puts on her best dress in anticipation of her son's visit, it is apparent that this mother would like to continue to be both intellectually and emotionally seductive with her son. The problem, however, is that Philippe has recently married. While his mother would very much like to erase his wife Irène from her mind, and from the world for that matter, this is somewhat difficult, particularly since Philippe is quite fond of his new wife. When the young couple cheerfully announce that Philippe has decided to stop working on his dissertation, to abandon plans for pursuing a university career like his mother's, and to take a lucrative position (which his father-in-law has found for him) in the business world, his mother feels betrayed. She interprets the decision as a rejection of the intellectual world which has been the focus of her life, and as a victory for the young and modern Irène in their tug of war over Philippe. She muses dejectedly:

> I am the one who fashioned his life. Now I will remain outside of it, a distant spectator. This is the fate common to all mothers; but who has ever found consolation in the fact that her fate is shared by others?[29]

She realizes that she has been deluding herself into thinking that Philippe might one day come home again to stay. In many ways she acts like a rejected lover, slamming down the phone and swearing that she will never see her son again, that everything is over between them. In one poignant scene she goes into her son's old room, tears up his papers, throws away many of his things and packs the rest away in suitcases to put it all out of her sight. Her pride is wounded both by Philippe's defection from her academic world, and by his allegiance to Irène: "Married. Gone over to the enemy."[30] Philippe consciously plays his role in their relationship and enacts what is expected of him. In his attempt to defuse his mother's anger, he pleads, "My little one, my beloved, I beg of you, don't hate me. I can't live without you. I beg of you. I love you so."[31] Strange words with heavy sensual overtones for a recently married young man to be addressing to his own mother.

29. "L'Age de discrétion," *La Femme rompue*, 27.
30. Ibid., 41.
31. Ibid., 54.

The mother in "Age of Discretion" eventually comes to accept her son as a separate entity in whom her vested interest has turned out to be a disappointment. He will be neither an academic nor a liberal leftist. She also realizes that her emotional commitment during the remaining years of her life must be to her aging husband rather than to her grown offspring. Perhaps her contacts with former students and younger colleagues can lighten the burden of aging. Perhaps she can find a cause that will absorb the energy she once put into her relationship with the recalcitrant Philippe. Her attempts to be both emotionally and intellectually seductive with her son have apparently in no way hindered his development into a normal and independent young man, but they have left her with a great void in her life now that he is married and she has retired from teaching. Like Monique in the title story of the collection, she too is in many ways "a woman destroyed."

Myth, mystification, mystique: all of these words have been used to describe the aura with which the modern world has suffused the idea of motherhood. From early childhood, Simone de Beauvoir resisted this mystique, insisting on imagining that her dolls were her pupils rather than her children. Her fictional works served to some extent as a testing ground for her very strong feelings about the societal pressures which had for centuries propelled young women into an unthinking acceptance of the role of wife and mother. For the first time in history, women of the midtwentieth century had access to safe methods of controlling their fertility. Simone de Beauvoir's fiction seems designed to make sure that, for her readers, motherhood will always be a conscious choice rather than a passive yielding to tradition.

In the characters Simone de Beauvoir created, she explored the extremes of varying approaches to the raising of children. She worked through her ambivalence about the mixture of love and domination with which her own mother brought her up as well as her rage at the manipulative possessiveness of Zaza Mabille's supposedly well-intentioned mother. She observed with a clinical eye the effect of an overabundance of maternal devotion on the self-respect and sense of identity of mature women. Manipulative, long suffering, perfectionistic, seductive: Beauvoir's fictional mothers are eloquent spokeswomen for the author's repeated warnings about the dangers of concentrating all of one's energy on one's husband and children. Along with *The Second Sex* and the volumes of her autobiography, Simone de Beauvoir's novels and short stories constitute a giant step toward the demystification of motherhood.

Beauvoir family. Printed with the permission of Hélène de Beauvoir.

CATHERINE PORTUGES

Attachment and Separation in *The Memoirs of a Dutiful Daughter*

> Mothers feel ambivalent toward their daughters, and react to their daughters' ambivalence toward them. They desire both to keep their daughters close and to push them into adulthood. This ambivalence in turn creates more anxiety in their daughters and provokes attempts by these daughters to break away.[1]

These words from Nancy Chodorow's *The Reproduction of Mothering* resonate in many of today's investigations—whether literary, theoretical, cinematic or poetic—of the origins and manifestations of female identity. As such, they join the contrapuntal voices of women throughout history who seek themselves by reenvisioning their mothers. In the French language alone, those voices are many and diverse, and I do not wish to conflate them into a single melodic line, or to harmonize their accounts of the vicissitudes of closeness and separateness between mothers and daughters. Quite the contrary: for these voices encompass both Madame de Sévigné's longing epistolary complaint to her rejecting daughter and Madame de la Fayette's portrait of the Princesse de Clève's dependence upon her mother; they include Colette's lyrical reminiscences of Sido as well as Marie Cardinal's searing tale of a daughter's psychic imprisonment by the internalization of her mother's madness.[2] More recently, we have had the benefit of Nathalie Sarraute's explorations of her childhood. And Luce Irigaray laments in her own incantatory address to her mother, *Et l'une ne bouge pas sans l'autre* [And One Doesn't Stir Without the Other]: "You look at yourself in the mirror and already you see your own mother there. And soon your daughter, a mother."[3]

As a pioneer among contemporary French women writers, Simone de Beauvoir added her voice to this discourse more than twenty-five years ago in *Memoirs of a Dutiful Daughter*, the first volume of her

1. Nancy Chodorow, *The Reproduction of Mothering: Psychoanalysis and the Sociology of Gender* (Berkeley: University of California Press, 1978).
2. Marie Cardinal, *Les Mots Pour le Dire* (Paris: Editions Grasset & Fasquelle, 1975).
3. Luce Irigaray, "And One Doesn't Stir without the Other," trans. Hélène V. Wenzel, *Signs* 7, (Autumn 1981):56–67.

autobiography and a text of female development no less preoccupied with the "tangled vines" of the mother-daughter dynamic than those of her literary descendants.[4] Like her foremothers and their progeny, Simone de Beauvoir was then and is still compelled by the problematics of reading and writing as a woman, and hence desirous that this reconstruction of her life might serve to help others learn to read the text of their own. "I have always had the secret fantasy," she writes, "that my life was being recorded, down to the tiniest detail, on some giant tape recorder, and that the day would come when I should play back the whole of my past."[5] As a memorialist, she constructs and presents herself through language, aanouncing by the very title of the book an inversion of the traditional genre, governed in France by the code that entitles mainly important public lives—usually men's lives—to be inscribed for posterity. Instead, she offers the reader a seductive paradox, that of an avowedly "dutiful daughter" who nonetheless manages to escape, through the subversive act of writing, from the bonds of her socioeconomic and psychological milieu. As a text of female development, the *Memoirs* can be read profitably through psychoanalytic eyes, for it is laced through with the subjects at the heart of the psychoanalytic enterprise, subjects that anticipate many of today's feminist debates on gender and writing, the issues of separateness and relatedness among women and within the family, the exclusion of women from language, repression and desire. Simone de Beauvoir's observations are often framed by the ironic distance earned by the vantage-point of middle age from which her recollections are situated.

Seldom even uttered except as a single entity, in a single breath, testimony to the mother-daughter bond has grown so persistent as to be nearly obsessional. Its ramifications are evident in professional conferences and academic curricula, the Broadway stage and the Hollywood set, the learned journal and even *People* magazine. We should, however, not be surprised to realize to what extent Simone de Beauvoir anticipated such widespread popularization, and as we honor her here in 1984 we celebrate not only the passionate writer of fiction and the scrupulous analyst of women's social condition, but also the prescient and generous memorialist, intent on elucidating, long before it was fashionable or even acceptable to do so, this highly charged and mysterious phenomenon. And, although *Memoirs of a Dutiful Daughter* is but one of

4. Simone de Beauvoir, *Mémoires d'une jeune fille rangée* (Paris: Librarie Gallimard, 1958); *Memoirs of a Dutiful Daughter*, trans. James Kirkup (New York: Harper, 1959). References to this work will henceforth be given in the text.
5. Simone de Beauvoir, *La Force des Choses* (Paris: Gallimard, 1963), v. 2, 128.

her texts in which the subject is addressed—*A Very Easy Death* is perhaps a better-known contemplation of daughterhood[6]—I propose a rereading of the *Memoirs* in terms of contemporary psychoanalytic thought, with the hope of discovering in this classic fresh insights that may, in turn, cast new light on our theorizing of the feminine through the acts of rereading and writing.

Memoirs of a Dutiful Daughter was written in 1958 by a daughter who had not become a mother, speaking at that point in her life from the position of a successful fifty-year-old writer. The book covers the first twenty years of a life (1908–28) marked by sustained efforts to know, understand and fulfill itself. Beauvoir has said that she wrote the book in part to set down the odyssey of her initiation as a writer, as well as to repay the obligation she felt she owed to Elisabeth Mabille (Zaza), the cherished friend of her youth. The book in fact concludes with Zaza's death at twenty, and hence suggests that its title is meant also to apply to another daughter who tried—and failed—to please her mother. Zaza reappears at the conclusion of each of the four chapters of the *Memoirs*, leaving a lasting impression of her centrality in the formation of Simone de Beauvoir's personality and literary vocation

The memorialist's voice, however objective she may have thought it to be, is colored, like all first-person narratives, by the defenses and inadvertent subtexts inherent in the project of presenting the self on the written page. The volume is infused with an aura of passionate discovery, and resounds with the writer's intense search for happiness, her devouring stance toward life. Simone de Beauvoir's transformation from the comfortable, complacent centerpiece of a secure household to a young woman forced into awareness of the dangers of being a dutiful daughter constitutes the psychological "work" of the text. Its structuring device is the family photograph album, which provides the occasion for the writer's retrospective gaze as it attempts to penetrate beneath the surface of the conventional images.

If indeed psychoanalysis can be seen as a narrative—the repeated stories told to the self and retold in the transferential situation—it is appropriate also to read this memoir in terms of its implications of the self and its inner objects enacted through language as well as in the world. Family and early friendship are its ostensible pretexts, and as we look beneath the text we can discern something of the shaping power of these primary relationships in the mature self. By focusing my inquiry through the lens of recent feminist psychoanalytic theory, which re-

---

6. Simone de Beauvoir, *Une Mort Très Douce* (Paris: Gallimard, 1965).

casts Freud's theories of female development to give primacy to the pre-Oedipal phase, with its strong maternal attachment, rather than to the Oedipus complex, I mean to suggest the formative influence of Simone de Beauvoir's relationship with her mother—and the mothering elements of other, subsequent attachments—on her own psyche and her view of women.[7] And, by concentrating specifically on the questions of attachment, ambivalence and separation, I am aligning my reading with the work of theorists concerned with the quality of "object relations" who stress the cathexis of the pre-Oedipal stage. In their view—and here I draw from Margaret Mahler, D. W. Winnicott and, secondarily, Nancy Chodorow—the child's early conflicted desires for autonomy and dependence are imagined as internalized representations—or images—of the nurturing adult, most frequently the mother.[8] In its emphasis on the primordial role of dependency conflicts as a major force in the development of the self, object relations theory throws into bold relief the psychic material feminists have long accused Freud of minimizing or altogether misunderstanding: the story of the mothering relationship, as lived out by the daughter, in the shaping of identity and its impact upon the processes of separation and individuation.[9]

Calling especially upon the work of Margaret Mahler, we can examine this pre-Oedipal attachment and its later strivings for autonomy by listening attentively to the unconscious discourse of the mother-daughter dialectic (and here I do not mean only the relationship of the actual mother and daughter but also the maternal anf filial elements incorporated into the self and reenacted with other objects).[10] The context in which this drama unfolds in *Memoirs of a Dutiful Daughter* is not, obviously, limited to females. But it becomes rapidly clear that women in Beauvoir's account prevailed over her early life:

> Being a child filled me with passionate resentment; my feminine gender, never. With regard to the grown-ups, my experience was rather ambiguous. In certain respects Papa, grandpapa and my uncles appeared to me to be superior to their wives. But in my everyday life, it was Louise [her governess], Mama, grandmama and my aunts who played the leading roles. [55]

7. See also Melanie Klein and Joan Rivière, *Love, Hate and Reparation* (New York: Norton, 1964).

8. For an overview of the contributions of object relations theorists, see Jay R. Greenberg & Stephen Mitchell, *Object Relations in Psychoanalytic Theory* (Boston: Harvard University Press, 1983).

9. Margaret Mahler, *The Selected Papers of Margaret S. Mahler*, vols. 1 & 2 (New York: Jason Aronson, 1979).

10. Ibid.

Further, she writes:

> I thought of grown-ups essentially in their relationships to childhood: from this point of view, my sex assured my pre-eminence. . . . In all my games, my daydreams, and my plans for the future I never changed myself into a man; all my imagination was devoted to the fulfillment of my destiny as a woman. [56]

Thus the stage is set for strong female attachments, with their attendant ambivalence, love, envy, jealousy and disappointment; the strongest among these, we soon learn, are to be those among equals, also equally laden with maternal and filial affects: Simone de Beauvoir's sister Hélène, called Poupette, and her friend Zaza, whose friendship was "the great drama of my schoolgirl life: I never had any other real friends after her" (56).

Let us therefore extend the mother-daughter paradigm, as I have suggested, to embrace the world of sisters, paradigmatic as it is within feminism and, perhaps not surprisingly, noticeably absent from feminist theorizing. The relationship of sisters is often emblematic, and perhaps also determinative, of later interpersonal relationships, and holds a special imaginative power for many of us. The ambivalence Chodorow invokes with respect to mothers applies also, I believe, to sisters, and in Simone de Beauvoir's story the latter played a decisive role in the family:

> I was glad, too, that I was not entirely at the mercy of grown-ups; I was not alone in my children's world; I had an equal: my sister, who began to play a considerable role in my life about my sixth birthday. [42]

In the eyes of the young Simone, this sibling

> was someone like myself, only a little younger; she was grateful for my approval, and responded to it with an absolute devotion. She was my liegeman, my alter ego, my double; we could not do without one another. [42]

On the very first page of the *Memoirs*, in fact, the writer informs us that she was two-and-a-half years old when Poupette was born:

> I was, it appears, very jealous, but not for long. As far back as I can remember, I was always proud of being the elder: of being first. . . . I had a little sister: that doll-like creature didn't have me. [42]

She goes on to amplify her reading of the sisters' mutual psychological dependence while asserting her appreciation for an occasion to wield power over another: in their games together, the secret life they shared,

Poupette was "my accomplice, my subject, my creature." The younger sister is described in pedagogical metaphors as a virgin mind upon which truths could be impressed, resulting in the creation of something real. Having until then responded dutifully to the protection and care lavished upon her by family, teachers and confessors, Simone de Beauvoir at last felt herself to be useful to someone else. Images of instrumentality pervade as she describes the siblings as bound by the same kind of "durable bond" that presumably exists between teacher and student: ". . . by sharing my knowledge with another, I was fixing time on another's memory, and so making it doubly secure" (42). Through her sister's existence Simone claims her right to personal freedom: "I was breaking away from the passivity of childhood and entering the great human circle in which everyone is useful to everyone else" (45). Endowed with authority by virtue of Poupette's obedience, the young Simone, so preoccupied with pleasing others, declares that a partner was absolutely essential to her ability to bring to life the imaginary stories of childhood play. In so doing she gives credit to Poupette for helping her "to save my daily life from silence; through her I got into the habit of wanting to communicate with people" (44).

Here, as at other points in the text, we can only wonder how the "other," characterized with such admirable certainty by the writer, might have seen things. Irigaray's title, *And One Doesn't Stir Without the Other*, comes to mind, transposed from the maternal to the sororal sphere. In contrast it is striking to note the 1978 filmed interview with Simone de Beauvoir, made by Malka Ribowska and Josée Dayan:[11] in one sequence the writer appears with her sister Hélène (Poupette) to engage in chilhood recollections. Poupette remembers Simone's penchant for playing the teacher and for imagining herself as a saint; she says: "At five you were a good teacher; you were a heroic woman, a saint who dominated me!" Although Simone de Beauvoir herself evokes both real and mythological heroines with whom she identifies in the *Memoirs*—Joan of Arc, Mary Magdalene, Saint Blandine, Geneviève de Brabant and Griselda—she reacts in embarrassment and even displeasure to Poupette's revelations, while the camera tracks obediently away from the formerly silenced sibling who had finally had her say.

As we read retrospectively from the perspective of current theorizing on the construction of gender, it is well to remember that, in her

11. *Simone de Beauvoir*, a film by Malka Ribowska-Josée Dayan, 1 hr. 40 min., Red Ribbon, American Film Féstival 1982. References taken from screening notes.

rejection of certain assumed differences between masculine and feminine, Simone de Beauvoir is a precursor of contemporary theorists such as Chodorow and Dorothy Dinnerstein, who assert that the assymetry of male/female psychic development arises from the fact that women in our culture are the primary caretakers of children,[12] and hence remain the primary objects of love, gratification and rage. So too can sisters cathect one another in an analogous constellation of affects that may, like the primal unity with the mother, remain permanent inner objects carried throughout life. Simone de Beauvoir continues her reflections in the *Memoirs* on childhood games with her sister by offering telling glimpses into her childlike self: she acknowledges her preference for active, "phallic" fantasies, describing, for instance, her pleasure in playing the role of the nurse who gathers the wounded on the battlefield but refuses to pursue the dull caregiving required afterwards. When she and Poupette play house, responsibility and power elicit her excitement, while domestic tasks are contemptuously dismissed as routine acts of unredeemed drudgery:

> I refused to let a man deprive me of my rightful responsibilities; our husbands would travel. . . . I knew very well that in life things were quite different: the mother of the family is always under the surveillance of her husband; a thousand thankless tasks weigh her down. When I imagined my future I regarded this state of servitude as so onerous that I balked at the prospect of having children; what mattered to me was molding minds and characters; I decided to be a teacher. [55–56]

Thus Poupette enables her elder sister, simply by virtue of her existence, to pursue the single-minded search for self-realization that is one of the subjects of the *Memoirs*. Of her sense of purpose in writing the book Simone de Beauvoir remarks:

> I had long wanted to set down the story of my first twenty years, nor did I ever forget the distress signals which my adolescent self sent out to the older woman who was afterward to absorb me, body and soul. Nothing, I feared, would survive of that girl, not so much as a pinch of ashes. I begged her successor to recall my youthful ghost, one day, from the limbo to which it had been assigned. [55–56]

In recalling that "youthful ghost," she brings to life a sense of self connected to the world, continuous with others, particularly mother,

12. Dorothy Dinnerstein, *The Mermaid and the Minotaur: Sexual Arrangements and Human Malaise* (New York: Harper, 1976).

sister, and Zaza, and secondarily aunts and governess. Let us return now to the earlier stage of bonding with the mother that contemporary theorists postulate as often narcissistically defined, that is to say characterized by fluid ego boundaries in which both mother and child experience each other as extensions of the self. As Melanie Klein has noted: "The creative artist is impelled by the desire to rediscover the mother of the early days, whom he has lost actually or in his feelings."[13] For it can be argued that a central motivation for writing the *Memoirs* is an act of reparation to the mother and sister cast aside in favor of the freedom promised in the person of Zaza, a retrospective desire to understand the rebellion and obedience of youth without sentimentalizing its negative or even brutal aspects. If indeed the "dutiful daughter" is also Zaza, who suffered at the hands of a rigidly pious mother and was, in Beauvoir's somewhat ambiguously expressed view, driven to her early death by the strictures of conventional bourgeois mortality, then the *Memoirs* serve a triple reparative function. The book's final sentence substantiates such an assumption as Beauvoir comes to terms with Zaza's death:

> Together we had fought against the revolting fate that had lain ahead of us, and for a long time I thought I'd paid for my own freedom with her death. [503]

The overall movement of the book may indeed be seen as working toward the writer's detachment from her early relationship perceived as both omnipotent and symbiotic, and as a struggle to come to terms with the double, paradoxical impulse of attachment and individuation. It is, after all, the text of a woman writer, a feminist intellectual impelled by the desire to define herself both in relation to and separate from the mother and her "introjects." Madame de Beauvoir is depicted as both pathetic and formidable, a woman whose "behavior complied with her beliefs; quick to sacrifice herself, she devoted herself entirely to her family" (40). In its single-mindedness, her portrait of her mother is reminiscent even of the orthodox Freudian analyst Helene Deutsch's description of ideal motherhood:

> . . . [the sine qua non of normal motherhood is] . . . the masochistic-feminine willingness to sacrifice [whose] chief characteristic is tenderness. All the aggression and sexual sensuality in the woman's personality are suppressed and diverted by this central emotional expression of motherliness.[14]

13. Klein & Rivière, op. cit.
14. Helene Deutsch, *The Psychology of Women*, vol. 2, "Motherhood" (New York: Bantam, 1973), 18–20.

In the face of such a similarity, we can scarcely be astounded when Simone de Beauvoir writes: ". . . maternity was something I couldn't entertain" (42).

The motif of devotion, apparent in the title and throughout, echoes elsewhere in Beauvoir's work: here *le dévouement* is meant at once as attachment, devotion and self-sacrifice of the daughter-mother relationship, with emphasis on the self-sacrificial and masochistic elements. It is obvious that Madame de Beauvoir's sense of duty aroused her daughter's suspicions and later mistrust, culminating in the derision with which she regarded religion thereafter. Her bias against altruism is evident in her essay *Pyrrhus et Cinéas* in which she concludes that *le dévouement* is both undesirable and impossible, a total renunciation of healthy egoism: "Devotion," she writes, "first appears as total resignation in favor of another person" (71).

As we follow the sweep of the *Memoirs* this theme is taken up repeatedly, yet its most powerful incarnation is in the person of the memorialist's mother. Margaret Mahler's work is useful here in illuminating the book's double movement between attachment and separation, as she discusses the manifestation of this process in the mother-child relationship:

> The entire life cycle constitutes a more or less successful process of distancing from and introjection of the lost symbiotic mother, an eternal longing for the actual or fantasied "ideal state of self," with the latter standing for a symbiotic fusion with the 'all good' symbiotic mother, who was at one time part of the self in a blissful state of well-being.[15]

Early in this chronicle of childhood and adolescence, Simone de Beauvoir alludes to the all-powerful symbiosis which Mahler describes. Invoking her mother's importance to her, she says:

> Any reproach made by my mother, and even her slightest frown, was a threat to my security: without her approval, I no longer felt I had any right to live. . . . At every instant of the day she was present, even in the most secret recesses of my soul, and I made no distinction between her all-seeing wisdom and the eye of God himself. [38–39]

Mahler too speaks of such omniscience as it is experienced by the infant:

> This phase of dim awareness of the "need-satisfying object" marks the beginning of the phase of symbiosis in which the infant behaves and

15. Mahler, op. cit., vol. 2, 119.

functions as though he and his mother were an omnipotent system (a dual unity) within one common boundary (a symbiotic membrane as it were).[16]

There is a psychic fusion within this symbiotic dual unity of representations of the self and representations of the mother, the first "object" who becomes grafted upon the infant's psyche to create an illusion of omnipotence in the child. Transposing this richly suggestive metaphorical language to the sphere of Simone de Beauvoir's childhood and early adolescence, we can retrace the trajectory of "dual unity" from her relationship with her mother, through her governess Louise, then to Poupette and finally Zaza. While Simone de Beauvoir reserves the language of symbiosis as such to apply to dependence upon her mother, there are equally powerful intensities experienced with the other "mothering" females:

> My feeling of unalterable security came from the presence of Louise. She used to dress me in the mornings and undress me at night; she slept in the same room as myself. Young, without beauty, without mystery—because she existed, as I thought, only in order to watch over my sister and myself—she never raised her voice, and never scolded me without good reason. . . . Her presence was as necessary to me, and seemed to me just as natural, as the ground beneath my feet. [5–6]

In contrast, her mother is seen as repressed and deeply conventional:

> Her childhood and youth filled her heart with a resentment which she never completely forgot. She suffered many sad disappointments in her adolescence; despite her great beauty, she lacked assurance and gaiety. . . . But with Louise, my sister and myself, she showed herself to be dictatorial and overbearing, sometimes passionately so. I did not look upon her as a saint, because I knew her too well and because she lost her temper far too easily; but her example seemed to me all the more unassailable because of that: I, too, was able to, and therefore ought to emulate her in piety and virtue. . . .Her hold over me stemmed indeed a great deal from the very intimacy of our relationship. [39]

Further in the *Memoirs* the author refers directly to her own attitude toward maternity, as mediated by her mother's ideas of it:

> My mother's whole education and upbringing had convinced her that for a woman the greatest thing was to become the mother of a family;

16. Mahler, op. cit., 169–81.

she couldn't play this part unless I played the dutiful daughter, but I refused to take part in grown-up pretense just as much as I did when I was five years old. [106]

It is only when she meets Zaza in school at the age of ten that such symbiotic and enmeshed relationships with female m/others is first challenged and then rapidly replaced. Through the person of her father, Simone de Beauvoir is seen finally as judging her mother and, heavily dependent as she was on his approval as well, she ends up feeling guilty for noting that her "real rival" was her mother. By the time she meets Zaza she begins to recognize that her sister no longer idolizes her unreservedly, her father considers her ugly and disappointing, and her mother is suspicious of the changes taking place in her adolescent daughter. From that moment on, she remarks,

I no longer looked upon myself as unique. Henceforward my self-sufficiency was tempered by feelings inspired by someone else outside my family. I had had the good fortune to find a friend. [106]

Thus Zaza is represented as offering a satisfactory integration of Simone de Beauvoir's desire for both closeness and differentiation, attachment and separation, a *point de repère* able to repair the schisms within her, and for that matter a way of interpreting and analyzing the world imposed upon her since birth. Her friendship with Zaza is the occasion for her to invest "so much weight to the perfect union of two human beings" (143).

It will not have escaped one's attention that Simone de Beauvoir's father is conspicuously absent from my reading of the *Memoirs:* in fact, as I have suggested, he does not figure prominently in the book. His importance to her psychological development may nevertheless have far exceeded the space she devotes to him in this volume, wherein it consists largely in her respect for worldly professional accomplishments. But she does admit to having been "dazzled by his superior character." His influence, too, no doubts elicits her assertion of preference for the prospect of working for a living to that of marriage: "at least it offered some hope." But M. de Beauvoir, she indicates,

was no feminist: he admired the wisdom of the novels of Colette Yver in which the woman lawyer, or the woman doctor in the end sacrifice their careers in order to provide their children and husband with a happy home. [104]

Yet as she grows older her passion for her father grows, and hence her envy of her mother's place in his affections. And love, she writes, is not envy: by the end of Book One she admits that she could think of nothing better in the world than loving Zaza: ". . . it was also true that I loved Zaza with an intensity which could not be accounted for by any established set of rules and conventions" (118).

Suspended thus between the individualism of her father and the rigid moral constraints of her mother's piety, Simone de Beauvoir's ambivalence about maternity, her unrelenting search for an authentic reconciliation of the masculine with the feminine are resolved through a process of differentiation from the mother, culminating in her love for Zaza: "This imbalance," she concludes, "which made my life a kind of endless disputation, is the main reason why I became an intellectual" (41). I suggest that, in large measure, we owe the abundant fruits of Simone de Beauvoir's intellectual life to her having faced and worked through this vexed question. For true feminism, as Julia Kristeva reminds us, " will not be possible until we have elucidated motherhood, feminine creation, and the relationship between them."[17]

17. Julia Kristeva, "La femme, ce n'est jamais ça, " in *Tel quel* 59 (Autumn 1974) cited in *New French Feminisms*, Elaine Marks & Isabelle de Courtivron, ed. (Amherst: University of Massachusetts Press, 1980).

IV. Toward Liberation:
Women Writing about Women

DOROTHY KAUFMANN

Simone de Beauvoir: Questions of Difference and Generation

For partisans and adversaries alike, Simone de Beauvoir's statement in *The Second Sex* that "One is not born, but rather becomes, a woman" has become the most familiar formulation of her position on sexual difference. It clearly defines her view of woman's Otherness as fabricated, imposed by culture rather than biology. If any doubts are possible about the pejorative implications of woman's difference for Simone de Beauvoir, they are immediately dispelled in the sentence that follows: "No biological, psychological or economic fate determines the figure that the human female presents in society; it is civilization as a whole that produces this creature, intermediate between male and eunuch, which is described as feminine."[1] Both "the feminine" and "woman," as she uses the terms here, are cultural signs for the male-created product she calls the second sex.

Simone de Beauvoir's feminism, which views sexual difference as necessarily a source of oppression, has been most seriously called into question by the theoretical writings that emerged with the French women's movement in the 1970s. For writers otherwise as diverse as Hélène Cixous and Luce Irigaray, it is precisely woman's difference, repressed by the phallocentric discourse of the Western humanist tradition, that is the source of her potential liberation. Although, so far as I know, there is no explicit reference to Beauvoir in the work of either Cixous or Irigaray, their theories of feminine specificity mark a complete break with the philosophical and cultural assumptions of Simone de Beauvoir's feminism. Against the existentialist humanism that informs her work, the starting point for Cixous and Irigaray is the post-

---

1. Simone de Beauvoir, *The Second Sex*, trans. and ed. H. M. Parshley (New York: Vintage Books, 1974), 301.

structuralist theoretical model that foregrounds language and de-constructs the notion of a coherent self. Lacan's psychoanalytic discourse defines the terms of their revolt even as their work seeks to subvert the Lacanian symbolic Father. Denouncing the rule of the phal-lus as privileged signifier, their writing attempts to celebrate and bring into being another signifier, that they call feminine difference.[2]

In the work of both Irigaray and Cixous there is a constant slippage in the meaning of feminine difference, from an affirmation of biological woman to woman as a metaphor for the unconscious of culture, every-thing that has been left out of the masculine libidinal economy. In relation to that ambiguous "woman," sometimes body and sometimes archaic signifier, Simone de Beauvoir's feminism inhabits another lan-guage and an earlier, more confident relation between words and things. Her focus is on referential women as they exist in the social order. In contrast to contemporary French discourse, there is still for her the assumption of a world outside the text; she can talk about reality and lived experience without quotation marks.

Despite that gap, Luce Irigaray has chosen to ally herself, however ambivalently, with the struggle that calls itself feminist. Indirectly al-luding to Simone de Beauvoir's model of feminism, Irigaray writes: "Women must, of course, continue to struggle for equality of salaries, social rights, against discrimination in employment, studies, etc. But that is not enough: women simply equal to men would be like them and therefore not women. Once more, the difference of the sexes would thus be annulled, unrecognized, covered up."[3] For Irigaray, then, the ide-ology of equality is necessary but insufficient. Her relative acceptance of Simone de Beauvoir's positive role is indicated by the fact that she

2. My purpose here is briefly to situate the theoretical framework of Luce Irigaray and Hélène Cixous in relation to Simone de Beauvoir. In the context of that comparison, their commonality is more striking than the differences between them. Irigaray's more directly psychoanalytic discourse contrasts with the more literary and Derridean strategies of Cixous's call to "écriture féminine," but their writing inhabits the same epistemological space. Both Irigaray and Cixous seek to break down "phallogocentrism" and to create a new language for women. Their sharpest opposition to each other is on the political issue of feminism. (See below.)

3. Luce Irigaray, *Ce sexe qui n'en est pas un* (Paris: Minuit, 1977), 150. Simone de Beauvoir is well aware of the problematics of women's success in a male world, noting that "women who have positions of importance often take on the same faults as men. They become like men, imbued with their own authority." (Quoted from my interview with Simone de Beauvoir, March 2, 1982.) Unlike Irigaray or Cixous, however, she does not conclude from this observation that feminine difference is a value in itself. "There is a very difficult dialectic," she said to Alice Jardine, "between accepting power and refusing it, accepting certain masculine values, and wanting to transform them. I think it's worth a try." *Signs* 5 (Winter 1979): 228.

recently contributed an essay to *Les Temps Modernes*, the journal founded by Sartre and Beauvoir.[4] Hélène Cixous, on the other hand, defines her position as against rather than beyond feminism, declaring categorically "I am not a feminist." As Cixous sees it, feminism is nothing more than a demand for power from the patriarchy and thus a cooptation of women by the system.[5]

The most virulent attack against Simone de Beauvoir from an ideology of difference appears in *des femmes hebdo*, the journal of the group originally called "Psychanalyse et Politique," which was closely associated with Hélène Cixous between 1975 and 1982. In their report of the twenty-fifth anniversary colloquium on *The Second Sex* held in New York in 1979, they feature its author as no less than the Big Bad Wolf. The article headlines this exchange with a gullibly feminist Little Red Riding Hood: "O grandmother, what fine concepts you have!" "The better to retard you with, my child!"[6] *Des femmes* mocks what it calls the "ambitious sons" of Simone de Beauvoir's phallic feminism, proclaims the nonexistence of feminist thought and asserts that the obvious source of women's oppression is not difference but the denial and scorn of difference.

A more suggestive context in which to consider Simone de Beauvoir's devalorization of feminine difference is provided by Julia Kristeva's 1981 essay on "Women's Time," in which she speaks of two generations of European feminist movements and looks to the possible forming of a third generation. Her use of the word "generation" implies not so much a chronology as a "signifying space," in which different generations can be parallel or interwoven. Existential feminists, in Kristeva's account, belong to the first generation beginnings, when women were aspiring to gain a place in social institutions on an equal footing with men. Part of the logic of that insertion into history, as Kristeva sees it, was the necessity of rejecting attitudes traditionally

4. Luce Irigaray, "Le Sujet de la science est-il sexué?" *Les Temps Modernes* 436 (Nov. 1982): 960–74.

5. Hélène Cixous, "Entretien avec Françoise van Rossum-Guyon," *La Revue des sciences humaines* 168 (1977): 481–82. Simone de Beauvoir offers her assessment of the value for women of Irigaray's and Cixous's writing in her interview with Alice Jardine. On Irigaray: "On the whole, I am interested in the kind of work she is doing and I found her book [*Ce sexe qui n'en est pas un*] very interesting. Still, she seems to lack audacity, which is necessary to demolish the ideas of Freud on feminine psychoanalysis." On Cixous: "I'm of an older generation. I can't read her, understand her. And I think it's wrong to write in a totally esoteric language when you want to talk about things which interest a multitude of women. . . . There is something false in this search for a purely feminine writing style." *Signs* 5 (Winter 1979), 228–29.

6. *Des femmes hebdo* 1 (9–16 Nov. 1979), 11–12.

considered feminine or maternal when they proved incompatible with political struggles. Kristeva's second generation links younger women who came to feminism after 1968 to women whose aesthetic or psychoanalytic experience led to what she calls an "exacerbated distrust of the entire political dimension."[7]

The attack against Simone de Beauvoir's devalorization of the feminine—characterized by "Psych et Po" and many others as misogyny—has tended to ignore the historical context in which *The Second Sex* was conceived. When she began to write her pioneering work in 1947, France was still emerging from the trauma of Occupation and the Vichy regime. It was only in 1944 that French women obtained the right to vote, legislated in part in reaction to the misogynist policies of Vichy and in recognition of women's active participation in the Resistance. However, male rejection of Vichy propaganda did not go so far as to consider women's right to control their bodies. In 1949, the publication date of *The Second Sex*, not only abortion but even the sale of contraceptives was still strictly illegal, going back to a law that was put in place in 1920 as part of France's natalist policies after the devastating losses of men in World War I. In spite of these policies, the birthrate in France continued to remain low, almost equaled by the rate of illegal abortions. After the defeat of 1940, a favorite refrain of Vichy was that the French lost the war because they didn't have children, that the Germans were making cannons and babies while the French were just having a good time.[8] After the war, pronatalist policies, in the form of subsidies to families, were continued by governments of both the right and the left. It was not until 1967 that the sale of contraceptives was made legal, but under such restricted conditions that in the early seventies, only seven percent of French women were using them. In 1974 the law forbidding abortions was repealed, due primarily to the militant activism of feminists—including Simone de Beauvoir who played a prominent role.

It has been noted, often with a sense of scandal, that Simone de Beauvoir begins her chapter "The Mother" in *The Second Sex* with a passionate polemic against the conditions under which women must undergo abortion in those countries where it is illegal. She points out that in France, at the time of her book, abortions were averaging about one million per year. That statistic achieves its full impact when we realize that in the United States, with a vastly larger population than

7. Julia Kristeva, "Women's Time," *Signs* 7 (Autumn 1981): 13–35.
8. See Evelyne Sullerot's account, "La Démographie en France," in *Société et Culture de la France contemporaine,* ed. Georges Santoni (Albany, N.Y.: State Univ. of New York Press, 1981), 64–86.

France, the estimated number of abortions performed annually was about two-thirds of a million.[9]

Simone de Beauvoir's consistent hostility to the biological as well as the cultural conditions of maternity is unmistakable. In *The Second Sex* she evokes the "quivering jelly which is elaborated in the womb (the womb, secret and sealed like the tomb)" and compares it to the "soft viscosity of carrion" (165). The pregnant woman is described as "ensnared by nature," "a stockpile of colloids," "plant and animal" (553). One aspect of her hostility to biological femininity, which I have discussed elsewhere, is her adoption of Sartrean existentialism and its rejection of the natural as antivalue.[10] Another crucial factor in this hostility is her sensitivity to the personal trauma of an unwanted pregnancy when abortion is not a legal option. In 1971 Simone de Beauvoir signed and collected signatures for the Manifesto of 343 writers and celebrities who declared that they were among those million French women each year forced to have recourse to dangerous and illegal abortions. At the controversial Bobigny abortion trial in 1973, she chose to incriminate herself further. Asked if she herself had aborted, she replied "Yes, a long time ago. What I have been doing for a long time and frequently since then is to help women who come to ask me how to abort. I give or lend them money and I give them addresses. Sometimes I even lend them my home so that the intervention can take place in good conditions."[11] When I asked her in 1982 about the gains of feminism during the seventies, her first response was to point to contraception and abortion, which she clearly sees as crucially important victories: "These are profound changes which completely alter women's lives." In answer to my question about the certainty of those gains should a right-wing government replace the Socialists, she compared the status of the right to abortion with the forty-hour work week (now thirty-nine hours) and the right to paid vacations, gains acquired in 1936 that have never been called into doubt since then, whatever the government in power.

Simone de Beauvoir's personal history illuminates her political priorities and her cultural assumptions. Growing up as a dutiful daughter

9. Cited by the translator of *The Second Sex*, 544.

10. See my essay, "Simone de Beauvoir, *The Second Sex*, and Jean-Paul Sartre," *Signs* 5 (Winter 1979): 209–33.

11. Quoted in Claude Francis and Fernande Gontier, *Les Ecrits de Simone de Beauvoir* (Paris: Gallimard, 1979), 513. My translation. As Marie-Claire Pasquier has pointed out to me, Simone de Beauvoir's statements do not necessarily indicate that she has had an abortion. They are intended as political expressions of solidarity, comparable to the May '68 slogan "We are all German Jews."

in the early part of the century, her childhood relation to her parents was in keeping with the traditional expectations and family structure of the time. Her mother took care of her moral welfare and day-to-day needs, while her father was the authority figure who embodied the Law and worldly knowledge. Françoise de Beauvoir, as evoked by her daughter, was a pious woman who lived her married life in accordance with the accepted middle class codes of propriety and devotion. Completely dependent on her husband, she resigned herself to his numerous trivial affairs as part of the inevitable double standard of marriage. She accepted without question her prescribed duties as wife and mother, renouncing any self-expression outside those roles.[12] Simone de Beauvoir describes her mother's growing resentment as she becomes aware of Simone's loss of religious faith and her beginning assertions of independence. She draws the portrait of her mother as a woman turned stranger to herself in the name of religious and moral principles of devotion. Françoise de Beauvoir becomes for her daughter a warning, the image of what she wants her own life not to be. The maternal, even as metaphor, will always look to Beauvoir like a trap, in which women lose their autonomy and their happiness.

In the recent film script about her life, Simone de Beauvoir is asked about her relationship with Sylvie Le Bon, a woman in her forties who has been her closest companion for the past several years. It is suggested

12. Simone's adolescent rejection of her mother's example did not include a rejection of marriage as part of her own future. As she points out in an interview with Alice Schwarzer, "At eighteen or twenty you get married for love, and at thirty it all hits you—and getting out of that situation is very, very difficult. It could have happened to me, which is why I feel particularly sensitive to it." *After The Second Sex: Conversations with Simone de Beauvoir*, trans. Marianne Howarth (New York: Pantheon Books, 1984), 73. She is referring to her adolescent relationship with her cousin Jacques, which could have led, had he so desired, to a conventional marriage and family situation, although she was more in love with love than with Jacques. Throughout her adolescence, as described in the *Memoirs of a Dutiful Daughter*, her rebellious determination to make her own life is counterbalanced by an almost Godot-like fantasy of waiting for the right man, the ideal companion who would justify her existence. In my interview with Simone de Beauvoir in March 1982, I asked her to compare her fantasy of love in the *Memoirs* with Sartre's fantasy of heroism in *The Words*: "The difference comes essentially from the difference in education and conditioning for men and women, at least at the time. It is precisely that realization which made me write *The Second Sex*. For a woman, given the models she had in front of her and the books she read, she couldn't think of herself as a heroine, or at least it was much more normal, more obvious, to think of herself as having the love of a man in her life, the man being seen if not as a protector, then at least as someone she could admire." Simone de Beauvoir's adolescent fantasy of love is clearly the model of what was to be her relationship with Sartre, however unconventional that relationship might have been in other respects. The problematics of love for women is a dominant and even obsessive theme in her novels; the problematics of male heroism plays a fundamental role in Sartre's theatre.

that their friendship could be considered a kind of mother-daughter ersatz. Simone categorically denies such a bond: "Absolutely not," is her response. "We have a much better relationship than what generally exists between mothers and daughters. . . . I have always been for chosen relationships as against those that are imposed."[13] Her response does not even consider any positive interpretation of the maternal metaphor, only the aspect of compulsion.

Simone de Beauvoir's fear of maternal engulfment is such that her early impulse of identification with her mother, the "petite maman chérie" of her early childhood,[14] is buried in her adult life. She releases those feelings only in a few unguarded spaces of A Very Easy Death, the most moving of her autobiographical writings. As her mother is dying of cancer, she suddenly falls into a spell of uncontrollable sobbing and describes her "stupefaction" at feeling such overwhelming grief: "When my father died, I didn't shed a tear. I had said to my sister, 'It will be the same for mother.' Up to that night, I had understood all my sorrows. Even when they submerged me, I recognized myself in them. This time, my despair escaped from my control: someone other than myself was weeping inside me."[15] It is her surprise more than her despair that is revealing. At the end of the book she makes one of her rare allusions to dreams: "In my sleep," she writes, "where my father appeared very seldom and in an insignificant way, [my mother] often played the essential role: she became confused with Sartre, and we were happy together."[16] The dream then turns into a nightmare as she panics that she will again be taken over by her mother, as she was in childhood. The impulse toward maternal identification, with her mother and Sartre fused into one, is not explored further. Simone de Beauvoir's repression of the feminine, perhaps the deepest limitation of her writing, produces the kind of rationalist framing of her thought, the ordering of painful and ambiguous experience into neat and manageable categories, that theoreticians of difference now characterize as masculine.

The celebration of feminine difference in the name of women's liberation seemed to explode all at once in France in the mid-1970s. Cixous's "Rire de la Méduse" and La Jeune née, Leclerc's Parole de femme, Herrmann's Les Voleuses de langue, Kristeva's Révolution du langage poétique, and Irigaray's Speculum de l'autre femme and Ce

13. Simone de Beauvoir, un film de Josée Dayan et Malka Ribowska (Paris: Gallimard, 1979), 72. My translation.
14. Une Mort très douce (Paris: Gallimard, 1964), 147.
15. Ibid., 43. My translation.
16. Ibid., 147.

sexe qui n'en est pas un were all published between 1974 and 1977. Whether the feminine is understood in these writings as the unconscious, or the maternal body, or as a metaphor for the silences in Western discourse, the impulse is to give birth to that feminine difference. It is not by chance that these celebrations found expression in the midseventies when in the political domain, women were achieving control over their bodies for the first time in history. To experience the feminine as liberation, a necessary condition is to have the possibility to live one's sexuality freely and, if heterosexual, to be able to separate sexual expression from reproduction. The maternal metaphor can only be privileged as liberating if the social world permits the actual experience of maternity as choice and desire.

It has not yet been demonstrated that the textual inscription of woman's imaginary can have a revolutionary effect on the real, as the theoreticians of difference proclaim. What is already clear, however, is that the real changes in women's situation in the past decade have altered women's imaginary. To the extent that any woman can be singled out as inspiring those changes in women's situation, Simone de Beauvoir should be there first. *The Second Sex* is where contemporary feminism begins. Its totalizing theory, however problematic, allowed for translation into a political praxis to which it gave philosophical support. Since the publication of *The Second Sex*, she has been actively involved in all the major political struggles against women's oppression, in France and elsewhere. It is ironic that she should now be dismissed by so many as not really a feminist, or even as a misogynist. Such accusations willfully confuse her distrust of the feminine with hostility to women, ignoring her efforts on behalf of women throughout her writing career, from the campaign to legalize family planning in France in the late fifties to her preface in 1982 for a book that protests the still widespread practice of genital mutilation in many Third World countries.[17]

Simone de Beauvoir's identification with the world of women in struggles we usually call political emerged clearly and unexpectedly in my interview with her in June 1982. I asked her why, in our previous conversation, she seemed to disregard her commitment to feminism, insisting that she had never been very involved in politics. Feminism, she replied, is different: "It's politics, but it's the kind of politics that touches me deeply. Perhaps, in spite of everything. I've shared the reticence of many women in regard to politics because politics is a man's

17. Renée Saurel, *L'Enterrée vive* (Geneva: Slatkine, 1981).

world. I've never formulated it to myself in these terms but if I try to understand why I've had little interest in politician politics ('la politique politicienne'), it's perhaps because it's a world of men. Feminism is a world of women. It's the cause of women and that interests me passionately. I was loath to enter the politician world of men, whereas a feminist world of women's revolt—although I myself haven't had occasion in my adult life to rebel—that I understand with my heart, I'm completely in agreement and I can become wholeheartedly involved." In the *Memoirs,* Simone de Beauvoir expresses on a personal level this sentiment of preference for women's values, noting that in many respects she set her women friends above her men friends, "for they seemed to me more sensitive, more generous, more endowed with imagination, tears, and love"[18]—an indirect tribute to the "feminine" qualities her ideology does not allow her to acknowledge directly.

In the past decade, changing social conditions have produced new theories of discourse and new theories of the feminine that are not dreamed of in Simone de Beauvoir's philosophy. Her feminism does not take into account the role of language and of the unconscious as forces of oppression and of potential liberation for women. In that respect, as in so many others, she is a product of her generation.[19] She reflects on the individual in society and does not offer the seductions of a feminine text. In antithesis, the work of the new feminine discourse, which has transformed our thinking about texts and the symbolic order, has had little to offer to the referential suffering of women in the social order. Nor has this discourse been able to reconcile the contradictions between the demand for equality and the demand for the recognition of feminine difference.

Simone de Beauvoir's view of feminine difference as a cultural fabrication is consistent from *The Second Sex* to her most recent interviews. It is not easy to find in her writing even the suggestion of any

18. *Memoirs of a Dutiful Daughter,* trans. James Kirkup (New York: Harper Colophon Books, 1974), 296.

19. Speaking with Alice Schwarzer, Simone de Beauvoir muses that were she thirty or forty now, she would "very much like to do a work on psychoanalysis": "I would not take Freud as my starting point, but go right back to basics and from a feminist perspective, from a feminine rather than a masculine viewpoint." *After the Second Sex,* 88–89. Although existentialist ontology rejects the notion of the unconscious, at the heart of psychoanalysis, she has made this admission about herself and Sartre: "One of our inconsistencies was our refusal to accept the idea of the subconscious. Yet Gide, the surrealists, and, despite our resistance, Freud himself had all convinced us that in every person there lurks what André Breton called *un infracassable noyau de nuit,* [an indestructible kernel of darkness]." *The Prime of Life,* trans. Peter Green (Cleveland and New York: World, 1962), 107.

positive effects of that fabrication. One such suggestion does emerge in her "interview" with Sartre on women. Beauvoir asks him whether the status of woman's oppression has not developed in women certain qualities as well as certain faults that differ from those of men.[20] When I asked her for her own response to the question, she enumerated those qualities which she thinks have developed out of woman's situation, what she calls "qualities of heart and of compassion": "Women are often more altrustic; they have more the sense of others; they tend to have a more ironic sense of the human condition. These attitudes should be kept, outside a situation of oppression, and communicated to men as well." When I remarked that she rarely addresses these positive differences, she explained that her reticence was a question of "prudence": "If one insists too much on difference, even positive differences, one risks imprisoning woman once again in a feminine nature. And yet if we want to see clearly and look at things in their totality, without either fear or complacency, we have to admit that there are also feminine qualities." Insofar as feminine qualities are positive, they must become universalized as values rather than being used to perpetuate what she calls the "ghetto of difference."

In contrast to what Simone de Beauvoir sees as the regressive dangers of a claim to sexual difference, she presents the claim to equality as a demand having radical implications. The feminist struggle, in her view, is not an effort to become like men and take their place, but a way to change the world as it has been made by men. Women's access to all human potentialities would change the structure of the family, of work, of political and personal relations. "If women really did have complete equality with men," she asserts, "society would be completely overturned."[21] For Simone de Beauvoir, the alternative to sexual difference is not sameness, as her enemies insist, but for women to be "singular and universal at the same time."[22] It is a claim to liberate the plurality and unexplored possibilities of individual difference, independent of sexual definitions. From that perspective, *The Second Sex* has been an acknowledged source for such radical and radically heterogeneous utopian visions as Dorothy Dinnerstein's *The Mermaid and the Minotaur* and Monique Wittig's "One is not born a Woman."

French male theory of the past two decades, asserting itself against the ideologies of humanism, the self and representation, has sought,

20. "Simone de Beauvoir interroge Jean-Paul Sartre," in *Les Ecrits de Simone de Beauvoir*, 553–46.
21. Interview with Alice Jardine, *Signs* 5 (Winter 1979): 227.
22. Ibid., 235.

quite successfully, to overthrow the authority of the Father who dominated intellectual France in the 1940s and 1950s: Jean-Paul Sartre and
Sartrean existentialism. The daughters seem to be imitating the masculine model as they seek to overthrow the feminist Mother, in the
name, paradoxically, of feminine difference. Up to now, there has been
no translation of theories of difference into a politics of feminine praxis,
with the dubious exception of "Psych et Po."[23] Simone de Beauvoir's
feminism, inseparable from the struggle for sexual equality, speaks to
philosophic and cultural issues that are far from being resolved. As we
move through linguistic and psychoanalytic explorations of Kristeva's
"exploded, plural, fluid" feminine produced by the second generation to
a third generation of daughters, we would do well to keep alive the
connection with our first generation feminist Mother, even as we move
beyond her limitations.

23. For a history of "Psych et Po" in relation to the French feminist movement, see
my essay, "Politics of Difference: The Women's Movement in France from May 1968 to
Mitterrand," Signs 9 (Winter 1983): 282–83.

Simone de Beauvoir in her study (1975). Reprinted from *Simone de Beauvoir et le cours du monde* with the permission of Janine Niepce Rapho.

ISABELLE DE COURTIVRON

From Bastard to Pilgrim: Rites and Writing for Madame

Violette Leduc and Simone de Beauvoir met in Paris shortly after the end of the war. At the time, the Sartre-Beauvoir couple was at the center of the Parisian intellectual stage. *L'Invitée* had appeared in 1943, *Pyrrus et Cinéas* had just been published, and *Le Sang des autres* had been accepted by Gallimard. Beauvoir was rehearsing *Les Bouches inutiles* and working on *Tous les hommes sont mortels*. Her personal relationship and intellectual collaboration with Jean-Paul Sartre were secure; her future as a writer appeared promising. Leduc's life presented the antithesis of Simone de Beauvoir's success story. Haunted by a lifelong obsession with her illegitimate birth and a physical appearance that she considered grotesque, scarred by a succession of hurtful love affairs with women and men, Leduc was suffering from an unrequited infatuation with the homosexual writer Maurice Sachs. Together, they had hidden out in Normandy during the Occupation, until he abandoned her there, in pursuit of more lucrative ventures. Their brief cohabitation, however, had not proven altogether detrimental. Exasperated by Leduc's compulsive monologues about her unhappy childhood, Sachs forced her to write down these reminiscences. In "obeying" him, Leduc discovered what was to become the single most important direction of her life: becoming a writer. Sachs also initiated her into black-marketeering, an activity that temporarily brought Leduc material comfort, companionship, and a sense of independence and strength—all of which she had been acutely lacking during the first thirty-five years of her life. Hence, the Liberation that so exhilarated Simone de Beauvoir had the opposite effect on Leduc for whom the war had represented a form of respite, and who found herself once again plagued by loneliness, marginality, and poverty. Such were their *situations*, then, when the former *jeune fille rangée,* now solidly anchored to the most influential

milieus of her time, was introduced to the self-proclaimed *bâtarde*.[1]
The excesses of this former *jeune fille dérangée* could not have con-
trasted more blatantly with Simone de Beauvoir's reasonable and ra-
tional attitudes—attitudes that she developed, in part, by gradually
learning to control the feelings of violence, the fits of rage, and the crises
of despair that are frequently mentioned in the earlier volumes of her
memoirs.

This encounter, the major turning point in Leduc's life, is related
succinctly by Simone de Beauvoir in *La Force des choses*: "During the
autumn, through my companion, in a cinema queue on the Champs
Elysées, I met a tall blond woman with a face both brutally ugly and
radiantly alive: Violette Leduc. A few days later, at the Flore, she handed
me a manuscript. 'Confessions of a woman of the world,' I said to
myself. I opened the book: 'My mother never gave me her hand.' I read
the first half of the story without stopping."[2] The slim manuscript
which recounted Leduc's bittersweet childhood in a village of Northern
France resembled in no way the "socialite's confessions" that Simone
de Beauvoir had anticipated. Impressed by Leduc's talent, Simone de
Beauvoir made helpful suggestions and published excerpts of the reminiscences in the newly created *Les Temps Modernes*. She then drew the
attention of the publisher Gallimard to Leduc's volume, and *L'Asphyxie*
was published in the collection *Espoir* directed by Albert Camus.

During the next twenty-seven years, Simone de Beauvoir was the
driving force behind Violette Leduc's life, the main catalyst of her inspiration as well as of her despair. She demanded the hard work, the
perseverance, the painful crafting of language that gradually took Leduc
from writing down random childhood associations to creating full-
fledged literary works. The two met every other week to review whatever Leduc had written. Simone de Beauvoir's perennial question:
"Have you been working?" would send Leduc into alternate crises of

1. This is how Jovette Marchessault described Violette Leduc when she made her the
subject of her play, *La Terre est trop courte, Violette Leduc* (Montreal: Editions de la pleine
lune, 1982), 13. "Femme laide, bâtarde, obsédée sexuelle, voyeuse sado-masochiste, para-
noïaque, pleureuse chronique, assoiffée de luxe, voyeuse à l'étalage, trafiquante durant
l'Occupation en France, vestale des homosexuels littéraires parisiens, putain, matricide,
maquereau, délateur, ni ouvrière ni bourgeoise, ni intellectuelle mais mendiante humi-
liée, passionnée, démesurée." [Ugly, a bastard, a sexual obsessive, a sado-masochistic
voyeur, paranoid, a chronic weeper, starved for luxury, a shop-window voyeur, a trafficker
during the Occupation, a vestal for Paris's literary homosexuals, a prostitute, a matricide,
a pimp, an informer neither worker, bourgeoise, nor intellectual, but a humiliated, passionate, immoderate beggar.]
2. Simone de Beauvoir, *Force of Circumstance*, vol. 1 (N.Y.: Harper and Row, 1963),
19.

paralyzing insecurity and renewed determination. Simone de Beauvoir's support reached every aspect of Leduc's existence. She assisted Leduc financially by arranging a small monthly stipend ostensibly paid by Gallimard during the years of extreme poverty. She also introduced Leduc to her network of friends, in the hope of alleviating her protégée's acute isolation. She fought Gallimard, albeit unsuccessfully, when the publisher decided to censor one hundred and fifty pages of Leduc's third work, *Ravages*, which it considered too sexually explicit. When the mutilation of this book and its subsequent disregard by the public drove Leduc to erratic extremes, Simone de Beauvoir judged that Leduc's behavior had become dangerously self-destructive and convinced her to enter a clinic. There, she underwent shock therapy and a sleeping cure. Leduc found the strength to write again upon Simone de Beauvoir's suggestion that she start an autobiographical project. When Leduc completed the first volume of this project, Simone de Beauvoir's forceful preface to *La Bâtarde* helped promote the book publicly. *La Bâtarde*, the provocative autobiography of a middle-aged woman who aggressively proclaimed her ugliness, her convoluted sexual adventures, her poverty and her social failures, became a best-seller in 1964. Its success justified Simone de Beauvoir's faith in Leduc's talent and her long support of this obscure and despairing writer. Finally, it was Simone de Beauvoir who edited the third part of the autobiography that Leduc completed just before she died in 1973. Although she never became the close friend Leduc ardently hoped for, Simone de Beauvoir replaced Violette's mother, Berthe, as the powerful maternal figure in her protégée's imagination. Unwittingly, she fueled the fantasy life from which some of Leduc's best writing was produced. Most important, she remained her principal literary adviser and her most discerning reader.

Along the way, Simone de Beauvoir evolved not only into Leduc's lifelong mentor, but into her muse as well. This double role underscores the exceptional nature of their bond. Indeed, not only is mentorship between women a rare occurence in light of their common powerlessness, but, as Carolyn Heilbrun has so aptly remarked: "Muses are for men . . . the muse has been progressively seen as male property and male inspiration. The question of who is woman's muse, and what is that muse's sex, has not been asked until recently."[3] It is clear, however, that for Violette Leduc the question of the woman writer's muse led directly to another, more famous, woman writer. Indeed, the presence of Simone de Beauvoir permeates Leduc's adult years and dominates most

3. Carolyn Heilbrun, *Reinventing Womanhood* (N.Y.: W. W. Norton, 1979), 153.

of her works. *Ravages* is dedicated to her. *L'Affamée* is a diarylike account of Leduc's passion for Madame—a thinly disguised Simone. The narrator of *Trésors à prendre* addresses Madame repeatedly, although the latter is not physically present in the text. And, of course, Simone de Beauvoir is ubiquitous in the autobiographical volumes for which Leduc gained notoriety.

Simone de Beauvoir was not the first of the real-life figures to whom Leduc became fervently attached and whose portraits are central to her predominantly autobiographical oeuvre. However, she provides the most striking illustration of an emotional pattern that structures the life of the character Violette and the works of the writer Leduc. I shall briefly outline this particular mechanism in order to illuminate the representations of Simone de Beauvoir that are woven throughout the works of Leduc.

In *La Folie en tête*, the second volume of her autobiography,—and a text in which Simone de Beauvoir is omnipresent—Leduc provides a key to understanding her failure to establish enduring relationships with other human beings: the metaphor of the binoculars. "Binoculars cut you off from people by bringing you close to them. You close in on what's happening far from you but without participating in it."[4] Violette approaches others as if she were observing them through binoculars, perceiving them as very close when in fact, as in the case of an optical illusion, they are extremely distant from her. When the binoculars are removed, she is overwhelmed by the reality of distance and by her hopeless estrangement. The disappointment is fierce. It provides relief, however, from a closeness that entails asphyxiation. The frustration that runs throughout Leduc's writings is a product of Violette's habit of repeatedly holding to her vision, then brutally snatching off the binoculars of her imagination. A correct perspective is never found. Jarring distortions and mistaken estimates alter Violette's view of every person to whom she is attracted. Indeed, the titles of Leduc's first three books, *L'Asphyxie, L'Affamée,* and *Ravages*, epitomize the paradox of a character starving for attention and suffocated by it, a character both devastated and relieved by separation from the loved one, longing for a closeness that inevitably ravages her. At the source of this tension is the narrator's ambivalent relationship to the dominant figure in her life, her

4. Violette Leduc, *La Folie en tête* (Paris: Gallimard, 1970), 231. All the translations in this study are my own, although I often consulted the existing translated works by Derek Coltman.) As of the present time, *L'Affamée, La Chasse à l'amour* and *Trésors à prendre* are not translated.

mother Berthe who, like Simone, is present in virtually all of Leduc's works.

Nancy Chodorow's object-relations theory, developed in *The Reproduction of Mothering*, sheds light on Violette's exceptional difficulty in achieving individuation from her mother.[5] Indeed, not only did the little girl not have a father to help her break the primary unity with and dependence on the mother; but the latter certainly treated her daughter as an extension of herself, imposing on the child Violette all of her own fears, concerns and passions, as well as her bitterness about her experience of womanhood. Lifelong issues of merging with and separating from others, which dominate the life of Leduc's autobiographical narrator, can be understood in the light of Chodorow's description of the subconscious psychic structures that result in women's less defined and more fluid ego boundaries. Unable to free herself from this original unity, Violette internalizes its complicated manifestations. The bond with the adored being whose dutiful but distant attitude throws Violette into paroxysms of despair serves as a paradigm for all subsequent relationships. The same pattern is reenacted with all of Leduc's fictional and autobiographical characters, but it takes on a distinct configuration in the two works that focus on the representations of Simone de Beauvoir (Madame) in *L'Affamée* and *Trésors à prendre*.[6]

L'Affamée, written directly after Leduc's first meeting with Simone de Beauvoir, provides the most striking illustration of the narrator's obsession with what she calls "the identical mirages of presence and absence" (188). Its main theme is hunger: the soul famished for attention and tenderness, devouring itself because it cannot devour the other, yearning for complete absorption, frightened by this compulsion yet frustrated by its failure.

L'Affamée opens with the narrator's encounter, in a café, with the person she calls Madame. It traces her tortured mental states during regular meetings with Madame, and during the latter's absences on trips. And it concludes with a fragile acceptance of the reality and limitations of their relationship. The text is written in the form of a monologue, divided into scenes that expose the narrator's fear, joy, despair, anguish, anger, frustration, adoration, and frenzy in the presence of

5. Nancy Chodorow, *The Reproduction of Mothering: Psychoanalysis and the Sociology of gender* (Berkeley and Los Angeles: University of California Press, 1978).

6. *L'Affamée* was published by Gallimard in 1948. *Trésors à prendre*, also published by Gallimard, was written in 1951 but did not appear until 1960. While these two works are not as well known as *La Bâtarde* and *Thérèse et Isabelle*, it is this critic's opinion that they are Leduc's finest literary achievements. References to these works will henceforth be given in the text.

Madame. Apart from a very few factual indications, this work is almost entirely composed of the narrator's richly imaged fantasies. Most of these revolve around the themes of death and destruction, for *L'Affamée* is Leduc's most violent work. Through extremely short sentences and constant repetition, Leduc communicates frustration and rage, and renders the feelings of being tracked, disconnected, possessed, stifled. The entire work reads as a jarring and tortured voyage, dominated by images of persecution and imprisonment. Nevertheless, the narrator's inner journey ends on a note of reconciliation with her situation: she has learned to recreate and transform her love through the act of writing. *L'Affamée* concludes with the narrator's adoring contemplation of Madame, who is reading peacefully in her café. The perfect distance has been found. Separated by a glass pane, they are apart yet near:

> She was reading. She turned a page in her book but it did not startle me. That arm, that hand half folded under her chin moved me deeply. Whenever I listen to an andante I think of that arm, of that hand. She turned another page. It became the close unfolding of the past. I received the rhythm of her reading as an illumination in the most intimate part of my soul. I was afraid to tarnish her radiance. I am not familiar with the way she breathes. She is the slave of her breathing. At that thought, I swelled with tenderness. I stood up because I was disarmed. . . . If I could have heard the sound of the page being turned, I would have been rich. I sat down once more, then I stood up. Estrangement and nearness. Through the glass pane, I could see her face more clearly. The speckled veil in front of her face, I had often imagined. That veil evoked the hundreds, the thousands of studious hours of her existence, that veil tempered her beauty.
>
> I slipped away softly. I stood tall in my hovel. I did not speak to the walls. I put on my apron. I tightened my leather belt. I did not have to wait for long. The nape of my neck was being uncovered, the collar of my apron was pulled back, a rivière of diamonds was clasped around my neck.
>
> To love is difficult but to love is a grace. [*L'Affamée*, 253–54]

The quasi-religious tone of the closing underscores a leitmotif set up at the very beginning of the work. The first meeting with Madame, to which she refers in *L'Affamée* as *l'événement*, clearly serves as the awakening of the narrator to the consciousness of divine reality:

> The light struck in a café during the month of February. Lightening and laceration. The first time she spoke to me, the other sounds receded. I became the stunned hiker who cannot wrench herself from

the hunting trap in which she has been caught. I was caught. While I gave her my sheets of paper, a cloud nestled inside of me. I stretched my face out toward her. I was invaded even faster. In spite of myself, a grave event had been created for me. The dazzling light was spreading. I received it as a stained-glass window would receive it. I leaned against the back of the seat but I did not surrender. She left the café. I was bewildered by an inner rumbling. I still remember the fatal sound of the door which closed by itself. The noises returned. I pondered over the event, I dreamed while others around me grew distant. . . . I knew then that what was happening to me was a beginning. [L'Affamée, 236–37]

This "conversion"—a traditional structural device of the auto-biographical genre—is not unlike the first stage of mystical experience described by the scholar Evelyn Underhill as "a disturbance of the equi-librium of the self, which results in the shifting of the field of con-sciousness from lower to higher levels, with a consequent removal of the centre of interest from the subject to an object now brought into view . . . mystic conversion is a single and abrupt experience, sharply marked off from the long, dim struggles which precede and succeed it. It usually involves a sudden and acute realization of a splendor and adora-ble reality in the world."[7] Madame, the creator of this new being, exac-erbates the narrator's sense of her own shortcomings. This response, too, resembles the mystic's attitude toward the greatness of the deity that has just been revealed. Indeed, for true mystics who have been awakened: "the Self, aware for the first time of Divine Beauty, realizes by contrast its own finiteness and imperfection, the manifold illusions in which it is immersed, the immense distance which separates it from the One. Its attempts to eliminate by discipline and mortification all that stands in the way of its progress toward union with God constitute Purgation: a state of pain and effort."[8]

In the same way, Violette's exaggerated emphasis on her lifelong inadequacies leads her to seek out any punishment that would make her worthy of Madame: "Let her order me to remove my shoes, let her order me to run on rocks, on nails, on pieces of broken glass, on thorns" (L'Affamée, 74). But Madame does not request such physical proofs of devotion. What she demands from Violette is the "purgation" of creat-ing works.

The next stage in the traditional mystic's way is described through

7. Evelyn Underhill, Mysticism (New York: New American Library, 1955), 176–78.
8. Ibid, 169.

the allegory of the pilgrimage—the quest for detachment, for movement from the material to the spiritual world. In accordance with this paradigm, Leduc's narrator becomes a pilgrim seeking out purification. *Trésors à prendre* constitutes the link between *l'événement* of *L'Affamée*, and the narrator's entry into the order of literature.

Trésors à prendre takes the form of a travel journal that documents the author's trip in southwestern France, the same trip taken by Simone de Beauvoir and Sartre several years earlier. The text relates the narrator's adventures and misadventures, her discoveries and disappointments, and the landscapes and people she encounters, from the time she leaves Paris until her return there several weeks later. But *Trésors à prendre* is also a mystic's tale of pilgrimage. It is a homage to the same unattainable Madame of *L'Affamée*, a hymn to her spirit which accompanies the traveller throughout her wanderings. Violette, literally retracing the footsteps of her beloved, is able to enter into communion with her through the mediation of places that have been visited, appreciated, and recommended by Madame, and where the latter's presence is still felt.

In keeping with the religious mission of her voyage, Violette visits mostly churches, cathedrals, basilicas, abbeys. The smell of incense, the color of stained-glass windows, the silent presence of black-robed priests predominate during these sightseeing expeditions as, walking in the footsteps of her saint, the pilgrim seeks purification through discipline. Like a monk, she travels alone, divested of worldly goods and desires, eating humble fare on the side of the road, washing her clothes in village fountains, even climbing rocky hills on her knees. She undergoes mystical transes: the most intense occur when she discovers the plateau of Montpellier-le-Vieux and the cathedral of Albi, highly praised by Madame, and is seized by the ecstasy of entering into communion with her idol and protectress:

> I am standing on the plateau overlooking Montpellier-le-Vieux. I am standing for you, Madame. It was bestowed upon me that I should give myself to you for nothing, by renouncing you. Returning to you is a vast relief. My effort is great as I dedicate myself to you. Your head was lowered, you were writing in a café, you were ignoring me. Then came the miracle. You seized my heart and when you returned it, it was virginal and dependent, and all the while your head was lowered, you wrote in a café, you ignored me. You are my pilgrimage over five continents, you are my goal and my way-station, you are my seedbed from which I burst forth in order to give more. I open wide my blouse,

unbuttoned over my chest, I tear myself open. I need space. . . . You are neither dead nor alive. You are absent. I had made room for you in my entrails as I bid you goodbye, as I shook your hand like every other time, with moderation, and that is when I embalmed you. The taxi took me away into the night with my relics. . . . I began to build toward your resurrection. I will never be able to say who completed the work for me. . . . I waited patiently in my darkness until I was able to forget you, to forget myself, I waited patiently, wrapped in my large night mantle. I knew that I was close to the miracle I had desired when I opened my eyes, when my waiting apparel melted away. You arrived, you appeared to me in the middle of your everyday habits. I can see you again on the plateau of Montpellier-le-Vieux as I will see you again in Paris. You reappeared as you will reappear, carrying with you the centuries of reality with which I have entrusted you. [*Trésors à prendre*, 127–29]

Ultimately, Violette reaches Ars, a pilgrimage town made famous by Saint Jean-Marie Vianney, where she joins a community of true pilgrims for several days.

The narrator's religion, like that of a passionate mystic, is far removed from the routine of ordinary churchgoers. Never abandoning her status as a rebel and a pariah, Violette has nothing but contempt for the blandness of organized religion. She claims she does not even remember how to make the sign of the cross. She deplores the morbid sadness of Catholicism and its "instruments of torture," the somber crucified statues, and the gloom of confessionals. Instead, she fashions her own religion from art, literature, passion and madness, drawing upon a panoply of geniuses, madmen and homosexuals whom she invests with saintly status. If Madame (Simone de Beauvoir) is the reigning God(dess), Jean Genet, Vincent Van Gogh and Toulouse Lautrec—exemplars of visionary transgression—are the saints.

In *Trésors à prendre*, Leduc appeals directly to the allegory of the pilgrimage, detailing the wanderer's solitude and hardship alleviated only by occasional glimpses of the Beloved through illuminations and visions. As in *L'Affamée*, the narrator struggles to accept the fact that she will never mean anything to Madame except in their common enterprise, literary creation. As in *L'Affamée* also, she succeeds in transforming her desire into writing. The inclusion in her text of the letters addressed to Madame, then the very text of *Trésors à prendre* are the verbal creations that will simultaneously express their author's desire and draw her closer to the desired being by direct address.

Ultimately, Madame begins to lose her specificity, her very an-
thropomorphism. She becomes more diffused, permeating the colors,
sounds and sights on the pilgrim's road:

> I met you, Madame, in the color, in the shape, in the stone of a cathe-
> dral, in an Archbishop's palace, in the roses of the garden that lies
> between the cathedral and the palace. I was whipped by love, by as-
> tonishment, by beauty, to the point of collapse, turning into a heap of
> limp rags in my hotel room. You did not appear to me. We were no
> longer in Montpellier-le-Vieux. In the morning, at noon, in the eve-
> ning, at midnight, I stroked the texture of your skin with my fingers,
> with my eyelashes, with my cheeks. I, who become religious at the
> very thought of you, I brushed with my lips the ardent surface of the
> cathedral. You are this cathedral. You, Madame, by enduring beauty.
> [*Trésors à prendre*, 146]

Divine being, human being, Madame becomes a monument for Leduc,
the cathedral itself in which she worships.

Although some of Violette's epiphanies are described in terms
evocative of genuine mystics, the analogy must not be overextended.
For the tortured, self-centered Violette, there is no Unitive Life,[9] no
suppression of the self in the traditional mystical sense. What is accomplished by her pilgrimage, however, is the creation of offerings in the
form of literary works that usher her into the religion of literature, of
which Beauvoir/Madame represents the locus. In later works, when
Violette the protagonist evolves into Violette Leduc the writer, the
literary communication of her experiences becomes her most precious
gift to the unknown reader who ultimately replaces Simone de Beauvoir:

> 22 August 1963. This August day, reader, is a rose window glowing
> with heat. I make a gift of it to you. It is yours. One o'clock. I am
> returning to the village for lunch. Strong with the silence of pines and
> chestnut trees, I walk without flinching through this burning cathe-
> dral of summer. My bank of wild grass is majestic and it is full of
> music. Solitude presses fire against my lips.[10]

If one is to read Leduc's corpus as a single text organized by a central

9. The Unitive Life stands as the highest point of the mystical ladder which can be
realized by human spirits. It involves the disappearance of earlier strivings, visions and
ecstacies, a conquest of character, the transcendance of self, attainment of complete
humility, the final establishment of union with God. (See Evelyn Underhill, op. cit.,
Chapter 10.)

10. *La Bâtarde* (Paris: Gallimard, 1964), 634. References to this work will henceforth
be given in the text.

theme—the painful but redemptive act of writing—one can describe this process as a quest mediated by Violette Leduc's sanctification of Simone de Beauvoir. She is the primary catalyst, the marker who traces the road figuratively, (and literally in the case of *Trésors à prendre*), that leads Leduc from the mortification of the sinner-bastard to the discipline of the writer-novice. At the end of her last work, *La Chasse à l'amour*, the narrator describes herself as a nun in the order of literature. Her house in Provence is likened to a convent, and writing is a ceremony, an ascesis: "My bedroom, a secular chapel. Nothing in it but an antique closet. . . . My bed? A metallic boxspring, a gravelled mattress. . . . I trip on the tiles in the bedroom. Monastic intoxication. . . . The tiles become smoother and smoother if I sweep them for a long time. . . . My schedule is incorruptible. I have an iron discipline."[11]

From *L'Affamée* to *La Chasse à l'amour*, and despite the long purgatorial passage of *La Folie en tête*—which relates her bout with "madness" and her subsequent incarceration in a mental institute—Violette Leduc's trajectory has led her on a psychic and spiritual journey that concludes not in sainthood but in another, equally severe and equally sacred vocation—that of writer: "Writing. It meant entering the struggle, it meant earning my livelihood as a believer earns her right to enter heaven" (*La Bâtarde*, 486).

Although Leduc's narrator displays toward Madame many of the same tempestuous emotions that appear to varying degrees in all her other relationships, her love for Beauvoir/Madame is the most consistently positive thread in Leduc's entire corpus. Their lifelong rapport becomes almost harmonious. Learning to detach herself from a passionate fantasy without automatically triggering a brutal rupture with its real-life object is a unique achievement in Violette Leduc's life and writings. Beauvoir/Madame is the only person whose image has come out intact after being subjected to one of Leduc's anarchic passions. This is because she is more than a maternal figure or an object of sexual desire, more than the envied example of the woman Leduc never could be, more than a worshipped idol. Simone de Beauvoir is, first and foremost, a writer who has inspired, encouraged, guided Leduc and helped her develop into a writer. In doing so she contributed to the growth of self-respect in one who was painfully bereft of it. The key to her success is that she has always known how to find and maintain the correct *distance* from Leduc. "I established a certain distance from the very beginning," asserts Simone de Beauvoir when questioned about the

11. *La Chasse à l'amour* (Paris: Gallimard, 1973), 401.

unique place she has in Violette Leduc's work.[12] And Leduc confesses: "I shall never understand the meaning of the word love when it applies to her and to me. I do not love her as a mother, I do not love her as a sister, I do not love her as a friend, I do not love her as an enemy, I do not love her as someone absent, I do not love her as someone always close to me. I have never had, nor will I ever have, one second of intimacy with her. If I could no longer see her every other week, darkness would submerge me. She is my reason for living, without having ever made room for me in her life."[13] Simone de Beauvoir gave Leduc serious attention as a writer and encouraged the best in her, but she never allowed herself to be approached too closely by her voracious protégée. By providing the proper "combination of response, encouragement, expectation and utter detachment that helps to catalyze creative work,"[14] and by prudently maintaining this fragile equilibrium, Simone de Beauvoir saved Leduc not only from yet another disastrous emotional failure but from creative asphyxiation as well.

Her periodic consultations with Leduc over the years, her generous gift of time, and her shrewd editorial advice helped Leduc find identity and purpose as a writer. The contacts between the two women were mediated by literature and writing, which both respected above all. "I am the bark, you are the sap" (*Trésors à prendre*, 122), wrote Leduc's narrator to Madame. And for two-and-a-half decades, the sap never ceased to flow and to nourish the tree. In one of her last interviews, Leduc made this poignant acknowledgment: "At the end of my life, I will think of my mother, I will think of Simone de Beauvoir, and I will think of my long struggle."[15]

Surrogate mother, object of desire, goddess, model, mentor, muse, idol and inspiration—the roles filled by Simone de Beauvoir in Violette Leduc's life and imagination are manifold. What function, then, did Leduc serve for her mentor? The few passages in Simone de Beauvoir's memoirs that deal with Violette Leduc are terse, albeit admiring. Si-

12. Personal interviews with Simone de Beauvoir, June 1983 and June 1984.

13. *La Folie en tête*, 156. It is interesting to compare this quotation with Carol Ascher's equally ambivalent statement in her "clearing the air" letter to Simone de Beauvoir: "Unfortunately, you aren't that 'good mother' I long for in my weakest moments. Although you have always taken young women under your wing, I sense your aloofness." (*Between Women*, ed. Carol Ascher, Louise DeSalvo, Sara Ruddick, Boston: Beacon Hill Press, 1984, 89.)

14. Ruth Perry and Martine Watson Brownley, ed., *Mothering the Mind, Twelve studies of Writers and their Silent Partners* (New York: Holmes and Meier, 1984), 3–4.

15. Interview with Jacques Chancel for *Radioscopie*, 25 April 1970.

mone de Beauvoir's editorial skills undoubtedly found outlet and satisfaction in helping this most loyal and hardworking of students grow into a writer of national stature. It is also clear that she prized Leduc's discipline, her courage, and her endurance. Relating Leduc's horrifying hallucinatory experiences that led to a complete mental collapse, Simone writes:

> She has appeared to me so stricken that at a certain point I had become doubtful about her recovery. One of her oldest friends became so frightened of her that he stopped seeing her completely. But there was something so robust in her, she loved life so passionately that she finally managed to overcome her wanderings. . . . When one knows what effort is required by the confrontation with the blank page, what tension is demanded by the alignment of words, one remains stunned in the face of such energetic perseverence.[16]

And, most importantly, Simone de Beauvoir greatly appreciated Leduc's writing: "She had a tone, a style, a manner that appealed to me right away. She was a hard worker and her tenacity also appealed to me."[17]

Beyond these more overt reasons, Leduc's place in Simone de Beauvoir's life remains an ill-defined one. However, Michèle Respaut's eloquent description of Leduc's obsession with Simone may provide a clue to the more obscure dimensions of this unique relationship:

> What we can see in this desperate quest, beyond the homosexual connection, beyond the filial connection, is the old stereotype being revived. Reproducing once more what thousands of women have attempted, to "become the Angel," to reject what she knows to be and what they tell her is monstrous, ignoble, dangerous and mad—what the narrator seeks is her antithesis, what we may call her complement. The "dark" woman seeking out the pure one, the Monster seeking out the Angel: to possess this other, to lose oneself in her, and to become her.[18]

Conversely, Leduc may have incarnated for Simone de Beauvoir, and quite literally so, the "maddened double" of which Gilbert and Gubar

16. Simone de Beauvoir, *Tout Compte fait* (Paris: Gallimard, 1972), 59.

17. Personal interviews with Simone de Beauvoir, June 1983 and June 1984.

18. Michèle Respaut, "Femme/ange, femme/monstre: *L'Affamée* de Violette Leduc," *Stanford French Review*, Winter 1984, 371. "Nous pouvons voir dans cette quête éperdue, au-delà de rapports homosexuels, au-delà de l'amour filial, le vieux stéréotype reprendre vie. Reproduisant une fois de plus ce que milliers de femmes ont essayé de faire, 'devenir l'Ange', rejeter ce qu'elle sait être et qu'on lui dit être monstrueux, ignoble, dangereux et fou—ce que la narratrice recherche en fait c'est son antithèse, ou peut-être ce qu'on pourrait dire son complément. Femme 'noire' à la recherche de la femme 'blanche,'' le Monstre à la recherche de l'Ange: posséder cette autre, s'y perdre et la devenir.''

speak in *The Madwoman in the Attic*: "by projecting their rebellious impulses not into their heroines but into mad or monstrous women . . ., female authors dramatize their own self-division, their desire both to accept the strictures of patriarchal society and to reject them."[19] Such fearful identification with the "monster-woman" in the self can surely transcend its literary representations, and attach itself to real-life figures. Simone de Beauvoir, the writer, created "calm," "serious," "serene," "distant," and "austere" autobiographical heroines who found catharsis in moments of inebriation, and release in moments of illness—"acceptable" channels for anger and despair. The same writer also created foils to each of these proper heroines, in the form of women characters who sank into the madness of jealousy, dependency, eccentricity and anger. Simone de Beauvoir, the intellectual, refused to allow herself loss of control except when projecting her personal anguish onto nefarious political and historical forces. Finally, Simone, the woman, succeeded in remaining reasonable in the face of intense emotions such as jealousy. Therefore, it can be argued that just as Leduc projected her "angelic half" onto Madame/Beauvoir, so perhaps Simone de Beauvoir, trapped in her own dutiful image and in her permanent role of "petite conscience morale" for Sartre,[20] disciplined herself not to express her anxiety and rage for fear of shattering her carefully constructed image, or rendering useless the unique role with which she had identified herself. Hence, she may have found relief in splitting herself off to merge with the passionate and chaotic Violette, her other, darker side. The more controlled Simone de Beauvoir who, as a young girl, had defined herself as both "irreproachable and monstrous" and who, for years, bemoaned her "divided mind," admitted that she had "always striven fiercely to keep darkness and light apart."[21] In order to do so, she may have discharged, and thereby further contained, her "monstrous" side, so carefully repressed, onto the excessive and violent being whose writing exploded with the emotional risks she took, and next to which the established writer's own works seem chillingly lifeless. Indeed, the creative works and the personal lives of these two women could not have been more radically opposed, their autobiographies more divergent. In fact, Simone de Beauvoir's conventional autobiographical project could in no way provide Leduc's bolder creative vision with a female counter-

19. Sandra Gilbert and Susan Gubar, *The Madwoman in the Attic* (New Haven and London: Yale University Press, 1979), 78.
20. Jean-Paul Sartre, *Lettres au Castor, 1940–1963* (Paris: Gallimard, 1983), 180.
21. Simone de Beauvoir, *The Prime of Life* (New York: Harper and Row, 1962), 458.

model of the genre. Yet order and chaos, adaptation and transgression, decorum and violence, dutifulness and madness, bound them intimately, within their psychosocial heritage, as inseparable sides of the same Mythical Woman. In this respect, Simone de Beauvoir's preface to *La Bâtarde,* on the surface an existential analysis of Leduc's work, may adumbrate the unwitting function Leduc served for her: "Most writers, when they confess to evil thoughts, manage to remove the sting from them by the very frankness of their admissions. [Leduc] forces us to feel them with all their corrosive bitterness both in herself and in ourselves. She remains a faithful accomplice to her desires, to her rancor, to her petty traits. *In this way she takes ours upon her too and delivers us from shame: no one is monstrous unless we all are so.*"[22] Such an interpretation would also explain why, although it is tempting to speculate that Simone's generosity was not limited to Violette Leduc's case, this particular experience was in fact unique in her life, and why she "chose" the unlikely Violette Leduc as its sole recipient.

Sadly, the connection between these two women writers remains overlooked even in the most hagiographical works on Simone de Beauvoir. While *camaraderie virile* in literary enterprises is indelibly engraved in our cultural repertory, no language has been created to define the bonds that exist between two women if these are forged by neither sexual intimacy nor sexual rivalry. The long and tortured apprenticeship of a writer, an arduous vocation ultimately redeemed by grace, stagnates in the margins of literary history, written in invisible ink and hidden in the seldom-read pages of an eccentric peasant-bastard woman. For more than a quarter of a century, Simone de Beauvoir served as catalyst of Leduc's excessive emotions. In the pages she edited and refined,[23] she found herself imprisoned in her own reflection as the angelic Madame—a source of superb images, tortured visions, mystical crises, and exalted linguistic finds. Yet she never allowed this unsettling phenomenon to interfere with her supervision of the violent passages in which she so often played the central part: "I blocked myself," she says

---

22. Simone de Beauvoir, "Foreword to *La Bâtarde* (New York: Farrar, Straus and Giroux, 1965), xvii.

23. A study of the original manuscript of *La Chasse à l'amour* reveals that much of Simone de Beauvoir's editing consisted of eliminating a large number of passages which she judged to be repetitive or unnecessary. She therefore "contained" Leduc's writing as she did Leduc's emotions—much to the latter's simultaneous feelings of gratitude and resentment.

today, "I considered it exclusively as literature."[24] This unprecedented gift of time, of experience, and of the self, now merely a footnote in Simone de Beauvoir's much-examined life and feminism, will ultimately find its deserved place in the chapters yet to be written on women-helping-women-to-write.

24. Personal interviews with Simone de Beauvoir, June 1983 and June 1984.

DEIRDRE BAIR

Simone de Beauvoir: Politics, Language, and Feminist Identity

At the conclusion of a far-ranging 1983 interview on the situation of women throughout the world today, Simone de Beauvoir made a statement that would no doubt have astonished Jean-Paul Sartre. "I think," she said, "that when women really begin to consider liberating themselves seriously, they will take more of an interest in politics."[1]

Politics, he said, in a 1965 interview with a reporter for *Vogue* magazine, was the one aspect of Simone de Beauvoir that he could not fathom: "There's only one matter on which she completely staggers me, and that's politics. She doesn't care a damn about it. Well, it's not exactly that she doesn't care, but she just won't have anything to do with politics."[2]

Reflecting on Sartre's comment, Simone de Beauvoir remembers it somewhat differently: "Politics in every sense of that word, in all its ramifications—we talked, we argued, we agreed on much, disagreed on much else. For years, political action and political discussion consumed us."[3]

Readers of Simone de Beauvoir's four volumes of autobiographical memoirs are familiar with her statements about the development of the

1. Deirdre Bair, "Women's Rights in Today's World: an interview with Simone de Beauvoir," *1984 Britannica Book of the Year* (Chicago: Encyclopaedia Britannica, Inc., 1984), 28.

2. Madeleine Gobeil, interview with Jean-Paul Sartre, *Vogue* (American Edition), July, 1965; reprinted in Serge Julienne-Caffié, *Simone de Beauvoir* (Paris: Editions Gallimard, 1966), 38–43.

3. During January and February, 1982, Simone de Beauvoir gave a series of weekly and biweekly interviews for a critical biography which this author is now completing. Since then, she has cooperated in interview sessions about her life and work several times each year. All direct quotations, unless otherwise noted, are from these interviews.

major concerns of her life, particularly in the early volumes where there is much discussion of Existential philosophy and the concurrent idea of commitment or *engagement*. In the later memoirs, she writes at length about the developing stages of her introspective, self-examination as at first she groped, then moved firmly and directly toward formulating a personal feminist theory, and how it led to her outspoken support for feminist action. But despite Sartre's exasperated disavowal, politics, (a term used here as she uses it, in the sense of action or behavior by or on behalf of nations, states, communities of interest or other organized groups), has always been an area of major concern and activity for Simone de Beauvoir, although it has only recently begun to receive sustained analysis in critical evaluations of her life and work.

Both philosophy and feminist theory stand juxtaposed within her curiously ambivalent attitude toward any expression or form of political action. She has never written anything exclusively devoted to the explication of a personal political credo, and has always denied in the strongest language any interest or involvement in politics per se. Still, the curious thing about all her seemingly contradictory statements is how political they are and have always been. Hers is a political rhetoric that has sometimes led to charges that she advocates social anarchy, is clearly a misogynist, and has even lost touch with the realities of contemporary life for most of the women in the world.

Language, as recent literary theorists have so ably demonstrated, often obfuscates where it attempts to clarify. In the case of Simone de Beauvoir, this has been true more often than not. Although she has used the language of politics throughout her life, in the last fifteen or so years, it has dominated her expression, especially her feminist statements. It is, in her words, "old language" which to her means rhetoric not informed primarily by recent gender theory but by the language of cultural values, mostly those associated in Western cultures with men, all with a confrontational, militaristic caste.[4] One might argue that this is only natural, since she spent most of her intellectual life in the company of men as the only woman among them.

She has chosen her words carefully to take note of this difference:

---

4. In *The Second Sex*, she wrote: "Representation of the world, like the world itself, is the work of men; they describe it from their own point of view, which they confuse with the absolute truth." Evelyn Fox Keller uses this passage as preface to her introduction in *Reflections on Gender and Science* (New Haven: Yale University Press, 1985). On page 10, Professor Keller comments along the same line: "Our 'laws of nature' are more than simple expressions of the results of objective inquiry or of political and social pressures: they must also be read for their personal—and by tradition, masculine—content."

"Since [World War II], I have never ceased to be involved. But," she added pointedly, "I have never been militant."[5]

This "nonmilitant" involvement has led during the past fifteen years to what she considers a "cohesive unity of personal belief and public action which I suppose I must describe in the vocabulary of politics because that is the only language available to me now. Perhaps women should have a new vocabulary to describe Feminist action."

When asked if such a "new" vocabulary should be one of gender-related terms, she replied: "I am not sure that I understand exactly what those terms are, or even what they should be. It is difficult to describe new concepts and actions in existing words, but it is even more difficult to invent new ones. And yet, words must be put to the service of action, either real or contemplated: words are crucial weapons for feminism and must be chosen carefully and used wisely."

Her own use of words as "crucial weapons" shows an interesting pattern: until 1970, her life had been dominated "by two concerns: my commitment to Sartre and to my writing." For the most part, she followed him as he veered from being a writer with purely literary concerns to a philosopher who believed in writing as the logical and legitimate expression of political commitment. This she duplicated, and when he became a political activist she was mostly content to be at his side to explain his actions, positions and statements—but only when her opinions were solicited or she was provoked into speech. She was content with the role of follower, saying "I did not desire to play even the smallest political role, so that for me to read the same books as Sartre and to meditate upon the same themes would have been a gratuitous activity."[6] She kept her political opinions to herself, mostly because no one (generally this included Sartre) asked for them. She noted with asperity in 1949, when Sartre had begun to be a constant presence at political rallies: *"For once I gave him a piece of political advice:* not to go." [Emphasis mine].[7]

She must not have been as silent as she thought. Raymond Aron

5. Caroline Moorehead, "Simone de Beauvoir: 'Happiness is a snare when the world is a horrible place,'" *The Times*, 16 May 1974, 11.

6. Simone de Beauvoir, *Force of Circumstance*, trans. Richard Howard (New York and London: Penguin Books, Ltd., 1968), 268.

7. *Force of Circumstance*, 186. In the 1982 interviews, Simone de Beauvoir confirmed that during these years, she and Sartre had conversations and discussions about his political activity, but although she was open and direct in expressing her opinions, he considered them more as conversation rather than as serious advice. In *Force*, 100, she had offered the opinion that "in Paris, all conversations seemed to become political ones. . .," recognizing the pervasive quality of the subject.

was one among many who criticized Simone de Beauvoir, saying she could be compared to "a blind person who would not hesitate to discuss painting; she was simply demonstrating in her writings her ignorance of politics."[8]

She disagrees: "I was not very occupied with politics or philosophy. I never wrote truly political books. I hardly committed myself to political actions, and I can't say that politics took any of my time." Yet, in a 1960 interview with Madeleine Chapsal, Simone de Beauvoir seemed surprised to remember how much politics had interested her when she was young, and how much she had written about it as she reread her papers, journals and diaries while writing her memoirs.[9]

During this time she considered herself and others of like mind to be "in a period of political powerlessness," and found it imperative to try to construct "some sort of balance sheet" by writing her memoirs, to assess what she called "the realities" of her situation.[10]

In 1982, Simone de Beauvoir compared herself as autobiographer to "a policeman writing his report. Accuracy is paramount." Many statements from her memoirs show her steady evolution toward social activism and then more specifically to feminism. In the years immediately before and after World War II, she lived in a world of political solipsism, a contented self-containment shared by the small and tightly closed circle of friends whom she and Sartre came to call "The Family." Describing herself in the decade 1929–39, she wrote: "I was riddled with bourgeois idealism and aestheticism, blinded to political realities. But this blindness was not peculiar to me; it was a characteristic and almost universal failing of the period."[11]

From 1945–65, when Sartre became a center of political controver-

8. Raymond Aron, "Mme de Beauvoir et la pensée de droite," *Le Figaro littéraire,* 12 January 1956.

9. "Une interview de Simone de Beauvoir," by Madeleine Chapsal, *Les Ecrivains en personne* (Paris: Julliard, 1960), 17-37. Reprinted in *Les Ecrits de Simone de Beauvoir,* Claude Francis and Fernande Gontier, ed. (Paris: Editions Gallimard, 1979), 380–96, and cited here.

10. The *Editors' Note* to Catharine A. MacKinnon's article, "Feminism, Marxism, Method and the State: An Agenda for Theory," (*Signs* 7 (Spring 1982): 515–44, reads: "Central to feminist theory and feminist method . . . is consciousness raising. Through this process, feminists confront the reality of women's condition by examining their experience and by taking this analysis as the starting point for individual and social change. By its nature, this method of inquiry challenges traditional notions of authority and objectivity, and opens a dialectical questioning of existing power structures, of our own experience, and of theory itself." Simone de Beauvoir, through her memoirs, demonstrates the raising of her own unique consciousness, proving the validity of MacKinnon's thesis.

11. *Prime of Life,* trans. Peter Green (London and New York: Viking-Penguin, 1965), 363.

sy, Beauvoir described herself as "moving in some sort of blur." She was "incapable of doing anything but hating Nazism and collaboration."[12]

During these years, Simone de Beauvoir became established as a writer of fiction and as an influential, outspoken member of the editorial board of *Les Temps Modernes*. It marked the beginning of an interesting dichotomy: Simone de Beauvoir, the private writer, worked alone each morning on her fiction before joining Sartre each afternoon and evening to talk, argue and sometimes write together on subjects of public involvement and concern. While Sartre wrote feverishly to espouse causes and explain his political positions vis-a-vis his philosophy, she was turning her attention in an altogether new and different direction: toward herself, and an examination of her role and place in society. Thus, while Sartre turned from literature to social and political theory on a highly visible public level, Beauvoir became—to coin a somewhat contradictory expression—publicly introspective. The tremendous outpouring of support and acclaim that greeted *Memoirs of a Dutiful Daughter* when it was published in France so buoyed her that it led to the continuing self-inquiry of the subsequent volumes.

This "story of myself," as she described it in 1982, led her "quite naturally to the study of all women within society." Writing *The Second Sex* gave her unsought influence throughout the global feminist movement, which she says "came from all those women much younger than I who sought me out, who convinced me of my duty to take my place among them."

Simone de Beauvoir was the first writer on the subject of women who examined all existing systems of inquiry through the philosophical methodology of Existentialism. In 1949, when the first volume of *The Second Sex* was published, she posited the view that all theories were biased because women had been eliminated from the record since the beginning of history. Much later, after her public commitment to feminism, she labelled all existing theories biased and inaccurate because they had been devised by men and were therefore useless in any evaluation of women. However, she still wrote in "the language of men" and couched her feminist statements within a political context. She paid little attention to those who looked to the creation of a new, nonprejudicial language without categorization by gender, and gave no thought at all to the creation of any personal system or theory of linguistic revisionism.

She drew upon earlier feminist writers to develop her perspective

12. *All Said and Done,* trans. Patrick O'Brian (London and New York: Penguin, 1977), 33.

for *The Second Sex*, among them Virginia Woolf, with whom she shares the same view of the relationship between economic independence and intellectual freedom.[13]

More importantly, Simone de Beaovoir used the documentation of women themselves, referring to letters, diaries, personal psychoanalytic histories, autobiographies, essays and novels. In many ways, she is responsible for the development of scholarly attention in these heretofore neglected areas which are now such important sources in revising history to include women.

All this should have made *The Second Sex* a preliminary source for the study of European women's history and the historical development of feminism. Unfortunately this has not happened because much of what she wrote is missing from all translations. The translator, H. M. Parshley, a retired professor of Zoology at Smith College, deserves high praise for independently reading the book in the original French and then tenaciously insisting that the American publisher, Alfred Knopf, subsidize its translation. However, the exigencies of publishing finances, Simone de Beauvoir's unavailability and even perhaps her unwillingness to cooperate with Parshley in suggesting possible cuts in the translation, led to his decision that what could most easily be sacrificed was the capsule biographies and entire discussions of more than fifty women of history who were soldiers, artists, or leaders of early suffrage movements. Only readers of the original French know these sections, as no other translations contain them.

When *The Second Sex* was first published, in English as well as in French, it puzzled as much as it informed simply because it was so different, so impossible to categorize. Indeed, even Parshley sometimes called it "an early sex manual" and Knopf described it as follows:

> She certainly suffers from verbal diarrhea—I have seldom read a book that seems to run in such concentric circles. Everything seems to be repeated three or four times but in different parts of the text, and I can hardly imagine the average person reading the whole book carefully. But I think it is capable of making a very wide appeal indeed and that young ladies in places like Smith who can afford the price, which will be high, will be nursing it, just as my generation managed somehow to get hold of Havelock Ellis.[14]

13. "Yes, Woolf is among the writers whose works I admire and sometimes reread, but only her feminist writings because I don't agree with her novels. They don't have any center. There isn't any thesis."

14. Alfred Knopf to H. M. Parshley, 27 November 1951. Reprinted with the kind permission of the Humanities Research Center, University of Texas, Austin.

A chronology of the book's reception and influence can be summarized briefly: the initial public outcry was partisan and vocal, with attacks coming from both Left and Right. Women were as shrill in their denunciation as in their defense of the book, and men were hysterical. Simone de Beauvoir was insulted in cafés and reviled in print. The only sustained theoretical discussion was Francoise d'Eaubonne's *Le Complexe de Diane*, which was not much read and soon out of print. Readership became an underground one, mostly women who passed it among themselves; temporarily out-of-print, it practically disappeared until the beginnings of the Women's Liberation Movement in the United States when Betty Friedan dedicated *The Feminine Mystique* to Simone de Beauvoir. In 1977, Friedan wrote that through *The Second Sex*,

> I had learned my own Existentialism. *The Second Sex* introduced me to that approach to reality and political responsibility—that, in effect, freed me from the rubrics of authoritative ideology and led me to whatever original analysis of women's existence I have been able to contribute.[15]

Clearly, countless women agreed with her. It was a work ahead of its time, prescient in its identification of the concerns of contemporary women. Simone de Beauvoir wrote of the economic inequities of employment, the burdens and responsibilities of motherhood, the class-defined access to abortion, to child care and education—of all the issues that separate working class women and oppressed minorities from women of the middle and upper classes even today, and of the issues which separate all women from parity with men.

Although Simone de Beauvoir's public embrace of feminist issues occurred long after the publication of *The Second Sex*, the time to begin to try to trace her politicization, especially her advocacy of separatism, lies in its publication aftermath. She had been shocked by the furies the book unleashed but had been entirely unprepared for the response of "even men of the Left . . . the fascist who sleeps in the heart of many men of the left." She told Madeleine Chapsal that one of the major reasons she continued to write subsequent volumes of memoirs stemmed directly from the shocking discovery that her status, "political powerlessness," was no different from that of any other French woman.[16]

15. Betty Friedan, *It Changed My Life* (New York: Dell Publishing Company, 1977), 391.

16. Op. cit., 386 and 396.

By the time she was writing the conclusions to *All Said and Done*, she was tracing her own feminist evolution, saying that her "practice and tactics" had changed, but nothing had happened to convince her that the basic argument of *The Second Sex* was in any way different: "All male ideologies are directed at justifying the oppression of women . . . women are so conditioned by society that they consent to this oppression."[17] —This, says Mary Evans," is radical feminism with a vengeance."[18]

It is indeed remarkable that, while living in relative isolation from other women and their problems, without the knowledge or context of a feminist environment, Simone de Beauvoir succeeded in defining the central issues which are still the focus of international feminism today. The years between 1950–70 found her writing in a different genre almost every time she put her pen to paper, but even so, each of these works shows a growing political awareness of the problems faced by women within society.

In 1954, she published *The Mandarins*, but at the same time she was beginning to express herself on political and social issues. *Privileges* contained two essays of importance in the development of her political feminism. "The Thought of the Contemporary Right," an essay about right-wing politics in France, was ostensibly to be an attack on Mendès-France and his government, but it is also a clarification of her attitude toward the bourgeoisie both as an economic class and a theoretical body. Another essay in this volume, "Must we Burn Sade?" deals with pornography and sexuality. A short essay on Brigitte Bardot was later published as a separate book continuing the thought originally expressed in the "Sade" essay. She wrote the preface to Jean-Francois Steiner's *Treblinka* and after it was attacked, followed it with an intelligent defense in *Le Nouvel Observateur*. This led to a frenzy of political activity followed by articles, editorials and manifestos mostly stemming from Sartre's involvements.

Curiously, the woman whose theoretical reflections and autobiographical introspections had set off a chain reaction of women questioning themselves and their societies throughout much of the world was spending most of her life in the turbulent 1960s following Sartre everywhere from the Russell Tribunal in Stockholm to (among others) The Soviet Union, Cuba, Brazil, and Mainland China. She wrote about

17. Simone de Beauvoir, *All Said and Done*, op. cit., 483–84.
18. Mary Evans, *Simone de Beauvoir, A Feminist Mandarin* (London and New York: Tavistock, 1985), 74.

the successive disappointments engendered in Leftists of varying degrees by everything from Soviet actions throughout Eastern Europe to French conduct of the Algerian War. Her pen raced across almost as many different kinds of pages as Sartre's, all in the service of political and social justice.

But by 1966, the continuing question of her feminism or the lack thereof, became too strong for her to ignore. Francis Jeanson expressed the charge best when he accused Beauvoir of understanding the feminine condition only because she had escaped from it. She denied the charge, insisting that she had never written condescendingly of women, but had only used her writings to depict their true position. She insisted that "the only interpretations of my feminism that are false in my eyes are those that are not *radically* feminist. One never falsifies my views in drawing me towards *absolute* feminism."[19]

Several years later, she decided that the utopian revolutionary thought that had characterized much of the thinking of the French Left since the early years of the century had had no lasting effect and was a failure. Along with this came the concurrent feeling that all existing socialist models had been disappointments and could no longer serve, even as foundations for the next wave.

Christine Fauré, writing in *Signs* in 1981, speaks of a "metamorphosis in the meaning of politics" which aptly describes this period of crucial change in Simone de Beauvoir's life and thought:

> . . . recognition of the failure of existing socialist models, and of the necessity if not to create, at least to understand the revolution in new terms—swung extraparliamentary political thinking over to the side of the counterculture . . . the women's liberation movement has profited from this metamorphosis in the meaning of politics more than other movements. It was appropriate for us to undertake our liberation in terms of a changing consciousness, of a counterculture, thus forcing the dark side of our condition as oppressed people out of shame and ignorance into the light.[20]

Simone de Beauvoir finds this quote an appropriate explanation for the sudden and violent changes which transfixed Paris after May, 1968, but feels that it resonates even more in the Feminism of 1970 and later. 1968–70 was probably the most active period of her life in terms of "pure" political activity, first because of her association with Sartre and

19. Jeanson, 253. Simone de Beauvoir's emphasis.
20. Christine Fauré, "Absent from History," *Signs* 7 (Autumn, 1981): 82–83.

the *Gauche Prolétarienne*, then with the generic French women's liberation movement.

In the decade during which Sartre began the inexorable decline that led to his death in 1980,[21] Simone de Beauvoir began to make herself available for almost everything she was asked to do. Separate from Sartre on the matter of issues and causes for the first time in her life, she expressed her individuality through feminist "solidarity" (an increasingly important word in her vocabulary). Some major actions: she was one of the signers of the 343 Manifesto and a witness at the Bobigny abortion trial; when *Choisir*, the prochoice organization was created, she became its first president; for several years she participated in meetings at the Mutualité which were devoted to exposing and denouncing crimes against women. She became president of the League for the Rights of Women, which fights discrimination against women in the work place, and she has contributed time and money to fund shelters for battered and abused women. When the editors of *L'Arc* came to her in 1975 asking to devote an entire issue to her work on behalf of feminist causes, she endeared herself to many warring factions by refusing once again to become an ikon and insisted that it be made instead into a forum for differing feminist thought.

She soon realized that she was much more comfortable using the printed word as weapon and began to limit her personal appearances, not only because words have always been her chosen instrument of expression but also because her age was becoming a factor; in 1975, she was sixty-seven. She decided that long marches and interminable meetings were too tiring and she limited her presence to those she deemed most crucial. In the meantime, she became "directrice de publication" for *Nouvelles Féministes*, then *Questions Féministes*, and finally *Nouvelles Questions Féministes*, as various controversies resulted in splits and offshoots within that publication. She was outspoken in her dismay at the controversy over the official registration of the title and acronym of the *Mouvement de Libération des Femmes*, or MLF, by the faction "Psych et Po."

The fragmentation of the French women's movement has been a disappointment to Simone de Beauvoir, but even more is the recognition that French feminism since 1968 has been founded primarily upon an anthropological and psychological basis radically different from her

---

21. The correspondence between Sartre's physical decline and Simone de Beauvoir's rise to a position of prominence in the women's movement is only noted here. It will be discussed fully in the biography.

own philosophical underpinnings. She does not argue that hers is more correct, but only that she is suspicious of some of the more radical precepts of the others, and she admits freely that she has not made a serious or sustained study of them: "I read what [publications] women send me, but I do not seek these works out at this time in my life."

A feminist French politician, Brigitte Gros, speaks for many when she accuses Simone de Beauvoir of close-minded inflexibility, of holding fast to outmoded theories and ideas:

> The intransigent feminism of Mme Simone de Beauvoir is that of a woman from another time. The feminist solidarity of the women of my generation no longer has anything in common with that of our suffragist mothers.[22]

Gros's comment underscores the sad reality in contemporary France that young women in lycées and universities today hardly recognize Simone de Beauvoir's name and know little or nothing of her work. Perhaps a further indication of how she has been relegated to a lesser position among French feminists is the way "Le manifeste de 85," an appeal for the equality of women, uses the following introduction to describe each of the signers: ". . . 85 women, from Catherine Deneuve to Marguerite Duras, have chosen . . . to launch an appeal in favor of women's equality in salary, career and responsibility." Simone de Beauvoir's name simply appears on the list.[23]

But the late Jacques Ehrmann offered a thoughtful observation, one important for any lasting evaluation of her role in contemporary society:

> Simone de Beauvoir enables us to realize clearly something of inestimable importance, if we would understand current French intellectual history. Namely, that commitment has no precise meaning until it is placed in its historical and political context.[24]

Simone de Beauvoir, who had spent most of her life within various groups formed by men around Sartre's political concerns, found herself more comfortable in communal situations with women. When she assumed a leadership role, she felt that her voice could be even more powerful when it was the focal point for a larger movement. "My actions always arose from my commitment to women's issues," she said

22. Brigitte Gros, "Une autre époque," *Le Monde,* 27 January 1978. Mme Gros was then Sénateur des Yvelines (radicale), Maire de Meulan.

23. *Le Nouvel Observateur,* 29 November–5 December, 43.

24. Jacques Ehrmann, "Simone de Beauvoir and the Related Destinies of Women and Intellectual," *Yale French Studies* 27 (1961): 30.

in a conversation about how her feminist activity began, "By that I mean causes separate from masculine causes or movements, because I discovered that whenever men were involved, the causes and needs of women were minimized, if not ignored altogether."

In a 1976 interview, she said:

> . . . in mass action, women can have power. The more women become conscious of the need for mass action, the more progress will be achieved. And, as to the woman who can afford to seek individual liberation, the more she can influence her friends and sisters, and the more that consciousness will spread, which in turn, when frustrated by the system, will stimulate mass action. Of course, the more that consciousness spreads, the more men will be aggressive and violent. But then, the more men are aggressive, the more will women need other women to fight back. That is, the need for mass action will be clear. Most workers of the class world today are aware of the class struggle whether they ever heard of Marx or not. And so it must become in the sex struggle. And it will. A feminist, whether she calls herself Leftist or not, is Leftist by definition. She is struggling for total equality, for the right to be as important, as relevant as any man. Feminists are therefore, genuine leftists. In fact, they are to the left of what we now traditionally call the political Left.[25]

For Simone de Beauvoir, the recognition that women would have to assume male language and strategy stemmed from the 1968 demonstrations:

> Properly feminist attitudes arose when women discovered that the men of '68 did not treat them as equals. . . . They realized that they would have to take their fate into their own hands and separate their battles from the larger revolutionary rhetoric of the men. I agreed with them because I understood that women could not expect their emancipation to come from general revolution but would have to create their own. Men were always telling them that the needs of the revolution came first and their turn as women came later . . . and so I realized that women would have to take care of their problems in ways that were personal, direct, and immediate. They could no longer sit waiting patiently for men to change the society for them because it would never happen unless they did it themselves.[26]

How then did Simone de Beauvoir think "properly feminist" women should effect social change? Elected office, was not the answer, for it

25. John Gerassi, "The Second Sex: 25 Years Later," *Society*, January–February 1976, 84–85.
26. Bair, *1984 Britannica Yearbook* interview, 25.

would only result in the creation of women who would assume the attitudes of men and lose solidarity with other women:

> Look at Indira Gandhi, and especially at Margaret Thatcher—she can make war as well as any man. No, I don't believe that women as heads of state will make any significant change in society because . . . the moment a woman gets power, she loses the solidarity she had with other women. She will want to be equal in a man's world and will become ambitious for her own sake.[27]

"In her opinion, no political party then constituted, either left or right, offered a suitable forum for the concerns of women."[28]

But why then did she work for the election of François Mitterand? "—Because he promised, indeed fulfilled his promise, to create a Ministry for the Rights of Women." Does that mean that she has at least modified her earlier comment about the unsuitability of political parties and elected office for women?—Not necessarily; Like Virginia Woolf, she measures her "political consciousness" through feminism, which is "her only true politics."[29]

In a 1968 essay, C. B. Radford urged Simone de Beauvoir's readers to pay very careful attention to her feminism as the central feature of her fiction and thought. He accused her of having abandoned restraint and common sense, saying "there is little doubt that neither international relationships nor feminism is likely to benefit from Simone de Beauvoir's more extreme political pronouncements."[30] This is an opinion which should have provoked widespread discussion but which has largely gone unchallenged.

Simone de Beauvoir's pronouncements raise many questions without providing satisfyingly consistant answers. In recent years, they have grown increasingly radical and separatist, from the 1960 comment to Chapsal that "men are the enemy," to her recent angry rejection of Betty Friedan's "second stage," to her description of the present structure of society as "one of the great battlefronts for women today." She has continued to denounce childbearing and housework but offers as the only alternative for women the refusal to do either or both.

She sees the route to change happening not as Friedan would en-

27. Ibid., 27.

28. Pierre Viansson-Ponté, "Entretien avec Simone de Beauvoir," *Le Monde*, 10 and 11 January 1978, 1–2;2.

29. Phyllis Rose, *Woman of Letters: A Life of Virginia Woolf* (Oxford: Oxford University Press, 1987), 257.

30. C. B. Radford, "Simone de Beauvoir: Feminism's Friend or Foe," *Nottingham French Studies*, Part 1, 6.2 (October 1967) 87, Part 2, 7.1 (May 1968) 51.

courage, through a reconciliation of the personal with the professional, but through an initial separation in which women must change their lives radically:

> Women in greater numbers [should] refuse to allow themselves to be considered any longer as natural property to be controlled or dominated. Women will turn to feminism for their self-education, and the fight will begin. It will be a hard struggle because men will not easily surrender their freedom from housework and family responsibility and all the other burdens that typify women's lot today.

But how, then, does she think this radical behavior should be focused? What can such radical action be if not political? This is exactly the point where she considers true political action to become a necessity:

> I think that when women really begin to consider liberating themselves seriously, they will take more of an interest in politics. And since liberation is a democratic concept, they will become more democratic and thus more radical. Men must be made to understand that, in the final analysis, feminist behavior is not gratuitous but serious. Feminists are not useless and silly hysterics. They have studied and thought, and they want to make changes that will benefit all of society. Throughout the world, women are still being sold, beaten, raped and killed, so this is a struggle that must be in the minds of all women and be the basis of all female behavior. We can no longer tolerate antifeminist behavior, from other women or from men.[31]

Beauvoir offers no concrete answers in these remarks, no specific model or plan for action, no coherent theory upon which to build new forms of feminist behavior. Only one thing is certain: there has been no other woman, in contemporary literature who has been so completely associated with the major events, causes and actions of her society. Language is Simone de Beauvoir's chosen instrument; the rhetoric of politics on behalf of social change has been one of her most intriguing uses of it. Considered separately, most if not all of her remarks make splendid sense; seen together they create a crazy quilt kaleidoscope of image and reality, opinion and fact. Feminist ideology cannot ignore Simone de Beauvoir; her importance should be unquestioned and is undeniable. The real question will be how to assess her contribution, and what use to make of it in the future.

31. The last two quotations are taken from the *1984 Britannica Yearbook* interview, 28.

V. Beauvoir and Sartre

MARGARET A. SIMONS

Beauvoir and Sartre: The Philosophical Relationship*

Most philosophers, feminists and nonfeminists alike, see Simone de Beauvoir's philosophical perspective as defined by that of her lifelong friend, Jean-Paul Sartre. Indeed, most references to Beauvoir's work in the philosophical literature cite her primarily as Sartre's biographer. Few surveys of contemporary continental philosophy, even those focusing on issues in socio-political philosophy such as Beauvoir raised in both *The Ethics of Ambiguity* and *The Second Sex*, include discussions of her work.[1]

The presumption of Beauvoir's philosophical dependence and lack of originality can be found even in the area of ethics, where Sartre published little, and where Beauvoir's essay, *The Ethics of Ambiguity*, is well known. One example is in the 1975 edition of the popular ethics text, *Great Traditions in Ethics*. In the introduction to the selection from *The Ethics of Ambiguity*, the editors write that Beauvoir's close relationship to Sartre, "makes it difficult and, perhaps unnecessary, to distinguish between their separate contributions to ethics."[2] The editors' choice of title for this section, "Ethics as Radical Freedom," illustrates the misinterpretations that can result from a failure to differentiate Beauvoir's philosophy from Sartre's, a differentiation which must include Beauvoir's early criticism and rejection of Sartre's concept of absolute freedom.

---

* An earlier version of a portion of this paper appeared in EROS (Purdue University) 8:1, 1981.

1. Beauvoir, *The Ethics of Ambiguity*, trans. Bernard Frechtman (Secaucus, New Jersey: The Citadel Press, 1948); Beauvoir, *The Second Sex*, trans. H. M. Parshley (New York: Random House, 1952, 1974).

2. Ethel M. Albert, Theodore C. Denise, and Sheldon P. Peterfreund, ed., *Great Traditions in Ethics* (New York: D. Van Nostrand, 1975), 350.

A survey of the philosophical literature, furthermore, reveals that Beauvoir's work has seldom received the close analytic reading necessary for an understanding of her philosophical relationship to Sartre. Most critics who identify Beauvoir's perspective with that of Sartre are simply making an unjustified, and sexist, assumption.

Feminist philosophers have been responsible for the growing appreciation of Beauvoir's work within philosophy. The Society for Women in Philosophy (SWIP) has been a forum for much of the debate concerning Beauvoir's philosophy since 1970. But even among feminist philosophers, scholars such as JoAnn Pilardi Fuchs, Eleanor Kuykendahl or myself who worked on Beauvoir during the seventies were exceptions. Feminists working within the continental philosophical tradition typically drew upon male philosophers such as Sartre or Merleau-Ponty rather than Beauvoir in their research. The first session on Beauvoir's philosophy did not appear on the program of the Society for Phenomenology and Existential Philosophy annual conference until 1978.

The Second Sex was the sole text in many early women's studies and feminist theory courses. Perhaps it was in reaction against this early dependence on the text that feminist philosophers sought other contexts and sources for exploring women's experience. It wasn't until the 1979 New York University conference on *The Second Sex* that feminist scholarly interest in Beauvoir deepened. *Feminist Studies* published a series of philosophical articles on Beauvoir's philosophy in 1979 and 1980 including papers from the N.Y.U. conference. *Signs* also published important articles on Beauvoir in 1979, including Dorothy McCall's important article, "Simone de Beauvoir, *The Second Sex*, and Sartre".[3]

Since that time numerous fine articles and books have appeared on Beauvoir, written primarily from a literary rather than philosophical perspective, however. The 1984 University of Pennsylvania conference dedicated to a reexamination of *The Second Sex*, produced many excellent philosophy papers on Beauvoir, some of which appear in the special 1985 issue of *Hypatia: A Journal of Feminist Philosophy* on "Beauvoir and Feminist Philosophy." But few feminist philosophers, with the important exception of Linda Singer in "Interpretation and Retrieval: Rereading Beauvoir," see Beauvoir as philosophically challenging Sartre.[4]

---

3. See *Feminist Studies* 5 (Summer 1979); and *Feminist Studies* 6 (Summer 1980); and Dorothy Kaufmann McCall, "Simone de Beauvoir, *The Second Sex*, and Sartre," *Signs* 5 (Winter 1979): 209–23.
    4. Linda Singer, "Interpretation and Retrieval: Rereading Beauvoir," *Hypatia* 3, a special issue of *Women's Studies International Forum* 8, no. 3 (1985): 231–38.

Dorothy McCall was writing for many of us when she wrote in 1979 that she wanted to "subvert both the domestication of *The Second Sex* as a generally unread 'classic' and the dismissal of it as merely an imitation of Sartre."[5] But, as the recent comment of a feminist philosopher reveals, that subversive activity has yet to achieve its objectives. In response to a discussion of my project on Beauvoir, a feminist philosopher asked: "Why read *The Second Sex*? It's out-of-date, male-identified, and just Sartrean anyway!"

That the assumption of Beauvoir's identification with Sartre functions as a prejudice, rather than a hypothesis can be seen when critics prefer to cling to it even in the face of contrary evidence. In fact, one does occasionally hear professors of philosophy who are teaching Beauvoir's *Ethics of Ambiguity*, or even *The Second Sex*, complain that it fails to be consistent with Sartre's philosophy. Irritated by this evidence of philosophical difference, they charge Beauvoir with deviating from the existentialism of *Being and Nothingness* as though her philosophical originality, rather than their presuppositions were at fault.[6]

Once a closer study of the actual differences between Beauvoir and Sartre is undertaken, it becomes clear that the simplistic view reducing Beauvoir to Sartre is inadequate for a full comprehension of her work. And such a view, by ignoring the considerable influence that Beauvoir had on Sartre's work, obscures the interpretation of his work as well. An appreciation of Beauvoir's influence on Sartre can provide a helpful context for understanding the often puzzling transition in Sartre's work in the 1950s as he struggled to come to terms with the social and historical forces that Beauvoir had analyzed so effectively in her landmark work of 1948–49, *The Second Sex*.

But an analysis of Beauvoir's philosophical perspective is not without difficulties, one of the most serious of which concerns Beauvoir's attitude towards her own work and that of Sartre. Beauvoir has always seen herself not as a philosopher, but as a literary writer. She remarks in her autobiography that after graduating in philosophy she felt, like most women of her generation, that she lacked the requisite audacity for bringing the world into question, as philosophy demands. In fact, Beauvoir has written very few philosophical essays, and has, on occasion, taken on the role of defending Sartre's position, as in "Merleau-Ponty and pseudo-Sartreanism." Her assumption of the role of Sartre's de-

5. McCall, "Simone de Beauvoir," 209.
6. Jean-Paul Sartre, *Being and Nothingness*, trans. Hazel Barnes (New York: Washington Square Press, 1953, 1966).

fender complicates the problem of identifying her own perspective from that of Sartre, but it does not make it impossible. She assumed this role very seldom, and all of her most important essays are clearly written in her voice.[7]

Perhaps most problematic for a philosophic differentiation of her work from that of Sartre's, is Beauvoir's separation of literature and philosophy. In a 1979 interview Beauvoir answered my questions concerning her influence on Sartre's work by arguing that while her literary works had been created out of her own life experience, and were thus entirely free of Sartre's influence, her philosophical perspective was, on the other hand, completely influenced by Sartre, on whose philosophical perspective she could have no influence at all since she was not herself a philosopher. Beauvoir said in that interview:

> For me a philosopher is someone like Spinoza, Hegel, or like Sartre, someone who builds a grand system and not simply someone who loves philosophy, who can teach it, who can understand it and who can make use of it in essays. . . . Sartre is a philosopher, and I am not; and I never really wanted to be a philosopher. I love philosophy very much, but my work has not been in philosophy. I have created a literary work. My interest has been with novels, memoires, and essays like *The Second Sex*. But that is not philosophy. On the level of philosophy, I have been influenced by Sartre. Obviously, I could not have influenced him, since I did not do philosophy. I critiqued it; I discussed many of his ideas with him, but I had no philosophical influence on Sartre. But that he influenced me is certain. But he had no literary influence on me, because I wrote what I, myself, wanted to write.[8]

While it is certainly true that Beauvoir has defined herself through her work not as a philosopher but as a literary writer, surely it is not the case either that their literary works have been isolated from their philosophic work—immune from its influence or incapable of exerting it—or that one must be a philosopher in order to influence a philosopher's ideas. But since Beauvoir is willing to admit that she may have influenced Sartre by introducing him to certain important ideas or by chang-

7. Simone de Beauvoir, *Force de l'age* (Paris: Editions Gallimard, 1960), 46; Beauvoir, "Merleau-Ponty and pseudo-Sartreanism," in *Privileges*, Coll. Les Essais, 76 (Paris: Gallimard, 1955).

8. Margaret A. Simons and Jessica Benjamin, Interview with Simone de Beauvoir, Paris, France, March 13, 1979. Parts of this discussion concerning Beauvoir's view of Sartre's influence on her work were deleted from an edited version of the interview which was published in *Feminist Studies* 5 (Summer 1979), 330–45.

ing his perspective on reality in some ways, our disagreement may be merely a verbal one.

In fact, Beauvoir's own reports of her often heated arguments with Sartre as recorded in her autobiographies, provide the commentator with some of the best indications of the direction of their mutual philosophical influence. It should be noted that Sartre offers little help to the commentator in this regard, having seldom acknowledged or discussed Beauvoir's influence on his work, or on the development of his ideas over the years.

The unusual situation of this close personal relationship between two social philosophers, and their different roles in that relationship does cause certain difficulties of interpretation, but it also leads to interesting insights. Understanding the relationship between these two writers and theorists should be invaluable in understanding similar creative relationships in a society less restrictive of women's activities and writing. It can also highlight the different voices of men and women within a sexist society. For in spite of the often "feminine" quality of Sartrean description of sensuous lived experience in *Being and Nothingness*, and Beauvoir's espousal of "masculine" values in *The Second Sex*, both are writing from their very different experiences as man and woman. Beauvoir's relationship with Sartre has been at the heart of much of her writing, and her philosophic identification with him problematic. So have intimate social relationships formed a major focus of contemporary feminist philosophy; and so does the problem of separation and identity among women, and between women and men, remain one of the most serious feminist issues today.

An important area of Beauvoir's originality and influence on Sartre is in the relationship of the individual to the social, historical context of the individual's action. Beauvoir was the first one to address herself to the problem of the Other, a concern which later became so prominent in Sartre's work. Beauvoir also recognized earlier than did Sartre the limiting effects of the social-historical context, including one's personal history and childhood, upon an individual's choice. She found Sartre's early voluntarism exaggerated.

Here as well, Sartre's perspective shifted over the years following World War II, in a direction bringing him closer to Beauvoir's position. Sartre's growing interest in childhood, and in the effects of an individual's social-historical situation on consciousness are reflected in the *Critique*, and its better known prefacetory essay, *Search for a Method*, which he dedicated to Simone de Beauvoir. These interests are also reflected in *The Words,* and the too often ignored, *Saint Genet,* published in 1952, as well as his massive work on Flaubert.[9] Understanding Beauvoir's perspective and its influence on Sartre, can help make those writings of the later Sartre comprehensible. Although, as Beauvoir commented in one of our discussions, "you know, one receives influences only if one is ready for them."

A serious problem in the philosophical understanding of Beauvoir's work is the mistranslations of her texts into English. This problem, which I have discussed at length elsewhere, is most serious in *The Second Sex,* because of extensive unindicated deletions and the inaccurate and inconsistent translation of key philosophical terms.[10] This important text is available in only one English translation. In that 1952 translation, over ten percent of the material in the original French edition has been deleted, including fully one-half of a chapter on history and the names of seventy-eight women. These unindicated deletions seriously undermine the integrity of Beauvoir's analysis of such important topics as the American and European nineteenth-century suffrage movements, and the development of socialist feminism in France.

They also seriously distort her historical assessment of women's role in history. With the deletion of much of her survey of women's historical achievements, Beauvoir's claim that women have never acted in history takes on an entirely different meaning than it has in the original French edition. Her original intention, now masked, was not to contribute to the historical invisibility of women, and the ignorance of their actions, but rather to point out the oppression and inefficacy of women as a class within a patriarchal society.

Compounding the confusion created by the deletions, are mistranslations of key philosophical terms. The phrase, "for-itself," for example, which identifies a distinctive concept from Sartrean existentialism, has been rendered into English as its technical opposite, "in-itself." Such mistranslations obscure the philosophical context of Beauvoir's work and inhibit the understanding of her work by English-speaking readers. But as with the other difficulties, this problem must not be used as an excuse to ignore Beauvoir's work. It should instead become

9. Jean-Paul Sartre, *Critique of Dialectical Reason,* vol. 1, *Theory of Practical Ensembles,* trans. Alan Sheridan-Smith (London: NLB, 1976); Sartre, *Search for a Method,* trans. Hazel Barnes (New York: Alfred A. Knopf, 1963); Sartre, *The Words,* trans. Bernard Frechtman (New York: G. Braziller, 1964); Sartre, *Saint Genet,* trans. Bernard Frechtman (New York: G. Braziller, 1963): Sartre, *L'Idiot de la famille: Gustave Flaubert de 1821 à 1857,* 3 vols. (Paris: Gallimard, 1971–1972).

an additional motivation for scholarly research, and support for a scholarly translation of *The Second Sex*.

THE RELATION WITH THE OTHER

Sartre is well known for his study of the relationship with the Other in *Being and Nothingness* and in literary works such as *No Exit*.[11] But it is seldom noticed that Beauvoir in her earliest works focused on the relation with the Other, writing prior to Sartre's work in this area, and defining her description of the structures of this relationship on the basis of her own experience. For Beauvoir, the problem of the Other is multifaceted. One important aspect is the difficulty of retaining one's sense of self while experiencing a longing for complete union with the Other. This problem, which Beauvoir describes first in her deep friendship for her childhood friend Zaza, took on dramatic dimensions in the early years of her relationship with Sartre.

This was a time when her own sense of direction was confused, as she first began her adult life separated from the restrictive confines of her family and school, and outside the established social roles for women. She experienced a profound moral crisis in which she felt herself losing her sense of self, in her love for the Other. But along with her search for union with the Other, she also felt the moral necessity for assuming responsibility for her own life and her individual autonomy.

It was within the tension of these two conflicting demands, so characteristic of women's experience, that Beauvoir conceived of the possibility and challenge of an authentic relationship. It is a delicate balancing act few of the women in her writings, from *She Came to Stay* to *The Second Sex*, *The Mandarins*, and *Woman Destroyed* are able to carry out successfully.[12] But for all its elusiveness, it remains a central value in Beauvoir's social philosophy, offering the individual an opportunity for authentic justification unobtainable in solitude. Linda Singer, in "Interpretation and Retrieval: Rereading Beauvoir," sees Beauvoir's

10. Margaret A. Simons, "The Silencing of Simone de Beauvoir; Guess What's Missing From *The Second Sex*," *Women's Studies International Forum* 6 (1983): 559–64.

11. Jean-Paul Sartre, *No Exit and Three Other Plays*, trans. Stuart Gilbert (New York: Random House, Vintage Books, 1955).

12. Simone de Beauvoir, *She Came to Stay* (New York: Dell Publishing Co., 1954, 1963); Beauvoir, *The Mandarins*, trans. Leonard M. Friedman (New York: Popular Library, 1956); Beauvoir, *The Woman Destroyed*, *The Monologue* and *The Age of Discretion*, trans. Patrick O'Brian (London: Collins, 1969).

philosophy as "the voice of the ethics of otherness," descriptive of freedom emergent from a situation of relatedness and affinity.[13]

This element of Beauvoir's perspective marks a decisive difference from the early individualism she shared with Sartre. And her divergence on this point is partially responsible for the tension that characterizes the perspective of *The Ethics of Ambiguity*. This tension resulting from the strain of moving from this individualism to a social perception of human reality only becomes comprehensible when both her hesitations about defining her own philosophical perspective, and beliefs in both individual freedom and the ultimate limitations of solitary individualism are understood.

Another aspect of the problem of Otherness addressed by Beauvoir in her earliest writings which is also found in Sartre's writings is the problem of the threat posed by the image of one's self in the eyes of the Other. Beauvoir explains the genesis of her perspective on this problem once again in terms of her own life experience. During the period of great uncertainty in her life when she first began living independently of her family, she felt threatened by the presence of other persons whose values differed radically from her own, and yet whose presence forced itself upon her. In the eyes of those other persons, she felt her values negated. *She Came to Stay*, the novel in which Beauvoir first addressed this question ends with the annihilation of the threatening person, with the radical refusal of the negation of the self. It was a problem arising from Beauvoir's own experience; the passage from Hegel which opens the book, "Each consciousness seeks the death of the Other," came to Beauvoir's attention only in 1940, after the book had been written.[14]

Beauvoir's work, which was written from 1938–41, anticipates the writings of Sartre on confrontations with the Other, including the section on the "Look" in *Being and Nothingness*, where existence of others, however, is given a secondary, derivative ontological status. In Beauvoir's work, on the contrary, relationships with other people, and conflicts among them over separation and identity are central. Casual critics of Beauvoir's work, thinking of the famous line from *No Exit*, "Hell is other people," have concluded that Beauvoir's works such as *She Came To Stay* in which the problem of the Other plays a major role, reflect the influence of Sartre on her work. But as we have seen, the reverse would be a more plausible interpretation.

Beauvoir's most well-known application of the concept of the

13. Linda Singer, "Interpretation," 232.
14. Simone de Beauvoir, *Force de l'age* (Paris: Gallimard, 1960), 324.

Other is, of course, in *The Second Sex* written in 1948–49. Since Sartre had only a short time before, in 1944, written *Anti-Semite and Jew*, in which a phenomenon very similar to sexism and the oppression of women is studied, one might expect Beauvoir's perspective to be profoundly influenced by Sartre.[15] And, in fact, their perspectives do share certain common elements, especially an analysis of the psychological dynamics of self-justification and the search by both the sexist and the racist for security in superiority.

But one thing the two works do not share is the use of the concept of the Other. Sartre never writes of the anti-Semite seeing the Jew as Other, although he certainly might have done so. It is only in a work that followed the publication of *The Second Sex*, *Saint Genet*, written from 1950–52, that Sartre utilized the concept of the Other in the analysis of social oppression, in this case, society's labelling of the boy, Genet, as a thief.[16]

In this work, Sartre describes the process by which Genet came to see himself as a thief, just as Beauvoir had analyzed the process of socialization that brings young girls into conformity to a sexist society. Here is an even more striking example of Sartre's utilization of a concept first found in Beauvoir's work. It's also in *Saint Genet*, a pivotal but often ignored text, that Sartre first utilizes the concept of fraternity and links freedom with reciprocity, as Beauvoir had done earlier in *Ethics of Ambiguity*. The complex issue of whether Sartre's philosophical perspective ever encompassed an adequate concept of fraternity, of social identity, cannot be resolved in this fairly brief survey article. But it should be clear that any such discussion cannot ignore either the importance of *Saint Genet* or the influence of Beauvoir's work in *The Second Sex* on the development of Sartre's perspective.[17]

CHILDHOOD SOCIALIZATION

The problem of the Other was not the only area in which Beauvoir's ideas on the relation of the individual to society differed from those of Sartre, and at least in part, were to influence him. A second significant

15. Jean-Paul Sartre, *Anti-Semite and Jew*, trans. George J. Becker (New York: Schocken Books, 1965).

16. Jean-Paul Sartre, *Saint Genet*, trans. Bernard Frechtman (New York: George Braziller, 1963).

17. I'm grateful to James Edwards, whose paper "On *Saint Genet*," delivered at the Sartre Retrospective program offered by the Radical Caucus and the Society for Women in Philosophy at the December 1980 American Philosophical Association meeting, clearly demonstrates the pivotal importance of this work in the development of Sartre's thought.

area concerns the effect on an individual's freedom of the social-historical context, including the personal history of one's childhood. In her
1960 autobiography, *Force de l'age*, Beauvoir reports that in the early
years of her relationship with Sartre, they both held a "rationalist-
voluntarist" attitude towards reality and a belief in their radical freedom. As young teachers, Beauvoir comments, "circumstances permitted us a certain measure of detachment, free time, and lack of concern. It
was tempting to confound them with sovereign freedom." "It was our
conditioning as young petit bourgeois intellectuals that led us to believe
ourselves free of conditioning."[18]

But while their profession as teachers gave them a shared perspective, their childhoods had also provided them with profoundly differing
experiences with which they began adult life. At the onset of his teaching career, Sartre felt his freedom threatened with the end of his years of
childhood irresponsibility, the approach of his military service, and the
beginning of his career as a teacher, civil servant, and member of the
dreaded establishment.

While he and his closest male friends outlined the works they
would write, challenging and undermining the status quo, Beauvoir was
adrift, without a clear sense of direction, living outside the confinement
of social roles and expectations. She celebrated her first teaching assign-
ment as the fulfillment of her dreams of independence, as her victory
against the threats to her individual survival which had been posed by
her family, her teachers, and her close relationship with Sartre.

Simone de Beauvoir had experienced her adolescence as a struggle
for her freedom against the future of dependency to which she, as a
bourgeois woman, was destined. When her best friend Zaza died in the
midst of a struggle with her mother to escape an arranged marriage,
Simone de Beauvoir felt as though her own freedom had been won at the
cost of her friend's life. Thus along with a belief in her own individual
freedom, and in her capacity to will her own destiny, Beauvoir also had
an awareness of the power of social oppression, which Sartre's childhood experiences had not given him.

Their differing backgrounds also translated into a different attitude
towards their work, and extended to epistemological questions. Beauvoir admired Sartre's dedication to Literature which far exceeded her
own commitment as a writer, a profession which she, like Sartre, had

18. Beauvoir, *Force de l'age*, 26, 19, 24, 25. All passages are my own translations from
the French edition since serious problems exist in the English translation of this important text.

chosen at an early age. But she found her newly won freedom so exhilarating that her first commitment was to Life, to experiencing life in all its richness. That commitment set her at odds with Sartre, who assumed what Beauvoir felt to be an exaggerated subjectivist position. She asserted that the fundamental ambiguity of reality prevented it from ever being captured totally in a sentence or an essay. Sartre argued that reality coincided exactly with man's knowledge of it.[19]

Later in their relationship, the arousal of passions which astonished her by their intensity led Beauvoir to modify her psychological voluntarism. But Sartre continued to hold that position, arguing that Beauvoir had chosen to give in to her emotions, to the demands of the body, and that the will always retains its dominance. Thus, although both Beauvoir and Sartre shared many attitudes in common in the early years of their relationship, Beauvoir's experiences both provided a different perspective and led her eventually to modify her position in ways taking her further away from Sartre's position.

A critical problem for the commentator at this juncture is ·that Beauvoir began her career as a writer later than did Sartre, and at first wrote exclusively fictional works, short stories, and novels, thus making the task of comparing their early philosophical perspectives difficult. But Beauvoir's differing perspective does emerge from a consideration of their early works, notably in her references to the childhoods, the personal histories of her characters, and in her efforts to come to grips with the experience of Zaza's death.

Beauvoir developed the childhoods of her characters in almost all of her early writings, which focused on the problem of the relation with the Other. Her second novel, which is untitled and unpublished, is the story of a young girl's apprenticeship in life. In the novel, the main character learns to accept another person without idolizing her, and to consent to her own freedom without expecting the other person to support her existence.[20] Beauvoir also tried to tell the story of Zaza's death, where a character dies in a struggle to escape the bonds of bourgeois society. Her third unpublished novel, written in 1933–35, focuses on an oppressive childhood experience, the efforts of a young girl to avoid an arranged marriage and her subsequent difficulties in a relationship in which her independence and self-confidence were threatened by her feelings driving her impetuously towards another person.

Beauvoir wrote *La Primauté du spirituel*, a collection of loosely

19. Beauvoir, *Force de l'age*, 151.
20. Beauvoir, *Force de l'age*, 108.

connected short stories, in 1935–37. The collection was finally published in 1979 and translated under the title, *When Things of the Spirit Come First*.[21] This important early work, with its focus on relationships between women, anticipates the subject and style of her later books, *A Woman Destroyed* and *Les Belles Images*. All three works express a moral condemnation of the women responsible for the smothering socialization of the young girls in their charge. An important theme is a young girl's heroic quest to escape the moral and epistemological bonds of her childhood. The family is clearly the medium for the transmission of the ideology of bourgeois society to the individual, and childhood is the time.

In writing *She Came To Stay*, Beauvoir gave a lengthy account of the central figure's childhood which she later deleted from the published version of the novel. She also drew heavily on an account of the central figure's childhood in *The Blood of Others*, which again focuses on the problem of establishing a relationship of freedom to freedom with the Other. Although Beauvoir also felt the necessity of describing the childhood of another central figure in the book, she decided to indicate it only through several brief allusions. Thus Beauvoir's commitment to understanding the individual within the context of their childhood experiences is evident in all of her novels and short stories from 1931 through 1945.[22]

This concern, however, is in sharp contrast to Sartre's attitude at that time towards the significance of one's childhood, and the past in general. The for-itself emerges full blown in *Being and Nothingness*, with birth and development, and possible hindrances to development ignored. Nor are the childhoods of the characters in his novels often considered to be significant. In an interview in 1945 in which Sartre discusses existentialism and the problem of freedom in a novel, he contrasts his approach to that of Zola, saying that: "For Zola, everything obeys the narrowest determinism. Zola's novels are written in the past, while my characters have a future. . . . The childhood of Mathieu is of no importance."[23]

Consider as well Sartre's essay on *Baudelaire* where his interest is with both Bauldlaire's life and writings.[24] Even here, where Sartre be-

21. Beauvoir, *When Things of the Spirit Come First*, trans. Patrick O'Brian (New York: Pantheon Books, 1982).

22. Beauvoir, *The Blood of Others*, trans. Roger Senhouse and Yvonne Moyse (New York: Alfred A. Knopf, 1948); Beauvoir, *Force de l'age*, 325, 556.

23. Sartre, "Qu'est-ce que l'existentialisme? Bilan d'une offensive," interview article by Dominique Aury, *Les Lettres Françaises*, 24 novembre 1945; quoted in Michel Contat and Michel Rybalka, *Les Ecrits de Sartre* (Paris: Gallimard, 1970), 128.

24. Sartre, *Baudelaire*, trans. Martin Turnell (New York: New Directions, 1950).

gins with a discussion of Baudelaire's childhood, his treatment is perfunctory. Sartre's description of Baudelaire's childhood seems less interested in the actual experiences than in providing an occasion for an "original choice" as the theoretical starting point for the study of the adult and his writings.

Sartre did not write effectively about childhood until after Beauvoir had completed her monumental study of women, *The Second Sex*, which traces the effects of childhood socialization on inhibiting the development of the young girl's sense of personal autonomy and self-assertion. It was only in 1950, when Sartre began his essay on Jean Genet, that he first confronted the realities of childhood experiences. Although his approach to childhood, with its emphasis on the choice that gives childhood importance in the case of Genet, is certainly not identical to Beauvoir's, he has definitely gained an awareness of the significance of the family as mediator between society and the individual.

Both Beauvoir and Sartre continued to manifest their interest in childhood, Sartre increasingly so. In *Search for a Method* his prefacetory essay to the *Critique,* Sartre makes a complete about-face from his 1945 position on childhood quoted above. In *Search for a Method* he criticizes the so-called orthodox Marxists for writing as if "they were born at the age when we earn our first wages. They have forgotten their own childhoods."[25]

In *The Second Sex,* Beauvoir criticizes psychoanalysis for its masculinist bias, and its failure to understand the broader sociopolitical context of psychological gender differences. But rather than discard it, Beauvoir modified psychoanalytic theory using feminist, Marxist, and existentialist insights. She then utilized this revised psychoanalysis extensively as a mediator between the individual and society. Beauvoir saw the family as the locus of intersection of individual experience and historical forces operating in society. In *Search for a Method* Sartre arrives at a similar method, lacking only Beauvoir's feminist understanding. He joins the use of psychoanalytic and existentialist understanding of the individual with the Marxist analysis of the socioeconomic forces of history. Sartre's choice of the term "praxis" in the *Critique,* in substitution for "being-for-itself" of *Being and Nothingness,* takes his concept of freedom as concrete action rather than mere consciousness closer to Beauvoir's concept in *The Second Sex.*

25. Sartre, *Search for a Method*, trans. Hazel E. Barnes (New York: Alfred A. Knopf, 1963), 62. I am indebted to William L. McBride's insightful analysis of Sartre's contribution to social theory in *Social Theory at a Crossroads* (Pittsburgh: Duquesne University Press, 1980), especially p. 55 where he quotes this same passage from *Search*.

Beauvoir's influence is thus an important factor in understanding the shifts in Sartre's philosophical perspective from *Being and Nothingness* to the *Critique*.

CONCLUSION

This brief study of Beauvoir's philosophy, and her influence on Sartre, suggests more questions that it can begin to answer. Perhaps the most interesting period, the one richest in the interaction of their ideas, is the one left relatively untouched here. In our 1979 interview discussing Sartre's autobiography, written in the 1960s, Beauvoir commented that: "I was much more interested in my childhood than Sartre was in his. And I believe that, little by little, I made him realize that his childhood has also been important for him. When he wrote *The Words*, he understood that he had to talk about his childhood. And that, perhaps, was partially due to my influence; it is very possible." His study of Flaubert is in many ways the culmination of this interest, but also a return full circle to one of his first concerns. His work ended with a biography much as it had begun in the mind of his character from *Nausea*, Roquentin, finding justification for his existence in writing the story of another man.[26]

Beauvoir's work has similarly remained centered on life and the intimate relationships that have shaped it, with her friends, with Sartre, with her mother in her death. In spite of her recent involvement in the feminist movement, Beauvoir's work has not focused on political movements. In the *Critique*, Sartre contrasts the isolated actor with the social group, and makes a thoroughgoing study of social movements; it is the lack of just such an understanding of feminism as a social movement that contemporary feminists criticize in *The Second Sex*. In that work, Beauvoir wrote that women have never acted in history, a claim that is seriously distorted in the English edition, by the deletion of the names of seventy-eight women and stories of their achievements. She was not mouthing a misogynist claim of women's inferiority and lack of cultural contribution. Her point spoke not of the acts of individual women but of women acting as a group; that the sexist situation has conspired to deny women as a group either the concrete means or the individual freedom necessary for them to combat effectively their oppression as a group. That is where I think she failed to understand adequately the efficacy of the nineteenth-century feminist movement.

26. Sartre, *Nausea*, trans. Lloyd Alexander (New York: New Directions, 1964.)

But Sartre, as Beauvoir remarks, was always more politically active than she. Until the feminist movement of the seventies, she was the follower, and thus lacked the experience necessary for an understanding of social movements.

Beauvoir has been more cognizant of what might be called the forces of Nature on human experience than was Sartre, who "refus[ed] to attribute any causal efficacy whatsoever to nonhuman, or at least inorganic, phenomena." Beauvoir wrote a lengthy analysis of the effects of aging in one of the first major theoretical studies of the subject, *Coming of Age*. She wrote in intimate detail about the death of her mother, in *A Very Easy Death*, and about Sartre's final illness and death, in *Adieux: A Farewell to Sartre*. In *The Second Sex*, she locates the source of women's historical oppression in her "servitude to the species" in reproduction. The causal forces shaping the lives of women have originated outside of women, and apparently outside of men, for much of human history. Could men have done otherwise than subordinate woman in their initial conquest of nature and the creation of culture, Beauvoir asks in a very un-Sartrean voice. Could girls socialized to see themselves as Other, be said to have ever had a choice of freedom?[27]

Sartre and Beauvoir have influenced one another in a multitude of ways that their readers have only begun to appreciate. But they remain separate individuals, writers with unique voices, offering insights like those of none other of their generation. Understanding Beauvoir's and Sartre's works poses an exciting challenge of interpretation hardly begun by this brief survey. I hope that I have demonstrated that neither of these great writers can be reduced to the other, and that the understanding of their complex intellectual relationship must finally be opened.

27. McBride, *Social Theory*, 75; Beauvoir, *The Coming of Age*, trans. Patrick O'Brian (New York: G. P. Putnam's Sons, 1972); Beauvoir, *A Very Easy Death*, trans. Patrick O'Brian (New York: G. P. Putnam's Sons, 1965); Beauvoir, *Adieux: A Farewell to Sartre*, trans. Patrick O'Brian (New York: Pantheon Books, 1984).

Jean-Paul Sartre and Simone de Beauvoir. Reprinted from *Simone de Beauvoir et le cours du monde* with the permission of Gisèle Freund.

ELAINE MARKS

Transgressing the (In)cont(in)ent Boundaries: The Body in Decline

> *King Lear* is the only great literary work, aside from *Oedipus at Colonnus*, whose hero is an old man; old age is not conceived of in these works as the limit of the human condition, but as its truth: old age is the starting point for an understanding of human beings and the human adventure.—*La Vieillesse*

> In Paris, at the beginning of October, Sartre got up to go to the bathroom—he was in my apartment—and there was a mark on his chair.—*La Cérémonie des adieux.*—Translated by Patrick O'Brian.

Simone de Beauvoir, in 1985, is not only a writer. She is also, as we read her texts and consider the most appropriate modes for their analysis, a familiar photographer's model. From the baby in the carriage, admired by her family members, to the old woman seated despondently at Sartre's grave, thousands of photographs commemorate her activities and her travels, mostly with Sartre but also before and after him. These photographs document, in a profoundly moving way, the passage of time as it inscribes itself on a female body, marking, as my plagiarized title boldly states, "the body in decline."[1] It is as if this iconography illustrated, intentionally, what Simone de Beauvoir has been writing about as she tries to capture the signs of her own mortality and the signs of the mortality of those around her. The succession of photographs accomplish this without words, and ruthlessly. Because of such vivid picture books as *Simone de Beauvoir et le cours du monde*,[2] readers of the four volumes of her memoirs and the shorter autobiographical texts on the death of her mother and the death of Sartre occupy a privileged

1. The phrase "the body in decline" is from T. H. Adamowski, "Death, Old Age and Feminity: Simone de Beauvoir and the Politics of *La Vieillesse*" in *Dalhousie Review* 50, no. 3 (Autumn 1970): 395. I would like to acknowledge an unpublished paper by Kathleen Woodward, "Simone de Beauvoir: Aging and its Discontents," which I read with great interest. I would also like to thank Yvonne Ozzello for her invaluable suggestions.

2. *Simone de Beauvoir et le cours du monde*, ed. Claude Francis, photographs collected by Janine Niepce (Paris: Klincksieck, 1978).

182 Yale French Studies

position in relation to the world postulated by the images on one hand and the works on the other. Our narratological and theoretical sophistication does not prevent us from assuming that we have witnessed an "experience" free from mediation and that we are, in turn, not only adding to our repertoire of images, but having an "experience."

The first theoretical conundrum that faces readers of Simone de Beauvoir's texts concerns the question of "experience." This conundrum is not peculiar to the works of Simone de Beauvoir, although her writings and their resemblance to case histories aggravate it.

The question of "experience" dominates the feminist intellectual scene in the United States and has done so since the mid 1970s. Many of the earliest affirmations made by feminists in the United States during the late 1960s and reproduced in the titles of such books as *Of Woman Born: Motherhood as Experience and Institution*,[3] *The Female Experience: An American Documentary*,[4] *The Authority of Experience*,[5] assumed that there was an essential difference between males and females and that until the late 1960s Western culture had been organized around male experience universalized as human experience. Female experience, depending on one's theoretical perspective, was either marginalized, privatized and secret, or so repressed as to be invisible, unspoken, and unwritten. The feminist movements were seen as the occasion for female experience to write, paint, sing, embroider, think, organize itself as if its manifestations, once women's consciousness had been raised, would be spontaneous and clear. This concept of experience was slowly challenged by those theories and practices, transmitted from the European continent and from Third World Countries, that understood "experience" as always mediated by language and culture, as needing to be read through social constructs, texts, and material conditions.

The concept of "experience," as I understand it through the theoretical work of Teresa de Lauretis, involves thinking of sexuality and aging as social constructs that we interact with simultaneously through our language (which is also our culture) and our bodies.[6] Social constructs and bodies are not the same; neither are they separable. It is as if we were to try to apprehend "experience" not through some immediately available reality outside ourselves, but through the Lacanian orders of

3. Adrienne Rich (New York: W. W. Norton, 1976).
4. Gerda Lerner (Indianapolis: Bobbs-Merrill, 1977).
5. Arlyn Diamond and Lee Edwards (Amherst: University of Massachusetts Press, 1977).
6. *Alice Doesn't: Feminism, Semiotics, Cinema* (Bloomington: Indiana University Press, 1984), 159 ff.

the Symbolic, the Imaginary, and the Real all at the same time. There is no unmediated "experience," but there is a complex process in which the subjective and the social merge, producing the illusion of an original "experience." We shall see this process at work in *La Cérémonie des adieux* (1981) as we attempt to disentangle those discourses that Simone de Beauvoir's texts weave together.

If it is possible to salvage a notion of "experience" by way of a process of interaction between the individual and the social, it is more difficult to rescue the concept of "experience" as a solid yet developing block that inhabits individuals and that defines them. In the second part of *La Cérémonie des adieux*, "Entretiens avec Jean-Paul Sartre," Sartre says:

> There's one thing I've always thought—I spoke about it to some extent in *Nausea*—and that is the idea that you don't have experience, that you don't grow older. The slow accumulation of events and experience that gradually create a character is one of the myths of the late nineteenth century and of empiricism. I don't think it really exists. I don't have a life, an experience, behind me that I can turn into maxims, formulae, ways of living. So since I don't believe that I possess experience, I am the same at close on seventy as I was at thirty, as long as my body functions.[7]

Sartre's statements demystify rather convincingly the notion of age as the domain of the wise, of older people as somehow fuller in character than the young. There is, according to Sartre, no growing older; there are simply changes in the body. Sartre's questioning of the traditional discourses on aging and experience are radical in that they strip age of its privileges and strip history of its central position in our understanding of the human adventure in time. I shall also make use of this reasoning in attempting to rearticulate the discourses on sexuality and aging that traverse Simone de Beauvoir's texts.

The second conundrum that faces readers of Simone de Beauvoir's texts concerns the paucity of explicit discourses on sexuality in her memoirs and her shorter autobiographical works. I will propose that in her writing, sexuality emerges through the discourses on aging and that the uncontrollable body in decline is a body manifesting its sexuality. This sexuality, from the narrator's point of view, is always both disgusting and fascinating, and is presented with obsessive rhetorical strategies.

7. *Adieux*, trans. Patrick O'Brian (New York: Pantheon Books, 1984), 324. Titles in my text are given in French. Translations are cited in the notes.

I will suggest, tentatively, that at the center of the discourses on aging and sexuality there is a homo-sexual secret. What is the relationship, I will ask, between the contiguity of "Jean Paul Sartre's" *incontinence* and "Simone de Beauvoir's" "*Sylvie Le Bon*"? How can we analyze these unmentionables? And how can we maintain the problematic status of the proper names (I have used quotation marks)? Is it sufficient to insist that they represent textual figures?

Simone de Beauvoir was fifty years old in January of 1958, the year of the publication of *Mémoires d'une jeune fille rangée*. Her written and published work lines up rather evenly on either side of this fifty-year mark. There are twelve separate volumes before this date and eleven after, without counting articles, prefaces, and interviews. The major difference in the works written and published after Simone de Beauvoir reached fifty lies in the number of autobiographical texts: the four long volumes of memoirs and the two shorter autobiographical texts. In the four volumes of memoirs, a discourse on sexuality enters into the text to mark rites of passage from childhood to adolescence, from adolescence to young adulthood, from young adulthood to middle age. Here, too, the link between aging and sexuality is maintained. In her novel *Les Belles images* (1966) and in the collection of novellas, *La Femme rompue* (1967), the social and psychological problems associated with aging play a central role in the lives of the female protagonists. These problems also serve as an opening to sexuality. Sexuality is spoken through the aging process rather than through the presentation of relationships that are sexual. In *La Vieillesse* (1970) old age and aging are officially at the center of the stage. The "Introduction" to *La Vieillesse* reiterates the narrator's awareness, and delight, in breaking "the conspiracy of silence" (10) in obliging the readers to "listen" to the presentation of this taboo subject. It would, therefore, be accurate to affirm that since Simone de Beauvoir's fiftieth year, her texts are preoccupied with questions relating to aging, even obsessed with them. At the same time as we have this objective evidence from the content, the autobiographical volumes provide us with the narrator's comments on her relationship to aging. One of the more significant passages occurs in *La Force des choses* (1963) at the opening of Part 2. The narrator is forty-four years old, the date is 1952, and she is preparing to recount the beginnings of her love affair with "Claude Lanzmann" who was then twenty-five:

> Young women have an acute sense of what should and should not
> be done when one is no longer young. 'I don't understand,' they say,
> 'how a woman over forty can bleach her hair; how she can make an

exhibition of herself in a bikini; how she can flirt with men. The day
I'm her age . . .' That day comes: they bleach their hair; they wear
bikinis, they smile at men. When I was thirty I made the same sort of
resolution: 'Certain aspects of love, well, after forty, one has to give
them up.' I loathed what I called 'harridans' and promised myself that
when I reached that stage, I would dutifully retire to the shelf. All of
which had not kept me from embarking upon a love affair at thirty-
nine [with "Nelson Algren"]. Now, at forty-four, I was relegated to the
land of the shades; yet, as I have said, although my body made no
objection to this, my imagination was much less resigned. When the
opportunity arose of coming back to life, I seized it gladly.[8]

In this passage the emphasis is on the doxa, on what people say, and the
difference between what they say and do. The narrator assimilates herself to all women and recapitulates her own itinerary and the discrep-
ancy between her words and her behavior. On another level, the text
sets up two oppositions: one between aging and sexual behavior, the
other between the body and the imagination. Does the taboo operate
against a woman who is over forty and who wants to appear young, who
flirts with men, who pretends to be younger than she is? Or does the
taboo operate against a woman over forty who makes love with an aging
body? The word "harridans" in English does not convey either the sense
of physical disintegration contained in the French "les vieilles peaux"
(literally, the old skins) or the sexual overtones mingled with disgust.
The opposition between the body and the imagination removes the
body from the suspicion of desire, from the realm of sexuality, and
attributes to the imagination some dream of romantic love, a dream that
is powerful enough to bring about a rebirth. In both cases the oppositions affirm that the body in decline is repulsive and, by contamination
and contiguity, so is sexuality. These are the terms in which discourses
on aging and sexuality will occur throughout Simone de Beauvoir's
corpus.

The four volumes of memoirs allow the reader to note the precise
moment at which "Simone de Beauvoir's" primary love affairs and long-
term intimate relations began: with "Jean-Paul Sartre" in 1929, when
she was twenty-one; with "Olga Kosakievicz" in 1934, when she was
twenty-six; with "Nelson Algren" in 1946, when she was thirty-nine;
with "Claude Lanzmann" in 1952, when she was forty-four; with "Sylvie Le Bon" in 1965, when she was fifty-seven. In each case, as in the
example of "Claude Lanzmann" quoted above, the discourse that ac-

8. *Force of Circumstance,* trans. Richard Howard (London: Penguin Books, 1968),
291.

companies the event is organized in terms of rebirth, renaissance, rejuvenation rather than in terms of sexuality. Privileged relationships have the effect of breaking routines associated with age and stagnation. "Jean-Paul Sartre" and "Nelson Algren" were contemporaries of "Simone de Beauvoir"; "Olga Kosakievicz," "Claude Lanzmann," and "Sylvie Le Bon" were considerably younger. There are significant echoes, from one text to another, across time and genders: On the importance of her meeting with "Jean-Paul Sartre," the narrator writes in *Mémoires d'une jeune fille rangée*: "And then, I had been given a great chance: I suddenly didn't have to face this future all on my own."[9] On the importance of her friendship with "Sylvie Le Bon," the narrator writes in *Tout compte fait* (1972): "I was wrong in 1962 when I thought nothing significant would happen to me anymore, apart from calamities; now once again a piece of great good fortune was offered me."[10] The French in both texts is strikingly similar: "Et puis, une grande chance venait de m'être donnée," in *Mémoires d'une jeune fille rangée*; and in *Tout compte fait*, "une grande chance m'a de nouveau été donnée." The alternation between a male and a female suggests the bisexuality of the narrator and the contradictory, transgressive quality of her object choices. The repetition of "une grande chance" and "être [été] donnée," a passive construction, underlines the presence of a structure that is deliberately reduced to an expression of luck, chance, good fortune.

In 1973, in a book length essay entitled *Simone de Beauvoir: Encounters with Death*, I argued that Simone de Beauvoir was obsessed with mortality.[11] I attempted to describe how this obsession took the form of exploring encounters with death at the same time as these encounters were aborted by the construction of an ideology that emphasized commitment to a cause. In the dialectical movement between mortality and commitment, mortality was, temporarily at least, subsumed and obliterated, only to emerge again at a later moment in the same or another text. My 1973 essay apparently accused Simone de Beauvoir, the woman and the writer, of refusing to deal with mortality until the bitter end, as it were, and of veering off into a reassuring rhetoric.

In 1985 I take up some of my earlier positions and argue, but differently, that even though Simone de Beauvoir's texts do not go as far as I would have liked them then to go, they do go further than most. The

9. *Memoirs of a Dutiful Daughter*, trans. James Kirkup (New York: Harper Colophon, 1974), 345.

10. *All Said and Done*, trans. Patrick O'Brian (New York: Warner Brothers, 1975), 66.

11. New Brunswick: Rutgers University Press, 1973.

critical reception of *La Cérémonie des adieux* has obliged me to rethink my earlier interpretations and to conclude that *La Cérémonie des adieux*, like *Une Mort très douce* (1964), *La Vieillesse*, and certain passages of *Tout compte fait*, is a text that transgresses the (in)cont(in)ent boundaries. *La Cérémonie des adieux* goes beyond the limits of what is considered legitimate for a woman or a man to write. For aging and dying, when presented referentially, are taboo topics within phallocentric discourse: it is permissible to write about the sexual practices of a famous man; it is not permissible to write about his loss of control over his excretory functions. Through an analysis of the reviewers' discourse and of selected passages in Simone de Beauvoir's texts, I shall attempt to show what is involved in the systematic disparagement of this content and conclude with some generalizations on content, continents, incontinence. I shall also come back to the theoretical discussions that surround the death of the author, the death of the referent, and argue that for all their seductive subtlety they may also be a means of obliterating once again women, sexuality, old age, dying, and death.

While preparing the selection of book chapters, essays, and book reviews that will appear in a volume of *Critical Essays* on Simone de Beauvoir to be published by G. K. Hall, I have been reading and rereading what has been written about the author-narrator Simone de Beauvoir and about her corpus (the three are rarely differentiated). I am impressed by the repetition of the word "too," in the sense of more than sufficient, excessively. Whether the critics are French, British, or North American, whether they are Catholic, right-wing literati, left-wing intelligentsia, or devotees of *l'écriture féminine*, they seem to agree that there is a problem of excess: Simone de Beauvoir's texts are, in general, too long; there are too many lists in the volumes of memoirs; there are too many unpleasant details about her mother's body ravaged by cancer; too many repugnant details about "Sartre's" food spilling and incontinence (and the incontinence of their longtime friend "Camille" [Simone Jolivet]); too many anecdotes about characters in *Les Mandarins* who were on the borderline between the fictional and the factual (for example, Albert and Francine Camus); too many negative attacks on marriage and maternity; too much narcissism. Here are the words of some reviews: "Among other things, Simone de Beauvoir shares with Sartre, a tendency to write too much," in *Books Abroad*, 1965; "a merciless record of the trivia of death—old age and bed wetting, pubic baldness, enemas . . . ," in *Time*, 1966; "such an exhaustive and practically all-embracing manner," in *The French Review*, 1970; "she supplies a baker's dozen of facts, she provides exhaustive analyses," in *The Atlantic,* 1972; "excessively lengthy parts," in *The Economist,* 1972; "just short of five hundred obsessive and ultimately negative pages," in *The Spectator,* 1972; "the merciless realism of the description of the final degradation of her friend Camille," in the *New Boston Review,* 1977. As for *La Cérémonie des adieux,* from the moment it appeared the book created a furor. Simone de Beauvoir was accused of "captation d'héritage" [illegally seizing an inheritance], of voyeurism, almost of necrophagia in *Magazine Littéraire,* 1982. "Mme de Beauvoir spares us, and herself, nothing: the dribble on his shirt, the food spilt over his shoes, the wet patch on chairs, the soiled pyjamas at night," in *The Sunday Times,* 1984. Add to this the writer Nelson Algren, an ex-lover, now dead, who accused the woman, Simone de Beauvoir, of talking too much, even suggesting, in an article in *Harper's* (May 1965), that after a devastating atomic bomb explosion one voice would remain, indestructible, the voice of Simone de Beauvoir.

Other readers might agree with some or all of these charges of excess. These charges are usually couched in aesthestic terms and suggest that Simone de Beauvoir is not really an artist, or a novelist, or a philosopher, but over and over again an autobiographer, a label used pejoratively for women, or that she is, at her best, a memorialist. What interests me are the connections between the charges leveled at Simone de Beauvoir and those discourses that denigrate the importance of content and are uneasy (as we have all become) with unexamined common sense notions of language. The question is then: to what degree is Simone de Beauvoir being accused of transgressing boundaries established by both phallocentric discourse and the concept of *l'écriture féminine,* boundaries that have made and maintained certain content areas taboo: incontinence, old age, dying?

In a brilliant essay by Alice Jardine entitled "Death Sentences: Writing Couples and Ideology,"[12] a psychoanalytic reading uncovers violence against the mother in *Une Mort très douce* and the representation of Sartre as the phallic mother in *La Cérémonie des adieux.* These are challenging interpretations. The dream sequence in *Une Mort très douce* in which Sartre and the mother blend is a particularly convincing example of the blurring of gender lines and of the power of the pre-Oedipal mother. But, at another level, these interpretations might also be read as an example of theory trivializing "content," making it impossible for "new" or another content to emerge by immediately reducing

12. Susan Suleiman, ed., *Poetics Today* 6 (1985).

this other content to a familiar situation and paradigm. The problem then is how to write (about) aging, suffering, death in the first person without their being subsumed by those psychoanalytic concepts which demand a return to structures determined by childhood and which argue that the Real is not writable. The concerted attack against the conventions of realism, against the naturalizing of culturally constructed modes of thinking and behavior, and the insistence on the mediating role of language have undermined the importance of material life and its structuring influences on social life. The aging body, the body in decline, the dead body have no place in contemporary fictional and autobiographical texts read by poststructuralist, psychoanalytic critics because the apparent "story" is always secondary.

I would argue that to translate these texts on incontinence, old age, and dying into Simone de Beauvoir's "denial of the mother" or rage against the maternal function is perhaps to eliminate, with a very powerful and convincing theory, dramas other than those of the Oedipal family. I would not, therefore, so much argue against Alice Jardine's interpretations, but I would retrieve what is thereby excluded, the new kind of content that Simone de Beauvoir has been proposing and that almost no one has any desire to read.

Annette Kolodny, in her essay on Kate Millett's autobiographical text *Flying*, entitled "The Lady's Not for Spurning: Kate Millett and the Critics," contends that the critics had difficulty in dealing with Millett's text *Flying* because it pushed aside "the accepted boundaries of narrative content."[13] The introduction of a new content about women's lives was perceived as a transgression. We face a similar phenomenon in the critical response to many of Simone de Beauvoir's texts. A closer reading of these texts reveals that her tendency to transgress boundaries has always characterized her work. Indeed, the first narrative section of *La Cérémonie des adieux* with its particular examples of "Jean-Paul Sartre's" aging and incontinence recalls examples of the physical disintegration of women in other autobiographical or fictional texts, particularly "Camille" and "Violette Leduc" in *Tout compte fait*. In the second part of *La Cérémonie des adieux*, Simone de Beauvoir interviews Sartre on his relations to and with the big, embarrassing questions: the body, men and women, money, time, death, and God. These interviews remind us that in her fiction as well as in her essays Simone de Beauvoir

---

13. Annette Kolodny, "The Lady's Not for Spurning: Kate Millett and the Critics." In Estelle C. Jelined, ed., *Women's Autobiography* (Bloomington: Indiana University Press, 1980), 249.

Yale French Studies

has consistently broken with decorum and has written directly about those topics one does not write or speak about today except in the discourse of empirical social science, of jokes, or through metaphor. It could, therefore, be maintained that the originality of Simone de Beauvoir's discourse is precisely this act of trespassing. She has not obeyed the taboos placed by the institutionalization of specialized discourses on the body, sexuality, aging, and God; she has not remained within the acceptable boundaries marked by level of style or genre that tell the reader this is a poetic text, a scientific text, a philosophical text. The result is that Simone de Beauvoir has often been accused of "bad taste." Furthermore, the reaction against popular existentialism and against humanistic universalizing has added to the derogatory criticism of Simone de Beauvoir's discourse and to the accusation that she is, as a writer, incontinent with respect to topic, content, and style boundaries. Simone de Beauvoir, therefore, provides an excellent case study for one of the central problems that has emerged in Western Europe and the United States since the late 1960s and that continues to challenge theorists and critics: the relationship between language and ideology, on the one hand, and "le vécu," questions of sex, gender, race, class, age, and the possibilities of change, on the other. Although the emphasis on the signifier as the sign of the unconscious has relegated the signified, and with it the notion that language translates experience, to an ancillary position, Simone de Beauvoir remains one of the few major figures on the contemporary French intellectual scene to support the signified and its representations.

A few examples will reinforce these points and suggest others. In *Le Deuxième sexe* (1949) Simone de Beauvoir transgressed the boundaries of what was then considered permissible to write about male-female relations, about marriage and motherhood, and about female sexuality, particularly lesbianism.

In her chapter on "La Lesbienne" Simone de Beauvoir transgresses the boundaries of accepted discourse at several points: she writes against that common sense discourse whose reliance on nature and what is natural nullifies any serious analysis of ideology and makes political constructions impossible; she writes against the reigning determinist discourse of psychoanalysis with its case histories and its established categories of masculine and feminine; she opposes, by not mentioning it, any religious discourse in which procreation becomes the definition of woman's function. Her own negative attitudes toward reproduction, marriage, motherhood, and the nuclear family do not prevent her from imagining other living arrangements. At the same time, however, as these boundaries are transgressed, as official discourse appears to be shaken and sexual practices liberated from repressive patterns, other repressive habits are reinforced. If psychoanalytic theories are dismantled in Simone de Beauvoir's discourse, the examples of case histories from psychoanalytic literature, from Renée Vivien, Colette, Radclyffe Hall are used to illustrate the experience of lesbians in 1949 withiut any conscious attempt to understand the relation between the literary text and lived experience. Lesbianism, in this essay, continues to be viewed as an individual experience separate from any political and community considerations. And, as the most repressive of all possible gestures, throughout the essay reappears the figure of the ideal woman, the heterosexual, virile woman who lives and loves among men: Ninon de Lenclos, Madame de Staël. Must the reader add to this list another woman who prides herself on male connections: the narrator? Is this the way the narrator puts herself into the chapter? Men, throughout *Le Deuxième sexe*, are presented as the privileged class, outstanding men as the human elite. This does not change in the chapter on the "lesbienne," but it is more blatant there than elsewhere in the book. My reading is, of course, a 1985 re-reading, and my criticisms must be understood in light of the new research on homosexuality and lesbianism that has appeared since 1968. If I try to reconstruct my 1949 reading of "La Lesbienne," I can find again the radical, transgressive aspects of the essay. Indeed, in the history of discourses on lesbianism, Simone de Beauvoirs's "La Lesbienne" retains its status as precursor, as a text that has made it possible to formulate other discourses and to think against those that have been and continue to be in place. The fact that Simone de Beauvoir ventured into a new territory, even though she may have been holding the guiding hand of virile heterosexual women, has itself the status of a disruptive, discursive event.

In *Mémoires d'une jeune fille rangée* the narrator relates in the same paragraph the trials of puberty and the revelations made to her by her cousin Madeleine about how babies are produced; she ends with a comparison between herself and Gulliver:

> That year, when we moved to the rue de Rennes, I began to have bad dreams. Had I not properly digested the revelations made by Madeleine? Only a thin partition now divided my bed from the one in which my parents slept, and sometimes I would hear my father snoring: did this promiscuity upset me? I had nightmares. A man would jump on my bed and dig his knees into my stomach until I felt I was suffocating; in desperation, I would dream that I was waking up and

once again I would be crushed beneath the awful weight of my ag-
gressor. About the same time, getting up became such a painful ordeal
that when I thought about it the night before, my throat would tighten
and my palms would grow damp with sweat. When I used to hear my
mother's voice in the mornings I longed to fall ill, I had such a horror of
dragging myself out of the toils of sleep and darkness. During the day, I
had dizzy spells; I became anaemic. Mama and the doctor would say:
"It's her development." I grew to detest that word and the silent up-
heaval that was going on in my body. I envied "big girls" their freedom; but I was disgusted at the thought of my chest swelling out; I had
sometimes heard grown-up women urinating with the noise of a cata-
ract; when I thought of the bladders swollen with water in their bel-
lies, I felt the same terror as Gulliver did when the young giantesses
displayed their breasts to him.[14]

In *Tout compte fait* the pages on the narrator's new intimacy with
"Sylvie Le Bon," "She is as thoroughly interwoven in my life as I am in
hers" (72), are followed by the pages on the decline, the alcoholism, the
filth, and death of "Camille" (Simone de Jolivet, ex-mistress of Dullin
and of Sartre):

> One day when we were waiting for her in my flat we heard heavy
> uncertain footsteps in the street; they came nearer, then moved away.
> She took a quarter of an hour to find my door. She was staggering and
> she could not articulate properly. She went upstairs to the bathroom,
> and although she was usually so modest she left the door open: we
> heard her urinating loudly. [78]

Here the move from sexuality to urination and back to sexuality is
explicitly made. Urination, abundant, excessive urination by women
becomes the metaphor for everything that is embarrassing in sexuality.
The body grows on its own, so to speak, proliferates without permission, makes noises, in the same way as incontinence takes over the body
in decline. And the metaphor always involves the feminine. It is, therefore, not surprising that when Sartre's behavior is described in terms of
"his lack of aggressiveness and his resignation," it involves his metamorphosis into a woman as she is negatively defined both by culture and
cultural stereotypes and by Simone de Beauvoir in *Le Deuxième sexe*.
"Sartre," incontinent, is passive, incapable of transcendence, no longer
a creator but reduced like women to immanence and urinating in a
sitting position.

"Françoise de Beauvoir" is also incontinent in *Une Mort très dou-*

14. *Memoirs of a Dutiful Daughter*, op. cit., 99–100.

ce. She is the prey of a body in decline and ravaged by cancer. In this earlier text there are also reasons to evoke the family name Beau/voir of the narrator as the desire to see and not to see her mother's "bald pubis" and "the garden" (18) outside. Sartre is present in this text as a quiet witness of the narrator's unwitting imitation of her mother's mouth (28), and in the last chapter he appears in a dream with the narrator's mother: "She blended with Sartre, and we were happy together. And then the dream would turn into a nightmare: why was I living with her once more? How had I come to be in her power again? So our former relationship lived on in its double aspect—a subjection that I loved and hated."[15]

Une Mort très douce transgresses yet another set of boundaries. Simone de Beauvoir persists in her jibes against the institutions of marriage and motherhood that began in *Le Deuxième sexe* in 1949 and that continue through the interviews with Alice Schwarzer, *After the Second Sex*, in 1984. Simone de Beauvoir has not abandoned her earlier positions and her conviction that these institutions are traps for women. Her most significant example is the case of her mother, Françoise de Beauvoir, whose miniature biography as a "corseted woman" she presents in the second part of *Une Mort très douce*.

Both Mary Evans (*Simone de Beauvoir: A Feminist Mandarin*, London and New York: Tavistock, 1984) and Alice Jardine (1985) have read these challenges to the institutions of marriage and motherhood as symptoms in the writing and in the psyche of Simone de Beauvoir. Mary Evans reads them as a fear of female biology and of the irrational and the emotional. Alice Jardine, as we have seen earlier reads them as violence against the phallic mother whom Simone de Beauvoir needs to destroy and with her, the body of the man, Sartre. I would suggest that these readings, with their insistent accusations, miss or obscure the political and transgressive aspects of Simone de Beauvoir's text. Their critiques imply that she is immature, not yet an adult. For if, in our culture, famous men should not be seen as incontinent and out of control, mothers are even more sacred. The most famous French women theorists of the past fifteen years—Hélène Cixous, Luce Irigaray, and Julia Kristeva—have been adding to the sacred untouchable quality of the figure of the mother within our patriarchal Judeo-Christian tradition. In their desire to explore the pre-Oedipal stage of mother-child relations neglected by official psychoanalytic discourses, in their search for a feminine specificity, they have once again magnified the mother and moth-

15. *A Very Easy Death*, trans. Patrick O'Brian (New York: Penguin Books, 1983), 89.

erhood. Read as reading matter from their perspective, *Une Mort très douce* would indeed be a naive text.

In *La Vieillesse* Simone de Beauvoir once again transgresses the boundaries of what was then permissible to write about aging and death, about the attitudes that prevailed in nursing homes and in families towards the elderly. And once again the representatives of the official discourses on aging were shocked and offended that a nonspecialist had been audacious enough to theorize and sermonize about their materials.

With respect to women and aging, what characterizes Simone de Beauvoir's discourse in *La Vieillesse* is the revelation that sexism and ageism are embedded in the ideology and the language of Western culture. From the vantage point of 1985 what seems most interesting in her analyses are the ways in which sexism and ageism are intertwined. It appears, now, as if a discourse on aging could only have developed when it was possible to write a certain discourse of the body, when a certain discourse on women's body had been elaborated. (The fact that Charcot was giving lectures at the Salpêtrière in which he was putting both female hysteria and old age into discourse during the 1870s and 1880s requires further investigation.) The disgust and the fear provoked by the female body in Western discourses are related to similar effects provoked by old bodies. In both cases the reaction against contact with the woman is represented as abject, impure, and unclassifiable. Old bodies, in texts by Simone de Beauvoir, are always feminine or feminized bodies.

A detailed analysis of the paragraph in *La Cérémonie des adieux* in which "Sartre's" incontinence is first mentioned explicitly brings together, in anecdotal form. many of the questions we have been raising:

> When we came back [to Paris from Rome] at the end of September Sartre was in great form. "I like being back here," he said to me. Returning to my apartment pleased him. "As far as the rest is concerned, I don't care. But I'm glad to be in this place again." We spent some happy evenings there, and again I almost stopped worrying.
>
> But not for long. In the middle of October I once more became aware of the irreversible deterioration of old age. In Rome, I had noticed that when we went after lunch to eat Giolitti's wonderful ices, Sartre would hurry to the lavatory. One afternoon, when we were going along by the Pantheon, back toward the hotel, and he was walking very quickly ahead of us, he stopped and said, "Cats have just pissed on me. I went close to the balustrade and I was wet on." Sylvie believed him and laughed about it. For my part I knew what was the matter, but I said nothing. In Paris, at the beginning of October, Sartre

got up to go to the bathroom—he was in my apartment—and there was a mark on his chair. The next day I told Sylvie that he had spilled some tea. "You would say that a child had had an accident," she observed. The next evening, in the same circumstances, there was another mark. So I spoke to Sartre about it. "You are incontinent. You ought to tell the doctor." To my utter astonishment he replied in a perfectly natural voice, "I have told him. It has been going on for a long while now. It's those cells that I lost." Sartre had always been extremely puritanical; he never referred to his natural functions, and he carried them out with the utmost discretion. That was why I asked him the next morning whether he did not find this lack of control exceedingly embarrassing. He answered with a smile, "When you're old you can't expect too much, your claims have to be modest." I was touched by his simplicity and by this moderation, so new in him; and at the same time his lack of aggressiveness and his resignation wounded me.[16]

In *La Volonté de savoir* (1976) Michel Foucault writes:

But there may be another reason that makes it so gratifying for us to define the relationship between sex and power in terms of repression: something that one might call the speaker's benefit. If sex is repressed, that is, condemned to prohibition, nonexistence and silence, then the mere fact that one is speaking about it has the appearance of a deliberate transgression. A person who holds forth in such language places himself to a certain extent outside the reach of power; he upsets established law; he somehow anticipates coming freedom.[17]

I should like to change Foucault's the "speaker's benefit" to the "narrator's benefit" and begin to read the passage from *La Cérémonie des adieux* in relation to these sentences from *La Volonté de savoir*.

The reader of *La Cérémonie des adieux* reacts both to what is happening to "Sartre" and to the reactions of the narrator. What is happening to "Sartre," the signs of his incontinence, are localized in Rome and in Paris and are associated with Giolitti's ices, the Pantheon, cats, and a chair in "Simone de Beauvoir's" apartment. Perhaps, as her last name suggests, "Simone de Beau/voir" sees signs easily, or perhaps—*elle a beau voir*—no matter how or what she sees, she sees nothing, or she does not see that which is essential. The narrator in this

16. *Adieux*, op. cit., 33–34.
17. *The History of Sexuality*, trans. Robert Hurley (New York: Vintage Books, 1980),
6.

passage breaks the silence that surrounds "Sartre's" incontinence. First, to her friend, "Sylvie," whose presence in the text as an intimate friend of "Simone de Beauvoir's" appears to balance the list of "Sartre's" younger women friends: Arlette, Michèle, Wanda, Liliane, Melina. To "Sylvie," who had been duped (the narrator thought) by "Sartre's" story of the cats, the narrator lies. She lies as she lied to her mother in *Une Mort Très douce* and as she will lie, later on in this text, to "Sartre" about the seriousness of his illness. "Sylvie," whose family name is Le Bon, answers firmly but kindly, revealing that she knows. The narrator then breaks the silence a second time by confronting "Sartre" (as if he did not know) and as if he were a child and she, his mother: "You are incontinent. You ought to tell the doctor." The accusatory, peremptory tone of these sentences reveals the "narrator's benefit." Having broken the silence, having transgressed and spoken about what one should not speak about even if one knows, she assumes a maternal position of moral superiority. I know, and because I know, I can tell you what to do. But this benefit and the feeling of superiority that accompanies it do not last long. "Sartre" already knew; the silence had already been broken. From this point in the narrative until the end of the paragraph, "Simone de Beauvoir" as narrator and "Sartre" vie for the reader's attention. His puritanical behavior seems also to apply to her. His direct reply to her question that is asked in indirect style is not the last word. His plight cannot remain the focus of our attention. The narrator's reaction: "I was touched . . . wounded me" becomes as important as "Sartre's" incontinence and his reactions to it. At the end of the paragraph the "narrator's benefit" has been restored. If in "life" the silence has already been broken and "Sartre" has spoken to his doctor, in writing it down and showing it to the public, she comes first.

But there is something else going on in this paragraph. There is the suggestion, through the cats that piss and the strong odor associated with cats' piss, through the emphasis on "puritanical" and the presence of "Sylvie LeBon," that the narrator is keeping something hidden. The secret in this text, that which the narrator does not or cannot relate, is that the discourse on "Sartre's" incontinence is also "Simone de Beauvoir's" discourse on sexuality, on feminine sexuality, on her feminine sexuality. The name "Giolitti," *gît au lit*, perhaps contains the variety of possible bodily activities.

The Gods of the Pantheon eventually recall the gods of the title *La Cérémonie des* ADIEUX, and the SIMONIE [simony] in "Simone," the making of profit out of sacred things, may be read as another example of the narrator's benefit. What "Sartre" does with the members of his female entourage, what "Simone de Beauvoir" does with "Sylvie Le Bon," these are the taboo subjects that the narrator's text hides and reveals. They emerge, these taboo activities, in "Sartre's" "lack of control," which the narrator finds "exceedingly embarrassing." Lack of control, we remember from other texts by "Simone de Beauvoir" and particularly *Le Deuxième sexe*, is a sign of the feminine.

It is not my intention to enter into an analysis of the narrator's relationship to homosexuality and lesbianism. We have, in the interviews with Alice Schwarzer, her explicit and conscious remarks on this question.[18] But I am fascinated by and would like to pursue the relations between the repetition of the phrase "Sylvie and I" in *La Cérémonie des adieux* and passages from two other texts in which what is at stake is the production of another, like herself, a double.[19]

In his 1919 essay on "The 'Uncanny,'" Sigmund Freud wrote: "For the 'double' was originally an insurance against the destruction of the ego, an 'energetic denial of the power of death' as Rank says; and probably the 'immortal' soul was the first 'double' of the body."[20] We find striking examples of the "double" in the following passages:

> I resembled her [Maggie Tulliver in George Eliot's *The Mill on the Floss*] and henceforward I saw my isolation not as a proof of infamy but as a sign of my uniqueness. I couldn't see myself dying of solitude. Through the heroine, I identified myself with the author: one day other adolescents would bathe with their tears a novel in which I would tell my own sad story.[21]

The narrator is describing a series of displaced identifications with Maggie Tulliver, George Eliot, and her own future adolescent readers. In this case it is through the reading and writing of literary texts that a "double" may be produced, a double that would insure the continuation "of the ego." This is one of the ways in which writing, for Simone de Beauvoir, is a means of salvation.

The notion of the "double" who saves is particularly strong in these

---

18. *After the Second Sex: Conversations with Simone de Beauvoir*, translated from the French by Marianne Howarth (New York: Pantheon Books, 1984), 35–36, 112–13. In the earliest interview, "I am a Feminist," Simone de Beauvoir speaks harshly about "the sexual dogmas" lesbians "try to impose" (36). In the last interview, "Being a Woman is not Enough," she claims never to have had a sexual relationship with a woman but accepts homosexuality as a possibility for all women (112–13).

19. *Adieux*, op. cit., 85, 94, 95, 102, 109, 115, 118.

20. *The Standard Edition of the Complete Psychological Works*, trans. James Strachey, vol. 17 (London: Hogarth Press and the Institute of Psychoanalysis, 1955), 235.

21. *Memoirs of a Dutiful Daughter*, op. cit., 140.

concluding remarks about her new friend, "Sylvie Le Bon," in *Tout compte fait*:

> The better I knew Sylvie, the more akin I felt to her. She too was an intellectual and she too was passionately in love with life. And she was like me in many other ways: with thirty-three years of difference I recognized my qualities and my faults in her. . . .
>
> First she was posted to Le Mans and then to Rouen, in the same lycée where I had taught: when she spent the night there, she stayed in the hotel near the station where I had lived for two years, and she drank her morning coffee in the Métropole bar: all this gave me a certain feeling of being reincarnated. At present she has a post in the suburbs.
>
> This means that we can see one another every day. She is as thoroughly interwoven in my life as I am in hers. I have introduced her to my friends. We read the same books, we see shows together, and we go for long drives in the car. There is such an interchange between us that I lose the sense of my age: she draws me forwards into her future, and there are times when the present recovers a dimension that it had lost.[22]

"Sylvie Le Bon," it would seem, is more of a "double" than she is a disciple, a friend, a lover, or a daughter, although elements of these categories may be read into the relationship. She is less an other and different—aside from the difference in age—than she is the same. "Simone de Beauvoir's" particular kind of incontinence is related to her unabashed narcissism. This is the secret in *La Cérémonie des adieux*, and, by extension, it is also the secret of feminine sexuality. The reason why it is kept secret, the reason why it may be considered a transgression, is because this narcissism, in the universe of the atheist, is a source of power and of strength. The quotation from "The 'Uncanny'" recapitulates quite accurately the function of "Sylvie Le Bon" as "double." When the narrator repeats "Sylvie and I," she is informing her readers that she is not alone, that her posterity is with her, always. This doubling is confirmed at the level of their names: Simone de Beauvoir and Sylvie Le Bon. The similarity between the initial S and the initial B, the alliteration of Si and Sy, the ethical (masculine) resonance between Beau and Bon, even the particle and the definite article are similarly placed.

The presence of the double during the years of Sartre's final illnesses, when the readers might have expected the narrator to be alone,

22. *All Said and Done*, op. cit., 72.

gives further evidence of what, in the writings of Sarah Kofman and Elizabeth Berg, is referred to as the "scandalous . . . contradictions of the affirmative woman."[23]

I would read *Une Mort très douce* and *La Cérémonie des adieux* by maintaining both a psychoanalytic and a political reading. Incontinence is certainly closely allied to sexuality and to Simone de Beauvoir's uneasiness about feminine sexuality: its odors, its wetnesses, its sounds, and in particular, the difficulties in putting it into discourse, in breaking the silences with and for others. But incontinence is not only *old* sexuality. It is also a *new* continent to be written and a new continent to be explored. But that continent lies beyond the borders, and those who move beyond run the risk of being accused of acting in violation of the law of the fathers and of the mothers. Simone de Beauvoir, unlike many of the women writing on women since the late 1960s in France and in the United States, does not move from one position to another by *flying*. She transgresses, that is, she steps across, she trespasses. This makes her easier to track and to follow. What her writing is up to, and this must be a major source of the critics' malaise, is the affirmation that incontinence, like death, is a great equalizer. "Jean-Paul Sartre" with bed sores and incontinent is not very different from "Françoise de Beauvoir" with bed sores and incontinent. Between the old man who wets his chair and the old woman who wets her bed, the readers of both sexes who await their turn ("qui attendent leur tour," wrote Pascal) must read that, at the end, sexual difference fades and that the body that remains is the unrestrained, uncontrolled body of the old woman. It is precisely the body that Western culture and, ironically, Simone de Beauvoir herself have labored assiduously to hide.

There is a further transgressive aspect to Simone de Beauvoir's writing. In the "Preface" to *La Cérémonie des adieux* we read:

> I have spoken about myself a little, because the witness is part of his [sic] evidence, but I have done so as little as possible. In the first place because that is not what this book is about, and then because, as I replied to a friend who asked me how I was taking it, "These things cannot be told; they cannot be put into writing; they cannot be formed in one's mind. They are experienced and that is all [ça se vit, c'est tout]. My narrative is chiefly based on the diary I kept during those ten years; and on the many testimonies I have gathered."[24]

23. Elizabeth Berg, "The Third Woman." In *Diacritics* (Summer 1982): 20.
24. *Adieux*, op. cit., 24.

Simone de Beauvoir's project, whatever her disclaimers of false modesty, from the very beginning of her writing career and consciously assumed as the volumes of memoirs followed each other, has been precisely to put into writing what "cannot be told . . . cannot be put into writing . . . cannot be formed in one's mind." Writers who attempt this, whether in prose or poetry, usually turn to metaphor or to other deliberate deviations from the conventions of narrative and a common sense language accessible to all readers.

Simone de Beauvoir has refused to abandon these conventions and the immediate entrée to the text they guarantee. She has accepted the challenge of writing what cannot be written by relying on "the diary I kept during those ten years" and "the many testimonies I have gathered." The impossibility of the task is juxtaposed with the sources that made the narrative possible. The effects produced on the reader by this narrative should, in some measure, correspond to what "cannot be put into writing." Simone de Beauvoir succeeds admirably, I think, in replicating her position as an intimate observer and helpless witness and in providing the reader with sufficient openings for identification and distance for critical analysis. But in so doing, she transgresses what has become a ruling protocol for important writing in the 1970s and early 1980s: she revels in the referential fallacy and her writing remains readable. Having been moved herself, she attempts to move her readers.

There is a further irony. The reviewers' comments notwithstanding, references to incontinence in *La Cérémonie des adieux* are very few. If there has been so much made of them, it is because they come unexpectedly (in the text), and they are situated at a crossroads of feminist, antihumanist, and humanist discourses: sexuality, the body, sexual difference, control, dignity, public and private, subject and object, subjectivity and sociality, the Symbolic, the Imaginary, and the Real. It is as if the "real" had overwhelmed the reviewers, as if "pipi caca" and all the strains of toilet training had been released by Simone de Beauvoir's texts. It is as if she had made dirty, had sullied the white page. In 1954 Sartre is said, by Simone de Beauvoir, to have exclaimed: "La littérature, c'est de la merde." Simone de Beauvoir's example indicates how unpalatable it is to reverse the terms and exclaim: "La merde, c'est de la littérature."

VI. In Memoriam

MARGARET A. SIMONS

I was twenty-six years old and a graduate student in philosophy when I first met Simone de Beauvoir. It was 1972 and I had won a French government grant to work with her on my doctoral dissertation on *The Second Sex*. I sold everything I could to find to make the trip to France, my secretarial clothes, my car, my books. I was down to the essentials, my Red Wing boots, t-shirts and Levis. It sounds like a pilgrimage. But when a male philosophy professor in 1971 had first suggested that I try for a Fulbright to study in Europe, I had asked, "With Habermas?" When he replied, "No, with Simone de Beauvoir," I was stunned. How could I write a philosophy dissertation on *The Second Sex?*

As a feminist activist, I was committed to developing feminist theory, but had found it difficult to do in philosophy seminars. I had first written a paper on Simone de Beauvoir's ethics after a professor had referred to her disparagingly as Sartre's girl friend. I had once tried to present a seminar paper developing a critique of Habermas based on Shulamith Firestone's *The Dialectic of Sex*, but had been discouraged by the misogynism of the all-male classroom. By 1970 I had already begun presenting papers for the newly founded Society for Women in Philosophy on Simone de Beauvoir's feminist philosophy. But a dissertation . . . ?

Without the support of the secondary literature that a graduate student habitually leans on, without even a context within philosophy for defining the issues, how could I proceed? Philosophy professors in the all-male departments where I had learned how to do philosophy had never addressed a topic about women in any discussions or assignments. The few women philosophers we had read never discussed being women, Simone de Beauvoir herself denied being a philosopher and saw herself as a literary writer.

203

But I took up the challenge, and arrived in Paris with fantasies, soon to be dispelled, of sitting down to dinner with Simone and Jean-Paul. When I called her at the assigned time to arrange a meeting, she sounded brusque and impatient with my poor French. When I eventually found myself at the door to her apartment, I was very nervous. I walked around the block several times in an effort to arrive exactly on time. I was shocked when she opened the door. In spite of looking old and wrinkled, she had the audacity to wear lipstick and bright red nail polish! I was offended to the puritanical core of my radical feminism. During our interview we were both on edge. Chainsmoking, another affront to my "natural" values, she blew smoke in my face as I struggled to ask my questions in French. I wanted to ask her about the development of her philosophical perspective. I hesitantly posed my first question about the influence of the interpretations of Hegel by Kojeve and Hyppolite on *The Second Sex*. Of course she had read them, she replied, but I must remember, she said leaning towards me in emphasis, that the only important influence on *The Second Sex* was *Being and Nothingness* by Jean-Paul Sartre.

I was taken aback. Here was the forbidden name, the name that I had in angry reaction consigned to the footnotes in all my papers, moved back to center stage. Although I knew from her autobiographies that she saw Sartre as the real philosopher, I had hoped that as a feminist she would no longer see her philosophical work as merely derivative from Sartre's. I was unprepared for the forcefulness of her reply. It was impossible to see her in a passive role, as merely a follower of Sartre. Yet it was this very image of her work that she seemed to be defending so forcefully. Later I perceived her attitude as a defense of Sartre, who was still under attack for his late support of the May 1968 uprising. The fate of her own work concerned her much less. But how was I to proceed if she wouldn't go along with my efforts to trace the autonomous development of her philosophical position that was the focus of my dissertation research? I wanted her to be as docile as the texts that I studied in school. Dealing with a real person I could tell was going to be a challenge.

She enjoyed discussing feminist politics much more than my digging into the philosophical origins of *The Second Sex*. In our second interview she answered all of my questions in one word, either yes or no, and then asked eagerly, "tell me what's going on in the States." I threw up my hands and protested that I had spent three months working on those questions. I came to realize that it was a trade off, she'd put up with my probing questions about *The Second Sex*, in exchange for discussion of the women's liberation movement. But it was the last time I asked her questions that allowed for one word answers.

She wanted to know what I was reading, and when I left I gave her all the feminist books I had brought to France with me. I wanted to repay her generosity. I had never been included in those dinners with Jean-Paul. But she gave me all the help she could. Someone had sent her a manuscript with a detailed bibliography and she got down on her hands and knees to search through piles of manuscripts to find it for me. "I've lost my eyes," she complained in frustration as she tried to keep her glasses in place while she crawled across the floor. Once she lent me a book that she found particularly important; when I got back to the Cité I discovered that it had been autographed to her.

In our first discussions of feminist politics I took refuge from my intimidation in the supremacy of political correctness, especially when she told me that she was most in agreement politically with Juliet Mitchell's *Women's Estate*. As the weary veteran of painful years—well, months—of political struggle with leftist men at my school, I had abandoned compromise with socialism for the purity of radical feminism. I remember asking her with smiling condescension later that year if she still found the notion of feminine culture meaningless. Yes, she said, although she knew there were many feminists who disagreed with her. Only the fact that it was our last scheduled interview gave me the courage to state simply that I was one who saw nonservile feminine characteristics such as nurturance as part of a positive feminine culture.

In the years that followed, our relationship continued to grow. We met several more times for interviews and discussions of my various research projects. Once I had the pleasure of meeting Sylvie Le Bon, and sharing an interview with Jessica Benjamin, who helped me learn how to argue with Beauvoir about her work and its relation to Sartre. The publication of her book on Sartre's death came not long after my father's suicide and helped me deal with my grief. It also gave me the courage to talk with her in a more personal way about my feelings. In our last interview in 1985, after getting the tape recorder all set, I blurted out that I was still nervous after all these years of meeting with her. Her response was to offer me a Scotch. When I agreed she slowly got up from the sofa and walked, shuffling, bent over now into the kitchen for two glasses and back to the refrigerator where she kept an enormous bottle of Scotch. It makes me cry to think of her again; I wish she could have lived forever. I'm glad her death has brought together those of us who loved her so much.

YOLANDA ASTARITA PATTERSON

Some Personal Reflections

On Saturday, September 14, 1985, I was sitting in Simone de Beauvoir's apartment on the rue Schoelcher about to begin an interview, telling her of my determination to bring her sister Hélène's art to the West Coast. When Hélène de Beauvoir got off the plane at the San Francisco airport on Sunday evening, April 6, 1986, I was glowing with the satisfaction of a mission accomplished. Her oil paintings, acrylics and graphics were on display at Stanford University along with enlargements of some wonderful family photographs she had sent me. Invitations had been sent out for a reception at the Office of the President on the Stanford campus the following Thursday, and I was looking forward to sharing two weeks of my life and the beauty of the San Francisco Bay area with Hélène. A cloud hung over these anticipated joys, however. Hélène had almost not made the trip because her sister Simone de Beauvoir was in the hospital. She had asked me not to mention this to anyone; but at least there was someone with me with whom I could share my concern.

A telephone call the following Wednesday morning was reassuring: Simone de Beauvoir had been moved out of the intensive care unit. That Friday afternoon brought a disturbing telegram, however: she was back in the intensive care unit and there were pulmonary complications. The hours seemed to crawl by as we waited for an appropriate time to call Paris that night and see if Hélène should return immediately. No, Simone's condition had improved. No need for Hélène to cut her trip short.

Saturday was a very special day. Colleagues from all over the States were in town for the conference on Autobiography and Biography at Stanford, sponsored by the Center for Research on Women. Deirdre Bair came to our home on Saturday morning and she, Hélène de Beauvoir, Gloria Orenstein from U.S.C., Gloria's daughter Claudia and I sat around our kitchen table as Deirdre taped some questions she was asking Hélène about her childhood memories for the biography of Simone de Beauvoir she is writing. Somehow we all wanted to share and discuss memories that morning and Deirdre had to keep turning her tape recorder on and off. That afternoon we all headed to Stanford for a session on Simone de Beauvoir chaired by Hélène Wenzel. Deirdre spoke of her experience writing the biographies of Samuel Beckett and of Simone de Beauvoir, and I discussed her as biographer of the midcentury mandarins. Hélène de Beauvoir listened attentively to everything that was said and later remarked that she felt her sister's reputation was in good hands in the United States. The day ended with a conference banquet at the Stanford Shopping Center and a special toast to Hélène de Beauvoir and her art proposed by Marilyn Yalom, organizer of the CROW conference.

Sunday was a glorious clear day in San Francisco and all the sailboats were out dotting the Bay. We drove down Lombard Street, enjoyed the view from Coit Tower, and feasted at a restaurant on Fisherman's Wharf. That evening Hélène de Beauvoir and I looked over the slides of family photographs and of her art which we planned to use for a talk she was to give in San Francisco the next day.

Early Monday morning I was studying our map of the city trying to locate the offices of the *Journal Français d'Amérique*, where Hélène was to be interviewed at 11 A.M. The telephone rang, and I knew from the tone of the voice asking for Hélène de Beauvoir that the news was bad. When I called Hélène to the phone, I warned her of my premonition, and she too anticipated what that voice would say: Simone de Beauvoir had died at the Hôpital Cochin about an hour earlier. The number of details that needed to be taken care of immediately didn't give us much time to grieve, and before I knew it Hélène was back on a plane headed for Paris. When Hélène called that Wednesday morning and said that the funeral would not be until Saturday, April 19, I suddenly knew that I had to be there, had to share my sense of loss with others who knew who Simone de Beauvoir was and what an enormous influence she had had on twentieth-century thought. For the first and undoubtedly the last time in my life, I flew to Paris for the weekend.

After returning from the funeral, I was preparing a talk on Simone de Beauvoir to be given before a group of high school and university foreign language teachers. I thought of beginning by admitting that I really knew Beauvoir's sister much better than I knew her. Then I thought of all the hours I had spent reading and analyzing Simone de Beauvoir's works since the mid 1950s, when I chose *Les Mandarins* as the text for a second year French class I was teaching at Stanford. In her autobiography, Simone de Beauvoir stated that she wanted to be a writer in order to communicate with her readers, in order to share her life and her ideas with them. This is something she accomplished most effectively for me. I really felt as if she were talking to me personally as I read through her autobiography, her fiction, her essays. Someone commented in an article that appeared in *Le Monde* after her death that all of her readers wanted to be her friends. I think this was very true for many of us, even if we seldom had the opportunity to see her in person. She seemed always to be there, conscientious about responding to letters on her endless supply of graph paper, ready to comment, to express appreciation, to offer support, to fight for a worthy cause. Her departure leaves a huge void which can never again be filled in quite the same way.

JEAN PAUL SARTRE
1905 – 1980
SIMONE DE BEAUVOIR
1908 – 1986

The gravesite.

DEIRDRE BAIR

The details of her final illness are still sketchy: one evening in mid-March, Simone de Beauvoir complained of severe stomach pains to her friend and adopted daughter, Sylvie Le Bon. The pains persisted and intensified, so she was taken to the Cochin Hospital, where the initial diagnosis was possible appendicitis. The doctors decided to take tests and try to monitor her condition before proceeding further. After several days, when she seemed more likely to be suffering from an obstruction of the colon or possible colitis than from appendicitis, exploratory surgery was performed. Following the surgery. Simone de Beauvoir spent two weeks in the intensive care unit, where she recovered sufficiently to be moved into a private room.

Her doctors felt she was well enough to get out of bed, so they recommended a brief walk each day. Simone de Beauvoir had been taking kinesthetic massage on a regular basis since a previous hospitalization for pneumonia in December, 1984. Her doctors prescribed continuation of this therapy on a daily basis for the rest of her hospital stay, which they expected would be another two weeks.

The masseuse came, bringing the only amount of levity to a sad and tense time: despite all of Simone de Beauvoir's attempts to persuade the woman to vote for the Socialist Party, she had cast her ballot for Le Pen. But for the greater part of this time, Simone de Beauvoir was bored. She was too weak to read, and even though visitors were permitted one hour each day, she was too exhausted to receive them. Her friends, and especially her sister, Hélène, who lives near Strasbourg, depended on Sylvie's telephone calls to keep them informed. They had all agreed that Simone de Beauvoir's illness should be treated with strict secrecy to keep reporters, friends, and admirers from laying siege to the hospital staff or grounds. This small group of devoted people succeeded, which made the sudden, unexpected announcement of her death all the more shocking.

Of major concern to all of them was Hélène's situation: her husband, Lionel de Roulet, had just undergone difficult ear surgery and was recovering at their home in Goxwiller, Bas Rhin. He was planning to recuperate in the North African sunshine while Hélène traveled to Stanford University, where her paintings were to be exhibited in conjunction with a conference held by the Center for Research on Women. Since Simone de Beauvoir's condition was stable, although not as good as they hoped, Hélène and Sylvie decided that life should continue as normally as possible.

When Hélène arrived in the Bay area, news that Simone de Beauvoir's condition had destabilized awaited her. A related complication to the exploratory surgery, congestion in the lungs, was not responding to treatment. Throughout the time of the conference, daily telephone calls and telegrams passed between Hélène and Sylvie. In several critical instances, the exchanges were hourly rather than daily. Finally, by Saturday 12 April, even though Simone de Beauvoir had been returned several days previously to intensive care, it seemed as though her condition had stabilized once again.

That afternoon, Hélène attended a panel, and in the evening, was an honored guest at the concluding banquet of the conference. Only a few American scholars had been told about Simone de Beauvoir's hospitalization, and they too, had been sworn to secrecy. On 14 April, at approximately 4 P.M. (Paris time), Simone de Beauvoir died; the official cause of death was "pulmonary edema." An early morning (San Francisco time) telephone call from Sylvie Le Bon gave the sad news to Hélène de Beauvoir. She left for Paris that same day.

Meanwhile in Paris, Sylvie Le Bon (who would now be known as Sylvie Le Bon de Beauvoir), took charge of funeral arrangements, aided and comforted by Claude Lanzmann and Jacques-Laurent Bost (his wife, Olga, Simone de Beauvoir's long-time friend, had died in January, 1985.) It was decided that Simone de Beauvoir's body should remain at the Cochin Hospital until the funeral, scheduled for April 19 at 2 P.M. A viewing for family, close friends, and dignitaries, was to be held from 1– 2 P.M., after which a cortege would form and walk through the streets of Paris to the Montparnasse Cemetery.

The irony of Simone de Beauvoir's death occuring only hours before the 15 April anniversary of Jean-Paul Sartre's 1980 death, gave an even further ironic quality to her burial: she who had shunned marriage for more than fifty years of contingent fidelity, would lie beside her companion in the Montparnasse Cemetery rather than in the de Beauvoir family's burial plot at Père Lachaise with her father, mother, and other relatives.

On Saturday, a small group of people were permitted to file by her bier in the ampitheatre of the Cochin Hospital, where she lay in a scarlet turban and matching bathrobe. On her right stood Sylvie Le Bon de Beauvoir, flanked by Jacques Laurent Bost; on her left stood her sister Hélène, flanked by her friend, Claudine Serre. Claude Lanzmann moved quietly between them, and also among friends and relatives in the attached sitting room where Lionel de Roulet, still weak from surgery, also sat. Among the mourners were Simone de Beauvoir's cousins and childhood friends from Meyrignac, Jeanne de Beauvoir and Madeleine de Bisschof, with members of their families. Also there was her childhood friend Geraldine "Gégé" Pardo. Members of the present and past editorial boards of *Les Temps Modernes* were there, as were four former ministers of the Mitterand government: Yvette Roudy, Jack Lang, Laurent Fabius, and Lionel Jospin.

At the end of the hour, the coffin was closed and Simone de Beauvoir's body was placed in a hearse piled so high with flowers that they nearly doubled the height of the vehicle itself. Attached to the rear door was a wreath from the newspaper *Libération* so tall that it could be seen from the rear of the cortege.

Hélène and Lionel de Roulet went to the cemetery by car, but everyone else formed a procession behind the hearse and walked to the cemetery. In the courtyard immediately outside the ampitheatre, reporters and photographers swarmed with cameras of every sort, thrusting them into the faces of everyone in order not to miss anyone their editors might consider important. A crowd estimated at between three to five thousand people jammed the courtyard and the narrow streets that fed into the Boulevard du Montparnasse.

They composed a cross-section of society, so diverse and yet so united in the desire to grieve and pay respect all at the same time, that strangers struck up conversations and spontaneous small groups formed and reformed as the cortege proceeded slowly toward the cemetery. The thousands who marched included the famous and the unknown, among them a surprising number of young fathers bearing small children on their shoulders because they wanted them to be able to say some day that they had paid their respects to one of France's greatest women. Scholars and feminists from many countries marched, renewing friendships and making new ones. A large delegation of African women in native dress supported a cumbersome mass of flowers as they walked.

There were many old people, men and women whose dress and mien were of the working classes, some with small patches of the tricolor on their lapels, most carrying single flowers. Many older women of Simone de Beauvoir's generation walked along supported by middle-aged women who could have been their daughters, a great number crying real tears.

As the procession wound slowly down the Boulevard du Montparnasse all traffic was halted. One irate cab driver who left his car to bellow at the slowness of those who marched at the end of the procession was so chagrined when he found out whose funeral it was that he parked the taxi and joined the march. Many persons turned in silent homage as they passed by the Paris that Simone de Beauvoir loved so much: from her birthplace above the Dôme, to the Coupole where she danced and drank so many nights away, to the Rue du Départ and Boulevard Edgar Quinet, past the white apartment building that was Sartre's last home. Just as the streets were thronged, so too, were the balconies and windows of the houses along the way.

At the cemetery, guards fearing the crush of thousands of people among the fairly fragile tombstones, rushed to shut the massive iron gates. The crowd, sensing exclusion, surged forward, many climbing over the portable barriers in an attempt to get inside. Some enterprising photographers used the barriers to climb onto the high wall, where they ran back and forth snapping shots of the people inside and out. Light rain had begun to fall, but even though the gates were shut, no one left the procession. Those who crowded around the grave heard Claude Lanzmann read softly from the last few pages of Simone de Beauvoir's memoir, *Force of Circumstances*, ending with the moving last paragraph in which she rails against death, refusing to go gently into the annihilation which she never once in her life thought gentle. Periodically, the guards opened the gates and allowed more mourners to come in, but many of those already inside refused to move on, so it was difficult to see the grave itself. Cries of "circuler!" and implorations in several other languages rang out, as everyone seemed to have flowers they wanted to place on the grave.

The wrenching declaration of French writer and feminist, Elizabeth Badinter, "Women, you owe everything to her," was reflected among the flowers that covered not only Sartre's tombstone, but spilled over onto others nearby as well. Simone de Beauvoir was remembered by the Parti Socialiste, Section Montparnasse; internationally by Des Féministes de Grèce; the Women's Health Center, Woman Books, and Columbia University, all of New York; The International Simone de Beauvoir Society; The Campaneras du Instituto la Mujer of Madrid and Las Mujeres Andaluda; the Womens Studies programs of New South Wales, Sydney and Adelaide Universities of Australia. An African women's wreath carried the simple sentiment, "poor toi, Castor." Political realities appeared in a wreath which seemed to have been handmade with affection and care, bearing a touchingly misspelled ribbon attributing it to the "Association des Ecrivains Iraniens en 'Escil'."

Long after the principal mourners had left the cemetery, people still clustered in groups inside and out. There seemed to be a common sense of loss among those who stayed on in the rain. Among people who had known her well, worked with her, who had only seen her from afar, who had not known her at all, loss and bereavement were common and were shared. More than one person found it difficult to conceive of a world without Simone de Beauvoir.

Contributors

DEIRDRE BAIR is completing the biography of Simone de Beauvoir, to be published in 1987. From January, 1981 until three weeks before the writer's death, Bair conducted extensive interviews with Simone de Beauvoir, who considered this project to be her authorized biography. Deirdre Bair teaches English and Comparative Literature at the University of Pennsylvania. Her last book, the biography of Samuel Beckett, received the 1981 American Book Award.

JUDITH BUTLER is Assistant Professor of Philosophy at George Washington University. She has published papers on Sartre, Hegel, contemporary French philosophy and feminist thought in *International Philosophy Quarterly, Praxis International* and the *Berkshire Review.* Her book, *Subjects of Desire: Hegelian Reflections in Twentieth Century France* is forthcoming from Columbia University Press.

ISABELLE DE COURTIVRON is Associate Professor of French at MIT. She is co-author, with Elaine Marks, of *New French Feminisms* (1980). Her book on Violette Leduc (Boston: Twayne) appeared in 1985.

MARTHA NOEL EVANS is Associate Professor of French and Coordinator of Women's Studies at Mary Baldwin College in Staunton, Virginia. She has published articles on nineteenth- and twentieth-century French literature and psychoanalysis in *Sub-stance, Romanic Review, Littérature, La Revue des sciences humaines,* and the *Psychoanalytic Quarterly.* She has recently completed a book, *Writing and the Politics of Gender in Twentieth-century France* and is currently working on a book on hysteria.

VIRGINIA M. FICHERA is Associate Professor of Foreign Languages and Humanities at SUNY-Oswego and a Visiting Fellow in Peace studies at Cornell University. Her current research areas include American, French and German literature and theory with emphasis on gender, conflict, and subjectivity in the nuclear age.

DOROTHY KAUFMANN (MCCALL) teaches at Clark University where she is Associate Professor of French. Her publications include *The Theatre of Jean-Paul Sartre* (New York: Columbia University Press, 1969) and articles on Simone de Beauvoir and contemporary French feminism. She is presently studying the relationship of Simone de Beauvoir and Sartre in light of Sartre's *Lettres au Castor.*

ELAINE MARKS is Professor of French and Women's Studies at the University of Wisconsin-Madison. She has written books on Colette and Simone de Beauvoir and is coeditor with George Stambolian of *Homosexualities and French Literature* and with Isabelle de Courtivron of *New French Feminisms.* She is editor of the forthcoming *Critical Essays on Simone de Beauvoir* to be published by G. K. Hall.

FRANÇOISE C. MOINET is Agregée de Lettres Modernes from the Ecole Normale Supérieure at Sèvres, and is currently teaching at Stanford University.

YOLANDA ASTARITA PATTERSON wrote her Master's thesis on Simone de Beauvoir, whom she has interviewed on two occasions. She is the author of numerous articles on Simone de Beauvoir, has lectured extensively on her, and is currently completing a book on Simone de Beauvoir and motherhood. She recently received the Outstanding Professor of the Year award for 1986 at California State University, Hayward, where she has taught French, Spanish, Latin, Western Heritage and Women's Studies courses since 1965. She is a founding member of the Simone de Beauvoir Society, and currently serves as its President and as editor of its newsletter and its annual publication, *Simone de Beauvoir Studies.*

CATHERINE PORTUGES is Director of Women's Studies at the University of Massachusetts where she teaches in the Department of Comparative Literature. Her published work includes essays on the intersections of psychoanalysis and cinema; studies of gender and autobiography on Simone de Beauvoir, Marguerite Duras, and Colette; and interviews with Agnes Varda, Yvonne Rainer, and Nathalie Sarraute. Her coauthored book, *Gendered Subjects: The Dynamics of Feminist Teaching,* was published in 1985 by Routledge and Kegan Paul Ltd., London.

MARGARET A. SIMONS, Associate Professor of Philosophy at Southern Illinois University at Edwardsville, is editor of *Hypatia: A Journal of Feminist Philosophy*. She is currently working with Hélène V. Wenzel on a critical study and translation of the deleted and mistranslated sections in the existing English translation of *The Second Sex*, and a book on Simone de Beauvoir and feminist philosophy.

HÉLÈNE VIVIENNE WENZEL teaches French and Women's Studies at Yale University, where she offers classes in French Feminist Thought and an Introduction to Women's Studies and Feminist Thought. She has written on Monique Wittig, Luce Irigaray, Violette Leduc, and Simone de Beauvoir. She is on the editorial boards of *Signs, The Women's Review of Books* and *Feminist Issues*, and is especially interested in the politics of writing.

The following issues are still available through the **Yale French Studies** Office, 2504A Yale Station, New Haven, CT 06520.

19/20 Contemporary Art $3.50
23 Humor $3.50
33 Shakespeare $3.50
35 Sade $3.50
38 The Classical Line $3.50
39 Literature and
   Revolution $3.50
40 Literature and Society:
   18th Century $3.50
41 Game, Play, Literature
   $5.00
42 Zola $5.00

43 The Child's Part $5.00
44 Paul Valéry $5.00
45 Language as Action $5.00
46 From Stage to Street $3.50
47 Image & Symbol in the
   Renaissance $3.50
49 Science, Language, &
   the Perspective Mind $3.50
50 Intoxication and
   Literature $3.50
53 African Literature $3.50
54 Mallarmé $5.00

57 Locus: Space, Landscape,
   Decor $6.00
58 In Memory of Jacques
   Ehrmann $6.00
59 Rethinking History $6.00
61 Toward a Theory of
   Description $6.00
62 Feminist Readings: French Texts/
   American Contexts $6.00

Add for postage & handling

Single issue, United States $1.00
Each additional issue $.50

Single issue, foreign countries $1.50
Each additional issue $.75

- -

YALE FRENCH STUDIES, 2504A Yale Station, New Haven, Connecticut 06520

A check made payable to YFS is enclosed. Please send me the following issue(s):

Issue no.	Title	Price
_____	_____	_____
_____	_____	_____
_____	_____	_____
	Postage & handling	_____
	Total	_____

Name _____

Number/Street _____

City _____ State _____ Zip _____

The following issues are now available through Kraus Reprint Company, Route 100, Millwood, N.Y. 10546.

1 Critical Bibliography of
   Existentialism
2 Modern Poets
3 Criticism & Creation
4 Literature & Ideas
5 The Modern Theatre
6 France and World Literature
7 André Gide
8 What's Novel in the Novel
9 Symbolism
10 French-American Literature
   Relationships

11 Eros, Variations...
12 God & the Writer
13 Romanticism Revisited
14 Motley: Today's French Theater
15 Social & Political France
16 Foray through Existentialism
17 The Art of the Cinema
18 Passion & the Intellect, or
   Malraux
21 Poetry Since the Liberation
22 French Education
24 Midnight Novelists

25 Albert Camus
26 The Myth of Napoleon
27 Women Writers
28 Rousseau
29 The New Dramatists
30 Sartre
31 Surrealism
32 Paris in Literature
34 Proust
48 French Freud
51 Approaches to Medieval
   Romance
52 Graphesis

36 37 Stucturalism has been reprinted by Doubleday as an Anchor Book.
55/56 Literature and Psychoanalysis has been reprinted by Johns Hopkins University Press, and can be ordered through Customer Service, Johns Hopkins University Press, Baltimore, MD 21218.

The following issues are available through **Yale University Press,** Customer Service Department, 92A Yale Station, New Haven, CT 06520.

63 The Pedagogical Imperative:
      Teaching as a Literary Genre
      (1982) $12.95
64 Montaigne: Essays in Reading
      (1983) $12.95
65 The Language of Difference:
      Writing in QUEBEC(ois)
      (1983) $12.95
66 The Anxiety of Anticipation
      (1984) $12.95

67 Concepts of Closure
      (1984) $12.95
68 Sartre after Sartre
      (1985) $12.95
69 The Lesson of Paul de Man
      (1985) $12.95
70 Images of Power:
      Medieval History/Discourse/
      Literature
      (1986) $12.95

71 Men/Women of Letters:
      Correspondence
      (1986) $12.95
72 Simone de Beauvoir:
      Witness to a Century
      (1987) $12.95
73 Forthcoming Issue
      (1987) $12.95

Special subscription rates are available on a calendar year basis (2 issues per year):

Individual subscriptions $22.00
Institutional subscriptions $25.90

- -

ORDER FORM   **Yale University Press,** 92A Yale Station, New Haven, CT 06520

Please enter my subscription for the calendar year
☐ **1986** (Nos. 70 and 71)   ☐ **1987** (Nos. 72 and 73)

I would like to purchase the following individual issues:

_____

_____

For individual issues, please add postage and handling:
Single issue, United States $1.50
Each additional issue $.50
Connecticut residents please add sales tax of 7½%.

Single issue, foreign countries $2.00
Each additional issue $1.00

Payment of $ _____ is enclosed (including sales tax if applicable).

Mastercard no. _____

4-digit bank no. _____ Expiration date _____

VISA no. _____ Expiration date _____

Signature _____

SHIP TO: _____

_____

_____

- -

See the next page for ordering issues 1–59 and 61–62. **Yale French Studies** is also available through Xerox University Microfilms, 300 North Zeeb Road, Ann Arbor, MI 48106.